Imperial Cults

Imperial Cults

Religion and Politics in the Early Han and Roman Empires

REBECCA ROBINSON

OXFORD
UNIVERSITY PRESS

Oxford University Press is a department of the University of Oxford. It furthers
the University's objective of excellence in research, scholarship, and education
by publishing worldwide. Oxford is a registered trade mark of Oxford University
Press in the UK and certain other countries.

Published in the United States of America by Oxford University Press
198 Madison Avenue, New York, NY 10016, United States of America.

© Oxford University Press 2023

All rights reserved. No part of this publication may be reproduced, stored in
a retrieval system, or transmitted, in any form or by any means, without the
prior permission in writing of Oxford University Press, or as expressly permitted
by law, by license, or under terms agreed with the appropriate reproduction
rights organization. Inquiries concerning reproduction outside the scope of the
above should be sent to the Rights Department, Oxford University Press, at the
address above.

You must not circulate this work in any other form
and you must impose this same condition on any acquirer.

Library of Congress Cataloging-in-Publication Data
Names: Robinson, Rebecca (Assistant Professor, Department of History), author.
Title: Imperial cults : religion and politics in the early Han and Roman empires / Rebecca Robinson.
Description: New York : Oxford University Press, [2023] |
Includes bibliographical references and index.
Identifiers: LCCN 2023006048 (print) | LCCN 2023006049 (ebook) |
ISBN 9780197666043 (hardcover) | ISBN 9780197666067 (epub) |
ISBN 9780197666074
Subjects: LCSH: Han Wudi, Emperor of China, 156 B.C.-87 B.C.—Influence. |
Augustus, Emperor of Rome, 63 B.C.-14 A.D.—Influence. |
China—History—Han dynasty, 202 B.C.-220 A.D. | China—Politics and
government—221 B.C.-220 A.D. | Rome—History—Empire, 30 B.C.-284 A.D. |
Rome—Politics and government—30 B.C.-284 A.D. | Religion and
politics—China—History. | Religion and politics—Rome—History.
Classification: LCC DS748.16.H36 R63 2023 (print) | LCC DS748.16.H36 (ebook) |
DDC 931/.04—dc23/eng/20230307
LC record available at https://lccn.loc.gov/2023006048
LC ebook record available at https://lccn.loc.gov/2023006049

DOI: 10.1093/oso/9780197666043.001.0001

Printed by Integrated Books International, United States of America

Contents

List of Illustrations   vii
Acknowledgements   ix

1. Introduction   1
   - Comparative Ancient History   3
   - Comparing "Religion" in the Ancient World   9
   - Sources   10
   - Chapter Outlines   17

2. Transitions to Empire in Early China and Rome   23
   - From Republic to Empire in Rome   24
   - All under Heaven in Early China   27
   - Empire, Convergence, and Divergence   30

3. State Cult in Early China and Rome   34
   - Characteristics of Imperial Cult in Early China   35
   - Roman Religious Institutions   41
   - Conclusion   47

4. Reshaping Religious Institutions   49
   - New Men in Han China: The *Fangshi*   50
   - Priestly Colleges in Augustan Rome   52
   - Conclusion   58

5. Expanding Influence   60
   - Expanding Influence outside the Han Capital   61
   - Priestly and Political Power in Rome   69
   - Conclusion   74

6. Communicating Imperial Authority   75
   - Public Display as Media   76
   - Rebuilding Rome   78
   - Inspection Tours and Publicity in the Han   82
   - Conclusion   87

7. Redefining Ceremony	89
   Establishing New Sacrifices in the Han	90
   Reviving Festivals in Augustan Rome	97
   Epoch-Making Sacrifices: The *Feng* and *Shan* Sacrifices and
   the *Ludi Saeculares*	103
   Conclusion	114

8. Conclusion	116

Notes	125
Bibliography	169
Index	187

List of Illustrations

Table 4.1.	The *fangshi* under Emperor Wu	53
Table 5.1.	Consulships held by Priests	71
Figure 5.1.	Important sacrificial locations and the Five Sacred Peaks during Emperor Wu's Reign	64

Acknowledgements

This book has its origins in my doctoral dissertation, written at McGill University, and reached its end at the department of history at HKBU. Over the course of its life, from its inception by an overly ambitious PhD student to its completion by a rather more cynical assistant professor, the project has benefited from conversations, critique, and support from far too large a number of people to adequately thank in the space before me.

My foremost thanks go to the professors who have advised me over the years on this project. I have benefited enormously from a supportive doctoral committee who continue to generously offer their time and guidance beyond the PhD. Robin D. S. Yates was the advisor to both my MA and PhD theses, and he continues to offer generous guidance and support on my new projects. Hans Beck was willing to join the project as a co-supervisor to a student who at the outset had no training in ancient Mediterranean history or languages. The project has benefited from Griet Vankeerberghen's critical eye and assistance, and I have gained much from her support over the years. Carlos Noreña kindly served as the external reader for the dissertation and provided thoughtful comments and questions, which I have tried to address. I am grateful, too, to the two anonymous reviewers, whose constructive feedback has helped to shape the book. There are far too many people to whom I owe an intellectual debt to thank in this brief section; my thanks go to all who have contributed to the research and writing, directly or not, of this book. It is only the errors and omissions that I can truly claim as my own.

Funding for this project was provided by the Social Sciences and Humanities Research Council Canada (SSHRC), the McCall MacBain fund at McGill, the Canada-China Scholar Exchange Program (CCSEP), which allowed me to spend a semester working at Fudan University, and the HKBU Undergraduate Research Programme. My year as a postdoctoral fellow at the Louis Freiberg Center for Asian Studies at HUJI provided a much needed opportunity to clear my head by pursuing research that was not related to this book. Research assistants at HKBU, Rachel Cheng, Janice Ngiam, and Lo Wing Lam, Kammy, provided support in the final stages of the project.

At McGill, Brahm Kleinman and François Gauthier were always willing to answer my questions related to ancient Rome, though as of yet neither of them have been lured into the comparative project. My cohort at McGill provided another important source of support, both in terms of academic conversations and, perhaps more importantly, nonacademic distraction. Particular thanks go, in no particular order, to Rachel, Peter, Geoff, Angela, Wen-Yi, Erin, Matt, and Vita.

In Hong Kong, I have had the distinct fortune of joining the department of history at HKBU. Clara Wing-chung Ho is truly a force of nature, and my colleagues in the department and in Hong Kong have been an endlessly encouraging and supportive group. In particular, Catherine Ladds, David Schley, and Vincent Leung have been generous in offering their guidance in the revision and publishing process. My friends in Hong Kong, Lachlan, Celia, Catherine, David, Jessica, Dorothy, James, Vincent and Tim, have all contributed, directly or not, to the completion of this project.

Much of the book was written during the early stages of the COVID-19 pandemic, and I would be remiss if I did not thank the librarians at HKBU and around the world who helped me to access resources while the world was strangely disconnected. I'd also like to thank the authors who shared their publications with me when I was unable to gain access via university libraries.

My family, Dianne, Robbie, and Sarah, have supported me unwaveringly in this endeavour as they have all the others. Without them, completing, or even starting, this book would truly not have been possible, and it is to them I dedicate this book.

1
Introduction

In the *Shiji* (*Historical Records* 史記), the Han official Sima Qian 司馬遷 (d. ca. 86 BCE) described the sacrifices established by Emperor Wu (Han Wudi 漢武帝 r. 141–87 BCE):

> The sacrifices established by the present emperor are: those to Great Unity, Sovereign Earth, and the *jiao* sacrifice [to the High Gods] which is performed personally by the emperor every three years, the *feng* and *shan* to establish the house of Han; the *feng* is renewed every five years. [He also established] the five [sacrifices recommended by] Miu Ji: [those to] Great Unity and Three Unities, the Dark Ram, the Horse Traveller, and the Red Star, and those sacrifices [recommended by] Kuan Shu, which are performed by officials according to the correct seasons. These six [groups of] sacrifices are all under the supervision of the Director of Sacrifices.

> 今天子所興祠，太一、后土，三年親郊祠，建漢家封禪，五年一修封。薄忌太一及三一、冥羊、馬行、赤星，五，寬舒之祠官以歲時致禮。凡六祠，皆太祝領之。[1]

Eight thousand kilometres away, in 121 CE, the biographer Gaius Suetonius Tranquillus (d. after c. 122 CE) wrote of the ceremonies that the *princeps* Augustus (63 BCE–14 CE) revived during his rule:

> He also revived some of the ancient rites which had gradually fallen into disuse, such as the Augury of Safety, the office of Flamen Dialis, the ceremonies of the Lupercalia, the Secular Games, and the festival of the Compitalia. At the Lupercalia he forbade beardless youths to join in the running, and at the Secular Games he would not allow young people of either sex to attend any entertainment by night except in company with some adult relative. He provided that the Lares of the Crossroads should be crowned twice a year, with spring and summer flowers.

> *Nonnulla etiam ex antiquis caerimoniis paulatim abolita restituit, ut Salutis augurium, Diale flamonium, sacrum Lupercale, ludos Saeculares et Compitalicios. Lupercalibus vetuit currere inberbes, item Saecularibus ludis iuvenes utriusque sexus prohibuit ullum nocturnum spectaculum frequentare nisi cum aliquo maiore natu propinquorum. Compitales Lares ornari bis anno instituit vernis floribus et aestivis.*[2]

These new or revived ceremonies and sacrifices were recorded by the ancient authors as significant achievements in the reigns of the respective rulers and testify to the amount of attention Emperor Wu and Augustus paid to their religious institutions. These sacrifices and ceremonies were not the only changes made by the rulers; both also restructured their respective religious institutions, ensuring that they each had the final say over state-sponsored religious activities. These changes took place as they sought to solidify their authority—Emperor Wu sought to free himself from the restrictions of court officials and to regain control over semiautonomous territories within his empire that were governed by far-removed members of the royal family, while Augustus sought to establish himself as emperor of Rome in all but name, eliminating rival challenges to power in the tumultuous last decades of the Republic. Both rulers gained an impressive, almost unprecedented, amount of personal authority, and firmly established the foundations for centralized imperial rule in their respective states. *Imperial Cults: Religion and Politics in the Early Han and Roman Empire* argues that the reforms made to religious institutions and the newly established ceremonies and sacrifices placed each ruler at the centre of all religious activity, and that this was a fundamental part of securing the rulers' personal authority over their empires.

This monograph is interested in the relationship between religion and politics during the formation of empire in early China and Rome. Specifically, it looks at the changes made to religious institutions during the reigns of Emperor Wu of Han and Augustus in Rome.[3] During the reigns of these two rulers, significant changes to their respective political systems took place—in Rome, we see the establishment of a hereditary leader and the Julio-Claudian line, while in China, the Han empire consolidated its rule over semi-autonomous territories and expanded its territory to an extent not seen again until the Tang Dynasty (唐 618–907 CE). Both rulers enjoyed unprecedented authority; Augustus, while carefully avoiding claims to kingship or dictatorship, established himself as sole ruler of Rome; Emperor Wu asserted more personal authority than any Han emperor, bypassing the court officials, who held much bureaucratic power, and regional lords (*zhu hou* 諸侯) who governed their territories with a great deal of autonomy. While there were many factors that contributed to these two extraordinary reigns, this book is concerned with how the rulers used their respective religious institutions to consolidate their authority, secure support, and communicate their authority to the elite and commoners alike. The focus of the monograph is on the actions of the rulers themselves, rather than those around them. Both rulers were certainly assisted, or sometimes hindered, in their endeavours by many in their societies. Augustus, in particular, was voted many honours by the Senate which contributed to his elevated position in society. While interventions and contributions by elite were indeed important factors in shaping the two reigns, I chose to focus the comparison on the two rulers in order to highlight the initiative both rulers took in reforming religious institutions. *Imperial Cults* shows that the use of religion and religious institutions was a central component to the consolidation of one-man rule over a unified territory during the Western Han and early Roman empire. By comparing the expansion and reform of religious institutions, the book demonstrates that a comparative approach can not only reveal similar trends in the formation of ancient empires, but also that new perspectives on familiar material can be found be engaging in dialogue with other societies.

Comparative Ancient History

In recent years, there has been a growing interest in the study of the ancient world from a comparative perspective. The reasons for this are manifold, but stem in part from a desire to broaden the field of the study of the ancient world due to China's emergence as a world power in the twentieth century,[4] and its subsequent popularity as a field of study. It seems natural, therefore, to compare the civilizations of the east and west to which our intellectual, political, and cultural legacies are most indebted. And indeed, this is where studies of comparative history have been focused: beginning with Geoffrey Lloyd's pioneering work on Greek and Chinese science, historians have compared various elements of ancient Greek and Chinese societies, including art and aesthetics, historiography, philosophy, divination, ethnicity, and literary traditions.[5]

These studies aim to understand the differences between the development of science, philosophy, literature, and rhetoric in the two societies, while simultaneously exploring comparison itself: "to find a way of gaining from the joint study of two cultures understandings about each that would be unattainable if they were studied alone."[6] These works take as their starting point the fact that there are fundamental similarities between early China and ancient Greece; according to Geoffrey Lloyd and Nathan Sivin, both societies evolved "comparatively elaborate cultures, with languages and abstract conceptual structures that could be used to explore every aspect of individual and collective experience."[7] People in both societies also saw the need to inquire into the nature of the cosmos, the human body, or plants, animals, and the environment, and believed that the study of these diverse natural phenomena was essential to understanding man's place within the universe.[8] These studies of scientific inquiry, philosophy, literature, and rhetoric discuss the ways in which thinkers in each society understood and theorized their world, and how these inquiries and understandings were shaped by their cultural traditions. Scholarly interest in comparison has heretofore been primarily focused on the Sino-Greek comparison, with recent monographs on gender relations, divination, and ethnicity published in the last several years.[9] However, there has recently been an "imperial turn" in comparative work, turning to the study of empire and statecraft in Rome and China.

Moving away from the intellectual history orientation of the Sino-Greek studies, volumes comparing Rome and China have focused on questions related to empire, including comparisons of bureaucracy, monetary systems, trade, imperial courts, law, urban spaces, and gift circulation.[10] In so doing, these studies turn to the day-to-day operations of the empires, drawing conclusions about structural similarities and differences. Studies comparing the Roman and early Chinese empires seek to address questions related to state formation and longevity—why, for example, did the Roman empire endure, while the Han did not? Jane Burbank and Frederick Cooper's book on the persistence of empire as a form of political organization begins with a chapter comparing empire formation in Rome and China, setting the stage for the development of later historical empires. These comparative volumes, along with academic conferences and workshops, have demonstrated the usefulness of comparison in understanding the development of ancient societies, and have encouraged scholars to reconsider basic assumptions about their field through confrontation with the other. *Imperial Cults* contributes to this growing body of scholarship by examining the role of religious institutions and practices in the development of empire.

While comparative studies can attempt to answer large questions about human behaviour, civilization and state-formation, and cultural change,[11] the comparison of similarities and differences between civilizations also provides a new perspective on familiar material, and the comparative model can help scholars break out of the strictures imposed by centuries of historiographical traditions. As Walter Scheidel has put it, "comparison defamiliarizes the deceptively familiar,"[12] forcing historians to confront their sources with new questions and identifying important lacunae in the ancient records, as well as in more recent scholarship. The comparative project thus has two related goals: first, to seek to uncover similar processes in human behaviour under similar conditions from beneath the culturally specific characteristics and modes of knowledge and action. Second, to destabilize what we already know of these ancient civilizations, from both the ancient sources and the subsequent historical traditions that each field has engendered, by bringing the two civilizations into conversation. Comparative history is most useful insofar as it permits us to formulate new understandings of these civilizations, rather than to reinforce established understandings.

Following Walter Scheidel (2009; 2015) this monograph investigates what Jack Goldstone has termed "robust processes." A robust process is a causal explanation of events, given similar initial conditions, "a sequence of events that has unfolded in similar (but neither identical nor fully predictable) fashion in a variety of different historical contexts."[13] Goldstone, in his comparative study of the English and French revolutions with the Ottoman Crisis and the Ming-Qing transition, argues that big events, such as state breakdown, can be explained in part due to fundamental orientations in human behaviour, "knowing that, in a given situation, most people will react in some consistent fashion."[14] The focus on processes, rather than attempting to identify identical or universal structures in the ancient world, allows for more flexibility in comparison. It allows the historian to navigate the space between the overly general and the culturally specific. By seeking to understand the processes through which the early rulers consolidated their authority, the differences between the culturally specific characteristics of religious institutions become less important than the ways in which the rulers navigated them. We shall see that the strategies employed by the early rulers in transforming their respective religious institutions have many parallels, as the rulers adapted to challenges, and sought outside knowledge. The goal is not to create historical law, but rather to understand the parallels; thus, a robust process is less than a law but more than a limited historical generalization or analogy. It is a causal statement, asserting that a particular kind of historical sequence unfolds because individuals responded to particular, specified, salient characteristics in their respective historical situations.[15]

While Goldstone is interested in responses to crises, here I am interested in innovation, exploring the parallel developments in laying foundations of empires. Beginning with the initial observation that the rulers of the Han and Rome made dramatic changes to their religious institutions and used spectacular ceremonies to cement their rule, here we will examine how these changes took place, and to what conditions they responded. It matters little that the cult practices of the early rulers were dramatically different; the processes through which they were transformed are remarkably similar. This first goal of the comparative project is closely related to the second, and a thorough illumination of these parallel processes is only possible through a willingness to reinterpret established interpretations of historical events.

The second goal of comparative history is thus to destabilize what we know and think of the ancient world, particularly with regard to our sources and how they present their civilizations. The historical and archaeological records from early China and Rome differ dramatically in terms of both content and quantity. The written records from the Qin, Han, and Rome contain such different content that it quickly becomes obvious that the authors and archivists of these records—historians, religious specialists, statesmen, and others—of each civilization were concerned with radically different questions. The biases of these sources, have, understandably, influenced their respective historical traditions, and the two traditions diverge substantially in terms of the topics they have pursued. Rather than being an obstacle, this incongruity can be seen as an opportunity: by interrogating the Roman sources with questions asked by the Han scholars and the major discussions in the field of early Chinese history, we gain a different perspective on the ways in which the Romans wrote about their history, and how these sources have subsequently been written about. At the same time, reading the early Chinese sources through the eyes of a Romanist generates a wide range of questions about early Chinese culture and statecraft. To make a very broad generalization, we can say that the sources from ancient Rome tend to focus on military affairs, debates within the Senate, the opinions and actions of "big men," including writings on philosophy and legal affairs, while the sources from early

China trend towards questions about cosmology, good governance, and biographies of exemplary (or infamous) individuals and groups. In addition to the received literary and historical documents, we also have a wide range of excavated documents from early China, which give new insight into legal procedures and everyday life. While battle narratives, lauding the military achievements of generals, dominate the historical records of Rome, we have few such narratives from early China.[16] Discussions of correlative cosmology abound in the early Chinese sources, but are scant in Rome.[17] This is not to say that battle narratives were not told in early China, or that the Romans did not speculate about the nature of the cosmos, but simply that the authors of the historical texts that have become the dominant sources in each tradition, were not, respectively, as concerned with these questions. The Chinese histories were written about officials, "for officials by officials,"[18] and we can likewise perhaps say that the Roman sources were written "about *nobiles*, for *nobiles*, by *nobiles*." While it is, of course, impossible to read sources that do not exist, we can read between the lines, and try to understand these ancient sources on terms other than their own.

This type of comparison, however, raises several issues, most notably that of cultural specificity. It bears remembering that our comparisons between the ancient civilizations are not exclusively made between the two ancient civilizations, they are simultaneously a comparison with our own modern concepts of state, culture, and civilization. As Jeremy Tanner has put it, "one cannot take individual theories, for example the Greek theory of elements (*stoicheia*) and the Chinese theory of the five phases (*wu xing*), and compare them as answers to the same (probably modern) question about the 'nature of reality'."[19] These questions are particularly amplified concerning the question of religion and belief in the ancient world. There is no evidence to suggest that theories about the nature of society and the cosmos had their origins in one ur-civilization and were later adopted and adapted by disparate civilizations. The comparative approach is not a search for universality of belief or understandings of the world; it is an attempt to understand how actors in different civilizations approached similar problems under similar circumstances, and through a comparative analysis, to gain a different understanding of each civilization.

Comparative studies must necessarily operate in the space between broad generalizations and historical specificity. Comparative-historical analysis, according to Matthew Lange, allows the researcher to "balance idiographic and nomothetic explanations," and "gain knowledge about individual cases while at the same time pushing the envelope to explore whether explanations hold across multiple cases."[20] Individual case studies, when placed in comparison, are thus able to reveal larger processes at work in the formation of empires, while also providing detailed analysis of the individual cases. One of the difficulties in the venture is the balance between generality and specificity. A study that is too broad must ignore, or gloss over, important features of particular cultures and institutions, while a study that is too specific finds little ground on which to compare two societies. We must also resist the temptation to "fill in the gaps" of one society, and its historical record, with the material from another, seemingly comparable society. "There is never enough information," according to Bruce Trigger, "to explain all aspects of any early civilization, and this lack of information has stimulated many anthropologists to extrapolate what is known about one society to other, presumably similar ones."[21] It is not my intention, through the discussion of the parallel processes in reforms made to religious institutions in early China and Rome, to argue for any inevitable actions or results or to argue that because something happened in one place it must have also happened in the other; rather, through the juxtaposition of the two cases, I hope to demonstrate that, not only did the rulers make similar use of the opportunity to reform their religious institutions, but that the comparison can lead to different, and more nuanced interpretations of both cases. By using one society to "make visible" elements of the other that may be hidden or occluded in the historical record, comparative history reminds us that histories are the products of their societies, and present only one perspective on events and ideology. What comparative history has to offer, therefore, is not easy answers, but more challenging questions.

While comparative studies often begin with a search for similarities between societies, or for points of convergence on historical trajectories, the historian is, more often than not, confronted with more difference than similarity, more divergence than convergence. Given that the two societies under investigation developed independently from each other, this should come as no surprise. That there are great differences, however, does not jeopardize the comparative study; rather, it allows us to view familiar material in new, unfamiliar light. The comparative approach, rather than seeking to discover similarities in the minutiae of particular institutions, or the actions of individuals, can offer broad, causal explanations, while simultaneously forcing us to rethink and reargue some of the established orthodoxies in each field.

Comparing "Religion" in the Ancient World

The question of what constitutes "religion" in both early China and Rome has long frustrated scholars. While the word "religion" has often functioned as a catch-all term to describe any and all doctrines and practices from the ancient world that attempted to describe or engage with the extrahuman, our assumptions about what constituted religion are still very much reliant on the Abrahamic model. As we shall see in Chapter 3, the practices that we describe as religious in early China and Rome bear little resemblance to later religious traditions, both in China and the West. Additionally, as Filippo Marsili has recently argued, attempting to understand early Chinese traditions through the lens of Greco-Roman religious traditions only offers up more pitfalls, as we attempt to force Chinese theories and practices into the model of *polis* or state religion that dominated the ancient Mediterranean.[22] While some scholars have argued that ritual and religion are foundational to all societies, it is effectively impossible to come up with a definition of religion that encompasses all manifestations of what we refer to as "religion" in all societies.[23] It is not the intention of this monograph to create any such definition, nor to venture into the debate over what constituted religion in either early China and Rome, or both. In *Heaven is Empty*, Marsili convincingly argues for the need to understand early Chinese attitudes towards the extrahuman outside of Abrahamic models, as well as the need to be more cautious in comparisons with early Roman religions, the study of which has also long been influenced by Abrahamic religions and scholarly traditions.[24]

In particular, Marsili argues that one of the dangers of applying the Abrahamic or ancient Roman model to early Chinese religions is that it makes us assume that there was an "integrated, coherent system" for conceptualizing nonhuman phenomena.[25] As we shall see, there was not one approach to the extrahuman in early China, and the practices that we characterize as religious were subject to much experimentation. The early Chinese had, according to Kenneth Brashier, "many of the components that we may consider 'religious'—spirits, prayers, sacrifices, afterlife, and so forth—but they simply did not draw a circle around those components and then label the circle as we do."[26] Likewise, the ancient Romans had many of these components, and, unlike the Chinese of this period, an organized state religion, complete with clergy.[27] However, while the two share certain characteristics and components, the religious institutions of the Han and Rome remain specific to each society, and very different to later religions.

This monograph is thus not concerned with comparing the religions or religious characteristics of early China and Rome.[28] It is not concerned with the question of sacrality or secularity, of orthodoxy and orthopraxy, or even with the question of belief. Such questions are left to scholars of religion to debate.[29] Instead, this monograph is interested in comparing the ways in which rulers *used* their respective religious institutions to bolster their own authority. As we shall see, this involved the creation or adoption of new cults, the introduction of new men into positions of religious authority, and the use of religious ceremonies as communicative media. By focusing on the rulers' use of religious practices and institutions, we can compare the ways in which early rulers used their respective modes of engaging with the extrahuman to facilitate their claims to sole imperial authority. In so doing, rather than advancing any definition of religion as a cultural universal, *Imperial Cults* seeks to show that "religions," as culturally specific traditions, were manipulated by rulers for power; this practice being perhaps more of a cultural universal than religion itself. As such, this monograph is more about politics than religion, though at the same time it contends that neither society could have a politics without religion.

Sources

Our understandings of these religious institutions and practices have, of course, been shaped not only by contemporary religious traditions and scholarship, but by our sources for religions in the ancient world. Both cultures had a rich literary tradition, and writings about the state and society flourished in both empires. These sources were, largely, written by elites, themselves often members of court society or state bureaucracy. As such, the literary records are closely linked to the sociopolitical circumstances of the time, and in some cases, contributed to narratives of legitimacy.

Much ink has been spilled about written historical traditions in the ancient world and the goals and motivations of the historians. It is not my intention here to enter into this debate, but to highlight some of the salient features of the early Chinese and Roman historical traditions, as well as to draw attention to the areas where they resemble each other. Two generalizations may be made about the early Chinese and Roman histories, one more sweeping than the other. The first is that their authors, none of them professional historians, sought to investigate and reconstruct the pasts of their societies, in order to understand the present. In the early Han, the Grand Scribe Sima Qian, following precedent set by earlier annalistic works, searched for patterns; understanding those patterns would allow a ruler to rule according to the way of Heaven. In Rome, various Roman historians, including Livy, Polybius, Dio, and Tacitus, looked to the past to explain the rise and fall of the Roman Republic. The historians of the ancient world all attempted to provide a true reconstruction of the past; at the same time, they were explicitly aware of their own interest in present events. From this arises the second generalization: that, for the ancient historians, the writing of history required the historian to invoke his own judgement, whether explicitly or implicitly, freely or cautiously distributing praise and blame for past events. The writing of history was, and still is, a political act.

The topics that interested the historians, however, differed, as do the other sources that survive from the Han and Rome. Roman historians enjoyed sweeping their readers into the heart of battle and the shadows of intrigue, while the Han historians shied away from battles and tiptoed around scandals. Han histories provide detailed theories, calculations, and charts about cosmic patterns, such as calendars, while Roman histories force us to piece together the details of cosmology and calendrics, even though they were important parts of Roman life. Other literary sources likewise differ in their interests: texts from early China provide detailed instructions for, say, how to conduct a capping ceremony, allowing the modern reader to reconstruct said ceremony, should she so desire, while Roman sources allow us to imagine how it might have felt to hear a talented orator argue a legal case. Material culture from both societies greatly augments our understanding of the past, but while the Italian peninsula is seen to have largely revealed her secrets, the discovery of buried texts and important sites in China continues at a (for ancient historians, anyway) breath-taking pace. In what follows, I will discuss the relevant sources, from China and Rome, employed by this monograph. This is by no means a comprehensive survey of the two traditions, merely a brief guide to some of the relevant literature to facilitate readers who might be unfamiliar with one or the other traditions.

While there had been a long tradition of historical writing in early China, the genre took a particular form during the reign of Emperor Wu; a form which it would largely retain throughout imperial Chinese history. Started by the Grand Scribe (*taishi* 太史) Sima Tan 司馬談 (d. 110 BCE) and completed by his son, Sima Qian, who succeeded him as Grand Scribe, the *Shiji* was intended to be a history of the entire world, from earliest times to the reign of

Emperor Wu, during which it was written. This history, divided into imperial annals (*ji* 紀), tables (*biao* 表), treatises (*shu* 書), hereditary houses (*shi jia* 世家), and biographies (*lie zhuan* 列傳), set the precedent for subsequent history writing in China.[30] Rather than being simply a narrative history, the *Shiji* encompasses a vast amount of information about various subjects. The imperial annals provide a year-by-year overview of events during each emperor's reign, including omens and natural disasters, amnesties, imperial decrees, imperial travels, and military campaigns. The tables section includes chronological tables of important events and lineages, in order to clarify the different genealogical lines which existed simultaneously.[31] The treatise section contains chapters on diverse topics related to the empire; pertinent to this monograph are the chapters on ritual and sacrifice. The Hereditary Houses section provides information on the Zhou states, and contain a mixture of chronological and biographical information. Finally, the biographies section, the longest part of the text, is a collection of biographies of notable individuals; some notable for their connection to the imperial house, some famous statesmen or thinkers, and others, infamous for their crimes. The work is remembered as Sima Qian's greatest achievement, and his title *Taishi* is often translated, misleadingly, as the "grand historian" as a result of his work.[32] However, he was not employed by the court to write history, and this project was not directly related to his duties as Grand Scribe, which involved recording information and monitoring celestial phenomena, among other tasks.[33] His position gave him access to imperial archives and he also travelled to historical sites to gather materials and interview local officials, in order to present as comprehensive history as possible.[34] For the imperial records of the Western Han, it is reasonable to expect that his writing was based on materials from the imperial archive. The work was not, however, an attempt at purely objective history writing: in many cases it is a critique of the reign of Emperor Wu, out of whose favour Sima Qian had fallen.[35] The work was also a very personal project, as Sima Qian was perhaps attempting to position himself as a "second Confucius;" an assertion which in itself was an implicit critique on the legitimacy of the reigning emperor.[36]

Our second main source for the period, the *Hanshu* 漢書, completed in 111 CE, was written primarily Ban Gu 班固 (32–92 CE), with contributions by his sister Ban Zhao 班昭 (45–ca. 116 CE). This was also a project inherited from their father, Ban Biao 班彪 (3–54 CE). The *Hanshu* largely follows the model of the *Shiji*, comprised of imperial annals, chronological tables, treatises (*zhi* 志), and biographies (*zhuan* 傳). The Hereditary Houses section was not included, as it was not pertinent to the Western Han. Unlike the *Shiji*, the *Hanshu* was a history of a single dynasty—the Western Han. Written during the early Eastern Han, the *Hanshu* records the period from the founding of the Han dynasty to the end of the reign of Wang Mang 王莽 (45 BCE–23 CE), and his Xin Dynasty 新, in 23 CE. Much of the *Hanshu* repeats verbatim the text of the *Shiji*, yet it also builds upon the work of the Simas, not only extending the history to the end of the Wang Mang period, but supplementing many of the details from the reign of Emperor Wu.[37] Writing from a later period, the *Hanshu* provides a very different perspective of the events of Emperor Wu's reign, and is less interested in critique. This is not to suggest that it is free from its own bias, but that it has the benefit of historical perspective for this period. The *Hanshu* treatise that discusses Emperor Wu's ritual programme is largely based on that of the *Shiji*, though some modifications have been made. Throughout the monograph, I provide citations to both sources, noting the differences when pertinent.

In addition to these two histories, written during the Han, I make use of other texts from the pre- and early-imperial period, which provide more detailed explanations of ritual practices, or were intended as practical guides, such as the *Liji* (Rites Records 禮記),[38] *Lüshi Chunqiu* (*The Spring and Autumn Annals of Lü Buwei* 呂氏春秋), and *Huainanzi* (淮南子). These texts, particularly the ritual texts, can be tricky to employ in the study of Han institutions, for they were likely prescriptive texts, rather than representative of actual practice, and there is no indication as to what extent they were employed by scholars at court, though we know that they were consulted and in circulation in some form. These texts represent various types of knowledge available to the advisors to the emperor: at times they represent a consensus, and at other times a plurality of opinions on how ritual action should be undertaken.

Conspicuous by their absence in this monograph are the many texts and other documents that have been excavated or otherwise retrieved from tombs, wells, and antiquities markets.[39] These documents, primarily written on bamboo slips or wooden boards, offer a wealth of information about the Warring States, Qin, and Han societies that is not included in the historical or other received texts. In particular, the discovery of legal and administrative documents has reshaped our understanding of early Chinese statecraft.[40] Numerous documents, most notably those now classified as "daybooks" (*rishu* 日書) also shed light on popular religious and mantic practices, allowing us a glimpse of how nonelites might have interacted with the cosmic world in their everyday lives.⁴¹ Unfortunately for the present study, the excavated or retrieved texts do not, as yet, provide any insights into religious practices at the imperial level. While it is reasonable to suppose that the emperor and his advisors were aware of and even employed some of these mantic practices, there is no indication that they were a part of Emperor Wu's religious programme, or that they had any role in shaping his imperial vision. As such, excavated manuscripts will only be mentioned when they shed light on a particular topic or problem, and do not constitute a significant source-base for this study.

The texts whose authorship we can trace for this period were all produced by elite writers, many of them either directly employed by or closely affiliated with a court.⁴² While this is advantageous in that the historians, in particular, were able to include transcripts of imperial edicts, and had access to a wide variety of source materials, it does also mean that the histories are concerned almost exclusively with elite affairs, and pay scant attention to the common people. A similar situation is evidenced in Rome.

The Roman historical tradition was, like the early Chinese, long and rich. Developing from Roman antecedents, the Roman historians, some of whom were Greek, sought to not only provide detailed accounts of events of the past, but also to emotionally engage their readers. One of the earliest historians of Rome, the Greek Polybius Πολύβιος, argued that the most important type of history was what he termed "pragmatic history": history focused on the "deeds of people, cities, and rulers."⁴³ This type of history should be written to educate readers, and it is likely that his intended audience was aspiring politicians.⁴⁴ Furthermore, he stated that in order to write this type of history, one should be equipped with the necessary skills. Particularly, he suggested that hands-on political experience was necessary for the historian to understand politics and how to evaluate sources.⁴⁵ While not all of the historians, biographers, or other writers from Rome were themselves politicians, they were all connected to the ruling elite, and thus had not only close connections to the leading political figures of their time, but also the necessary education and access to sources to be able to write. These aims of history—to elucidate the past for the education of future leaders—remained important, and the authors' distribution of praise and blame reveals how they thought Rome should be run. There are many excellent overviews and detailed studies of Roman historical writing; as with the Chinese sources, this section will offer some brief comments on the main sources used in this book.⁴⁶

One of the most influential Roman historians, Livy (Titus Livius, 64 or 59 BCE–17 CE), wrote during the transition from Republic to Empire. Like Sima Qian, he wrote a history of the city of Rome from its earliest days, beginning with the founding of the city, up until his own time. Unfortunately for us, the Augustan sections of his *Ab urbe condita* are lost, but Livy's influence over later historical writing, as well as his parallels with Sima Qian, warrant his inclusion in this section. Like the Han historians, Livy was confronted with challenges with regards to his sources—in many cases, for the earliest histories, he relied on the principle of verisimilitude—that which is most believable—in order to avoid including fictitious or legendary stories from Rome's earliest history.[47] His history is conscious of making links between the past and the present, as well as including his own views on morality, and his history can thus be read, in part, as social commentary.[48] Livy was also closely connected with the imperial family; along with other notable literary figures, such as Virgil (Publius Vergilius Maro, 70–19 BCE) and Horace (Quintus Horatius Flaccus, 65–8 BCE), he was often a guest in Augustus' house, and even encouraged the future emperor Claudius, in his pursuit of history.[49] Despite their close relationship, Livy was certainly not a "court historian."[50] Although Livy's moral views often agree with those of the imperial family, historians believe that Livy "deeply believed in much of the 'Augustan program' on his own account,"[51] and that he was not influenced by Augustus to portray events in a particular fashion.[52]

Because Livy's history ends in the early Principate and many of the books have been lost to us, much of our understanding of the transition from Republic to Principate comes from the third-century CE *Roman History* Ῥωμαϊκὴ Ἱστορία of Cassius Dio (153–235 CE). The *Roman History* begins in legendary times, with the arrival of Aeneas in Italy (ca. 1200 BCE), and continues up to 229 CE. Of the original eighty books, only the books covering the events from 68 BCE to 47 CE (Books 36–60) are extant, making it an invaluable source for the late Republic and early empire.[53] Dio, like Livy, wanted to present a factual history of events in Rome, but he also included his own dramatizations of events, and composed speeches, inserting them into the mouths of historical figures, based on his own rhetorical training. This was common practice for Roman historians.[54] Dio was himself an elite and, without question, an elitist. Writing from the third century CE, during a period of decline, Dio admired Augustus' transformation of Rome from an immoral, conflict-ridden Republic to a peaceful and conservative Principate and empire.[55] His perspective, and his adoration of Augustus, must therefore be taken into consideration when reading this important source.

Cornelius Tacitus, writing from the late first to early second centuries CE, is one of Rome's most famous historians and a significant source for the first century CE. As a member of the Senate during the Principate, Tacitus was concerned with the changes that had taken place with the establishment of hereditary monarchy and the myth of the restoration of the republic. His *Annals* begin in 14 CE, with the death of Augustus, and reflect on how the transition from republic to empire came about, and at what cost. While the chronological focus of the *Annals* lies beyond the scope of this book, Tacitus provides valuable insight into the specifics of priesthoods and ceremonies that remained topics of interest and discussion in his own time. Other historians, such as Sallust, are not included, as their works, although significant sources for the Principate, have little to say about religious reforms.

Aside from the historians, other literary sources abound for the late Republic and early empire, in a variety of forms. Most important to us are the biographies, autobiographies, poems, and writings of statesmen which treat the topics of religion and politics. For the rulers, the most valuable literary sources for the historian are their writings about themselves, as well as the biographies, written in the second century CE by Suetonius (69–after 122 CE). These biographies, written in a thematic rather than chronological fashion, draw from a vast range of sources, unlike the histories, which tend to privilege only one or two. Ronald Mellor has described Suetonius as an "ancestor of the modern scholar" for his meticulous research, wide source base, and his tendency to include direct quotations, in both Greek and Latin, rather than to re-write them in his own style.[56] A contemporary of Suetonius, Plutarch Πλούταρχος (ca. 46–ca. 119 CE), was another important biographer writing in the first century CE. Plutarch's *Parallel Lives* Βίοι Παράλληλοι, juxtaposing the lives of important Greek and Roman men, was an overtly moralising exercise. Like Suetonius, Plutarch carefully researched the careers of his subjects, but was selective about which of their deeds he included, in part to make a more effective comparison, but also to bring to light characteristics of these great men that he thought were worthy of examination by his contemporaries.[57]

The rulers and eminent men also left behind writings about their lives and deeds. Augustus' *Res gestae divi Augusti*, engraved on bronze pillars after his death, provides not only a detailed list of the *princeps*' achievements, but also reveals to the reader what he himself considered to be a great deed, and what he hoped to be remembered for.⁵⁸ This point is important to emphasize, as it is clear that the "great men" of ancient Rome were conscious of their role, and that their lives would be written about. Cicero (Marcus Tullius Cicero, 106–43 BCE) makes this point in reference to Caesar, stating that in writing his commentaries, Caesar's aim was "to furnish others with material for writing history," and influencing how he would be remembered.⁵⁹ Cicero himself likely wrote with a similar idea in mind. As a prolific writer, the statesman and orator wrote with a surety that his works would be not only discussed during his own time, but remain influential in posterity. The Latin poets of the Augustan age and beyond provide valuable insights into festivals and religion during this period. Of particular note are Horace's *Carmen Saeculare*, Ovid's *Fasti*, and Macrobius' *Saturnalia*, which describe sacrifices, festivals, and religious orders in greater detail than the historians. Aulus Gellius' *Attic Nights*, a miscellany from the second century CE, includes some discussion of popular festivals. A final, fundamental, source for this book are the *fasti sacerdotum*, lists of the members of priestly colleges, that have been carefully and painstakingly reconstructed by Jörg Rüpke.

Chapter Outlines

The chapters of this book aim to place the early Chinese and Roman civilizations in as close comparison as possible, however, at times it is necessary to treat the material separately, in order to outline the different religious institutions and their historical evolution. *Imperial Cults* is a work of comparative history, so it is necessary to establish some basic foundations of early Chinese and Roman institutional history in order to provide a level ground for comparison. As such, much of the material in Chapters 2 and 3 may be familiar to the Sinologist or Romanist; specialist readers may choose to focus their attention on the topics with which they are less familiar. Chapters 4, 5, 6, and 7, which form the core of this study, place the changes made to religious institutions in comparison, and discuss the ways in which new imperial messages were shaped and publicized in China and Rome. The conclusion turns to look at the longevity and legacy of the transformation of religious institutions and the role of the rulers in each society. Unless otherwise indicated, translations of Chinese sources are my own; translations from Greek and Roman sources are taken from the Loeb Classical Library editions, unless otherwise noted.

Chapter 2, "Transitions to Empire in Early China and Rome," provides an overview of the historical development of the early Chinese and Roman states, up to the time of Emperor Wu and Augustus, respectively. Here we establish the ground for the comparisons made in later chapters by discussing the difficulties in each society in establishing an empire united under the rule of one man. In early China, although the principles of hereditary monarchy had long been established, until the Qin unification in 221 BCE, the lands of the Central States 中國 were ruled as independent kingdoms over a 250-year period of internecine warfare aptly named the Warring States Period (*zhanguo* 戰國 475–221 BCE). The short-lived Qin Empire (秦 221–207 BCE) briefly unified these independent states under the centralized authority of the former king of Qin, who adopted a new imperial title, proclaiming himself the First August Emperor of Qin (Qin Shi Huangdi 秦始皇帝).[60] Following the collapse of the Qin, the Han empire was established, but the founding emperor, Han Gaozu (漢高祖 nee. Liu Bang 劉邦 r. 206–195 BCE) did not wield full authority over his empire. Rather, he allotted kingdoms and commanderies to be governed by members of the royal family and loyal followers. Over the years, these kings and regional lords began to assert more and more autonomy from the central government, resulting, at times, in open rebellion. By the time of Emperor Wu, while much of this resistance had been suppressed, the central government did not have full bureaucratic control over the empire, and, moreover, it faced an external threat from the seminomadic Xiongnu 匈奴 confederation on the northwest border. Emperor Wu's ambition, as uncontested hereditary ruler, was to assume full authority over his empire and defeat the external threat.

The situation in Rome was almost the exact opposite: the central authority of the city of Rome was all but undisputed throughout the Mediterranean by the time of the late Republic, but the rule of one man was anathema to the ruling elite. Although the ancient city of Rome had been ruled by a series of kings—seven, to be precise—the tyrannical nature of the last kings resulted in their overthrow and expulsion in 509 BCE by the Roman elite, and with the downfall of the kings, royal authority was divided amongst elected officials, who shared power over one-year terms, so that Rome could never again fall under the rule of one man. The elected officials of Rome were generals as well as politicians and had to prove themselves both in battle and in civic duty, by advancing through the *cursus honorum* before being able to stand as candidate for the highest elected office, the consulship. The republican balance of power, lauded by ancient historians and early modern republicans alike, began to break down in the second century BCE, and power was contested between individual men and their cliques. This culminated in the civil war of the first century BCE, and Julius Caesar's rise to the position of dictator for life (*dictator perpetuo*) in 44 BCE. The political system was thrown into chaos after the assassination of Caesar (also in 44 BCE), and by the time Octavian Augustus, Caesar's heir, emerged victorious, the Roman political system lay in shambles. Augustus' ambition, then, was to become the sole ruler of Rome without appearing to do so. As we shall see in subsequent chapters, the different nature of the challenges facing Augustus and Emperor Wu required that they concentrate their efforts in different places: Augustus' efforts are primarily concentrated within the city of Rome, while Emperor Wu travelled across his empire, and spent comparatively little time in his capital at Chang'an 長安. This is not to say that Augustus did not make efforts to promote his authority in the provinces, nor that Emperor Wu did not care about his capital, simply that these efforts were not as closely connected to religious affairs.[61]

Chapter 3 discusses the salient features of the history of religious institutions in early China and Rome. In pre-imperial China, the chapter looks at the evolution of practices of imperial cult, where the emperor himself worshipped or ordered sacrifices, from the early state of Qin up to the time of Emperor Wu, following the history of these state sacrifices as outlined in our main source for the period, the *Shiji* "Treatise on the *feng* and *shan* Sacrifices" 封禪書. While our understanding of imperial cult in early China is heavily influenced by Sima Qian's portrayal of it, we can see how the cult practices of the Han followed from those established by the Qin in the early years of their state. The chapter demonstrates that, while Emperor Wu's expansion of imperial cult may have been unprecedented in scale, it followed precedent established by Qin and earlier Han rulers and therefore should perhaps not be considered as anomalous as it often is. Turning to Rome, we shall see how the relationship between Roman citizens and their gods was mediated by priests, organized into priestly colleges. With some exceptions, priesthood was not a full-time job; Roman priests, generally chosen from the same elite class as the magistrates, were active members of the political community, often holding magistracies or belonging to the Senate in conjunction with their priesthood. Membership in a priestly college was for life and granted the priests access to specialized knowledge concerning the gods and their relationship with the state. The priests could be called upon to advise the Senate and could therefore use their position to influence affairs of state. Membership in the colleges was limited, and so the priesthoods became another source of elite competition and patronage. In his "revival" of traditional Republican religion, Augustus focused his attention on the priestly colleges, and they became an important source of influence for him. Conspicuously absent from this chapter, and those that follow, is any discussion of the divinization of emperors, or the worship of the cult of the emperor. While Emperor Wu fervently pursued immortality and Augustus did little to prevent the worship of his person outside of the city of Rome, emperor worship was, at the period under discussion, less important to each emperor's immediate goals of centralizing authority.

Chapter 4, "Reshaping Religious Institutions," looks at the structural and personnel changes made by Emperor Wu and Augustus. Significantly, it finds that in expanding cult (Emperor Wu) and reviving neglected religious institutions (Augustus), both rulers surrounded themselves with "new men." In the Han case, these were the *fangshi* 方士, masters of esoteric arts, who flocked to the emperor to offer him instruction on the transmutation of cinnabar to gold, the secrets to immortal life, and the sacrifices that needed to be performed to attain it. The traditional reading of the relationship between these men and the emperor is that they manipulated him into following their advice for profit, without being able to deliver on any of their promises of immortality. In this chapter, I argue instead that while some of the *fangshi* certainly attempted to trick the emperor, Emperor Wu chose whose advice to follow based on his own agenda. Meanwhile, in Rome, Augustus "revived" the priestly colleges which had been all but emptied of members during the period of civil wars. He made himself a member of each college, an unprecedented move at the time, and co-opted new priests from among his followers. Chapter 5, "Expanding Influence," turns to look at how both rulers used their newly structured institutions to expand their authority; Emperor Wu expanded his cult across the empire, incorporating important spiritual locations into the imperial sacrificial programme, and thus assuming authority over them. In Rome, Augustus transformed the balance of power among the priestly colleges, elevating the college of *quindecimviri*, formerly a minor college, over the two most powerful, the *pontifices* and *augures*. The *quindecimiviri* would ultimately organize and preside over the largest ceremony of state, the *ludi saeculares*, discussed in Chapter 7, but most importantly, the college became an important political forum, and recruitment into the college, with the patronage of Augustus, placed one in good stead for a successful political career. Through these institutional changes, both rulers placed themselves at the centre of all cult activity, declaring their own authority over religious knowledge and access to the gods and spirits.

Chapter 6, "Communicating Imperial Authority," shows the ways in which Augustus and Emperor Wu communicated the message of their authority to the people. Again, our focus in Rome is on the city itself, while in the Han, the emperor's activities took place primarily outside of the capital. Drawing on ritual and architectural theory, this chapter demonstrates that through inspection tours (in the Han) and public building (in Rome), the two rulers were able to simultaneously announce their positions of power and to forestall any popular resistance against their rule. In the Han, Emperor Wu's inspection tours, echoing the practices of the sage kings of antiquity, had him travel across the empire, visiting important spiritual locations, offering sacrifices, and establishing shrines. While the emperor would not have been visible to all but a few elite, his presence was made known, as the tours and sacrifices were accompanied with gifts and amnesties, freeing local populations from taxation and labour services. These benefits not only informed the population of the munificence of the emperor but also encouraged them to cooperate with the state. In Rome, Augustus engaged in a campaign of public building on both large and small scales. Famously, he transformed the city of Rome into a city of marble, building and rebuilding temples and preventing other elite from contributing to the architecture of the city of Rome. Less noted is the sponsorship and erection of shrines throughout the city of Rome, shrines that were patronized by people of all classes, rather than just the elite. These local shrines were eventually woven into a network of shrines, and they came to share a name with the *princeps*. The *lares augusti* were one of the ways in which Augustus spread his influence and ensured that he had the loyalty and support of the citizens of Rome.

Chapter 7, "Redefining Ceremony," turns to look at the sacrifices and ceremonies performed by Emperor Wu and Augustus. This chapter focuses on the most important sacrifices and ceremonies and discusses the ways in which each ruler shaped their sacrifices and ceremonies in order to convey the message of their exalted positions. Through their performances, the emperors announced their new authority to both gods and men. In the Han, we will look at the expansion or creation of sacrifices to the High Gods (*Shangdi* 上帝), Great Unity (*Taiyi* 太一), and Sovereign Earth (*Houtu* 后土). Following the advice of the *fangshi*, Emperor Wu sacrificed to the highest spirits of Heaven and Earth in the hopes that he might bring peace to the empire and, through so doing, achieve personal immortality. The cults that he created drew upon local and foreign traditions, and demonstrated the emperor's access to spirits throughout the empire. In Rome, Augustus revived ceremonies that had purportedly fallen into disuse. These ceremonies, the Augury of Safety, the Lupercalia, and the Compitalia, had long histories in the Republic, and were shaped by cultural memory. Augustus' revival of these ceremonies was much more of a transformation; writing a new script that celebrated the new Augustan order. The final section of the chapter compares two spectacular ceremonies in the Han and Rome: the *feng* 封 and *shan* 禪 sacrifices and *ludi saeculares*. Through these ceremonies, the rulers ushered in a golden age, which was only made possible by their unprecedented authority.

In the conclusion, we will return to examine the comparative approach, as well as to examine the legacies of these rulers' reforms, as they had very different trajectories. Augustus' reforms were largely successful—his heir, Tiberius, was also a member of each of the priestly colleges and assumed the same honours and responsibilities as his adoptive father. The Julio-Claudian dynasty lasted only into the first century CE, but the emperorship lasted much longer, and many of the religious traditions established by Augustus continued. The system of imperial cult practiced by Emperor Wu, however, did not last long beyond his reign. During the early Eastern Han dynasty (25—220 CE), the lavish sacrifices that required the emperor to travel on lengthy journeys outside of the capital were abolished, and sacrifices to Heaven were firmly established in the suburbs of the capital—henceforth the spirits would travel to the emperor and not he to the spirits. While at first glance it may appear as though Emperor Wu's reforms failed while Augustus' succeeded, the conclusion will suggest that it was not quite so simple, and that both rulers were subject to external factors which impacted the longevity of their religious reforms.

2
Transitions to Empire in Early China and Rome

Concerned with the examination of similar processes in the formation of empire in the Han and Rome, this monograph is primarily focused on the "parallel lives" of Augustus and Han Emperor Wu, though some attention will be paid to their political forebears, Julius Caesar and the First Emperor. The reason for this choice requires some explanation, due to the generational gap between Emperor Wu and the First Emperor, Qin Shi Huang, and why I see Emperor Wu as the parallel to Augustus rather than the founding emperor of Han, Han Gaozu. The comparison of great rulers from Han and Rome has become an increasingly popular topic, with recent studies comparing the First Emperor with either Julius Caesar or Augustus.[1] In the realm of imperial cult, however, there is a much stronger connection to be made between Augustus and Emperor Wu, and, within the process of the consolidation of imperial power, it is Emperor Wu, rather than Han Gaozu, who is the heir to the First Emperor's vision of ruling All under Heaven, just as Augustus completed the transformation from Republic to Empire in Rome.[2] Augustus and Emperor Wu faced different sets of problems in consolidating their rule: for Julius Caesar and Augustus, Roman authority over the conquered territories was rarely disputed, however the rule of one man was much derided. For the First Emperor and Emperor Wu, although a monarchical system had long been the norm, the unity of territory under the capital was, for the First Emperor, a recent achievement, and during the reigns of the early Han emperors, significant parts of the empire were ruled by the regional lords and kings (*zhuhou wang* 諸侯王).[3] Despite these differences, the steps taken by the early emperors, especially in the realms of imperial cult and religious ideology, were remarkably similar. It is thus necessary to present the broad contours of the historical background to the imperial project in early China and Rome.

From Republic to Empire in Rome

Rome was not the only Mediterranean state that was belligerent, or capable of fielding a large army, but it eventually came to dominate the Mediterranean world, less due to its military superiority, as the long and protracted wars and sometimes ruinous defeats indicate, than due to its "ability to assimilate outsiders and to create a large and stable territorial hegemony."[4] For much of the Roman Republic, this incorporation was accomplished by granting citizenship (initially without enfranchisement) to the conquered peoples, while Roman culture gradually spread, allowing for closer cultural ties between Rome and its conquered territories.[5] It was not only Rome's territorial empire that was built on continual expansion; elite politics were tied to this process of conquest, and aristocrats achieved political success through military conquests.[6] The highest office in the Roman Republic, the consulship, was in large part a military office, granting the consul *imperium* over an army, as well as a designated sphere of engagement (*provincia*), awarded to them by the Senate.[7] The Senate, comprised of ex-magistrates, was an advisory body, which not only determined the theatres in which each consul would operate and which provinces would be given to magistrates to administer, but most importantly, controlled the state's finances. Ultimately, however, the election of magistrates and the passing of laws had to be voted on by "the people," a complicated political term, which broadly referred to the male citizens of Rome.[8] Such was the idealization of the Roman Republic in its last years—a state built on conquest, with an equal division of powers, and a constitution relatively unchanged from the expulsion of the kings in 509 BCE. While the idea of an unchanging Republic has been thoroughly refuted by modern scholarship, particularly the work of Harriet Flower, this is the concept that was accepted in later times.[9]

The vision of an unchanging Roman Republic, with its division of powers between the Consuls, the Senate, and the People, is most clearly expressed in Polybius's second century BCE account of Rome's "mixed constitution." Polybius describes the constitution of the Roman Republic to be equal parts monarchic (the consuls), aristocratic (the Senate), and democratic (the people), such that "it was impossible even for a native to pronounce with certainty whether the whole system was aristocratic, democratic, or monarchical."[10] Despite what Polybius described as a fair distribution of power, while there were limitations on the power of any one individual or group in the republican period, the system, from its earliest days, favoured the aristocracy, and the Roman state was much more an oligarchy than a democracy.[11] Indeed, although all male citizens were granted a vote, "the value of an individual citizen's vote depended on his social status, not only formally, but also in the actual practice of voting,"[12] due in large part to the structure of the voting system.[13] Roman politics was thus primarily a sphere of elite competition, and the changes that occurred in politics were largely due to opposing ideas about what elite power should look like.[14]

With the conflicts, violence, and period of multiple reforms in the second-half of the second century BCE, the republican system of a balance of power had begun to break down, paving the way for the Sullan reforms of the first century BCE, which dramatically limited the power of the people.[15] Sulla (Lucius Cornelius Sulla Felix 138–78 BCE), in his role as dictator, attempted to increase the power of the Senate and reduce the power of popular assemblies. While this new republican system lasted only a decade after its implementation, Sulla's usurpation of extraordinary powers through force set a precedent for the turbulent years which followed.[16] The decades from the 70s to the 50s saw a further breakdown of divisions of power, and the increase in the power of individual generals or small political cliques.[17] According to Flower, republican politics had effectively stopped functioning around 60 BCE,[18] and the decade of the 50s should no longer be considered to be a republic,[19] as the balance of powers so admired by Polybius had almost completely disintegrated. The middle of the first century was characterised by the consuls enacting supreme power over the state, in matters of both internal and external policy,[20] and throughout the 50s, there were many elections which failed to take place.[21] The last years of the decade would be marked by increasing violence, and conflicts between increasingly powerful magistrates.

The last century of the Roman Republic was characterised by the politicization of the office of consul and the dominance of a few key men, notably Sulla, Pompey (Gaius Pompeius Magnus, 106–48 BCE), and Julius Caesar. After the reforms of the Sullan era, it became common for the consul to remain in Rome for their year of office, and only to assume a military campaign after their consulship.[22] The amount of legislation introduced by consuls in this era increased, along with consular "intervention in senatorial debates, their support for or opposition to certain legislative initiatives, [and] their active participation in courts."[23] As such, the consuls began to take power into their own hands, and we see an increase in consular speeches, edicts, and legislature in the late Republic.[24] This was exemplified in the concentration of power in men like Pompey and Caesar, who not only had much support within elite circles at Rome, also had the support of large numbers of troops. The destabilisation and concentration of power continued, until the outbreak of civil war in 49 BCE, and the appointment of Caesar as dictator in 46.[25]

While several men had been angling for position and had taken on extraordinary powers, it was only Caesar who indicated that he had no intention of giving up those powers. He was appointed dictator in 46 BCE for a ten-year term, and given the title *dictator perpetuo* (dictator in perpetuity) in 44 BCE.[26] During this period, Caesar was given enormous honours and privileges, not all of which he accepted, including the naming of both a month and a tribe after him, public sacrifices on his birthday, and the post of censor for life.[27] The historian Dio Cassius suggests that some of these honours were bestowed upon him to make him look ridiculous, or that through these honours it was hoped that the people would come to hate him and thus bring about his downfall, yet ultimately it was his attitude towards republican institutions that brought about the most hatred. Although he had taken on these supreme honours, what provoked the most ire amongst his opponents was his flagrant disregard for the election of magistrates (on several occasions he appointed them at his will, and several years in advance), and his disrespect towards the Senate, particularly when he failed to stand when they came to him with honorary decrees in front of the temple of Venus Genetrix.[28] Animosity towards the dictator reached a breaking point, and Caesar was assassinated on the Ides of March, 44 BCE.[29]

The aftermath of the assassination resulted in yet another protracted struggle for power, with changing alliances, military campaigns, and assassinations, but ultimately, Caesar's heir, Augustus, emerged victorious, and in January of 29 BCE, closed the gates to the temple of Janus, signalling the end of the civil war.[30] In 29 BCE, the elite of Rome had been engaged in factional struggles for decades, and these long periods of disturbance had taken their toll on the people of Rome. After Caesar's assassination, and the wars which followed, a functioning Republic was nothing more than a memory, albeit a very powerful one, and the Roman political system was in disarray. What Augustus thus had to achieve was a way to make his sole rule palatable to those who still wanted to uphold the traditional republican balance of power, which, as we will see, was in many respects the opposite problem from his Han counterpart.[31]

All under Heaven in Early China

The trajectory to empire in early China was significantly different from that of Rome. While the Roman state could be understood as those areas which were conquered by, or submitted to, Roman armies and were administered by Rome, the Chinese case was far more complicated. In early China there was not the same idea of the need for "municipal self-government on the basis of civic freedom"[32] that linked together the diverse parts of the Roman empire. Rather, understandings of a unified China in this period are usually expressed in cultural, rather than political, terms. The Chinese cultural sphere is usually conceived based on a group's participation in the Zhou ritual system. The Zhou (周 1046–256 BCE), having conquered the Shang Dynasty (商 c. 1600–1046 BCE) in 1046 BCE, established nominal control over the central plains, and created a system whereby areas were ruled autonomously by rulers related to the royal household, but who paid ritual respect to the Zhou king. In the early years of the Western Zhou, this *fengjian* 封建 system, which granted territories to relatives of the royal family and others, worked quite effectively in the Zhou heartland, regulated as it was through an elaborate bureaucratic system.[33] By the mid-Western Zhou, as the court of the king began to lose control over the regional lords, other solutions were needed. This resulted in what Lothar von Falkenhausen has termed the "Late Western Zhou Ritual Reform" of ca. 850 BCE.[34] The ritual reform is primarily seen through the standardization of sets of bronze ritual vessels, which corresponded to one's rank, and signified the owner's relationship with the Zhou court.[35] Significantly in this reform, ownership of these vessels was not defined according to one's relationship with the ruling family, but according to one's position within the administrative system. As such, so-called "barbarians"—people from outside of the traditional culture sphere, could use Zhou vessels, provided they adopted the system wholesale.[36] The concept of what constituted the *Hua* 華, members of the culture sphere, and what constituted All under Heaven (*tian xia* 天下) was thus predicated on participation in a shared cultural system, rather than allegiance to a particular state or system of government, as in Rome. Early Chinese writings on "barbarians" as being outside of the cultural sphere reinforce this vision of cultural unity, and it was the ideal of cultural unity which endured throughout the period of division.[37]

While the Western Zhou was often seen as a golden age, it was one which did not last. The Western Zhou fell to the so-called "barbarians" in 771 BCE, abandoned their capital, and fled east, to the new capital at Luoyang 洛陽. This ushered in the Spring and Autumn (*chunqiu* 春秋 771–475 BCE) and Warring States (475–221 BCE) periods: periods of steadily intensifying internecine warfare which lasted until the Qin unification in 221 BCE. During these five and a half centuries, rulers autonomously governed their own states and the Zhou kings, while still residing at Luoyang, had little to no authority over their former fiefs. While the rulers of regional states were autonomous in their own regions, they ruled through powers that had been invested in them by the Zhou king, and it was understood that the king could remove the ruler from power, if he failed to provide military support or keep his state in order. The Zhou king could (and sometimes did) interfere in succession in these states.[38] However, with the collapse of the Zhou, what authority the king did have over the regional states quickly disappeared, and, beginning in 344 BCE regional rulers began to adopt the title king (*wang* 王) for themselves, marking their complete independence from the Zhou king. Over the course of the Spring and Autumn and Warring States periods, these regional states were ruled as autonomous units, fighting amongst each other, creating alliances, and securing their own territory and political systems.[39] These two periods are notable for a number of major transformations in the early Chinese political system. Over this long period, power shifted from being divided by the ruler and his family, who were often employed as his advisors, to being consolidated in the hands of a single ruler, who employed ministers to aid in governing.[40] The Warring States period saw the development of seven states each ruled by kings and their officials, which employed mass peasant armies and had their own bureaucratic institutions. This was a time of intense literary production and increased social mobility, as men of talent sought to secure employment at a court.[41] These seven states each developed their own systems of governance and competed amongst each other to recruit the best talent to help them rule.[42]

While there had been constant internecine warfare throughout the period, it was only in the mid-third century that the state of Qin, located in the far west, began a systematic program of conquest that would ultimately defeat and unite the other states in 221 BCE. The Spring and Autumn and Warring States periods are often referred to by scholars as "periods of division" with the implication that this division was somehow anomalous, and that the natural tendency of the states in the Central Plains was towards unity.[43] However, the reality facing the First Emperor of Qin, and later Han

Gaozu and Emperor Wu, was that these states had long been divided and accustomed to independent governance.

The Qin state, given its secure position in the west, had several geographical advantages over the other states. With the conquest of Shu 蜀 and Ba 巴 in 316 BCE, the Qin had access to the fertile Sichuan basin, which greatly facilitated Qin's ability to conduct long campaigns against the other states.[44] The Qin made important reforms in legal and administrative areas which gave them a stronger centralized administration,[45] and they conquered the six states in rapid succession between 230 and 221 BCE, quickly implementing an administrative system to govern the newly conquered territories. The First Emperor adopted a new temple to be used by his imperial house in perpetuity, while replicas of the palaces of the rulers of the former states were built along the Wei River 渭河, perhaps, as Mark Edward Lewis has argued, to create a microcosm of the empire at his capital.[46] The rulers of the former states were also moved to the capital at Xianyang 咸陽, to prevent future rebellion by removing them from their areas of influence.[47] Despite these achievements, and the First Emperor's proclamation that he had built an empire that would last ten thousand years,[48] the Qin Empire fell almost as quickly as it had been established, and the states of the central plain once again descended into civil war.

The reasons for the demise of the Qin are numerous. Following Han historical accounts, many have attributed their fall to overly harsh laws, punishments, and taxation, as well as the repudiation of tradition.[49] Especially during the reign of the Second Emperor, Er Shi 二世 (229–207 BCE; r. 210–207), pressure on the peasants was huge, and there was no regulation of court spending. The Qin had overextended themselves in attempting to rapidly assimilate these politically independent states that had developed their own administrative and cultural traditions, and in the rebellions that followed the death of the First Emperor, many of the rebels had close ties to the former ruling families of the Warring States. While the First Emperor made some attempts to culturally integrate the states, he ultimately failed to do so, and his unified empire did not long outlast his death. The task of cultural and territorial integration would fall eventually to the Han, and in particular, Emperor Wu.[50]

After emerging victorious in the civil war following the end of the Qin, the Han founder, Han Gaozu, needed to create a system that would both unite the fragmented empire and reward his supporters. The Han system was thus a combination of the Qin and Zhou models—a centralized imperial bureaucracy, inherited from the Qin, with a supreme ruler at the centre, but a territory divided into semiautonomous kingdoms, to be ruled by Liu Bang's family and allies, and commanderies, which were under the administration of the capital.[51] Throughout the years of the early Han, there were conflicts between the kingdoms and capital, and the kingdoms resisted attempts to limit their power and incorporate them into the central administration. The most notable of these, the Rebellion of the Seven Kingdoms in 154 BCE, during the reign of Emperor Jing 景帝 (r. 157–141), was a direct response to attempts made by the emperor to reduce the size of the kingdoms.[52] The Han successfully defeated the rebellion, and the failure of this rebellion limited the power of the regional kings.[53] This process of limiting the power of the kings begun under Emperor Jing would be continued by Emperor Wu, under whose reign "the last significant opposition to the centralized power was quashed."[54] The empire inherited by Emperor Wu was one teetering between centralization and fragmentation. While the elite of the Han were not opposed to monarchism, as were the *nobiles* of Rome, there was periodic, but fierce resistance to the spread of centralized administration throughout the lands formally part of the Han Empire, where cultural diversity inhibited unification. While military force was often required to wipe out resistance and enforce policy, these were not the only factors contributing to Emperor Wu's successes in centralizing the Han.

Empire, Convergence, and Divergence

After this discussion of the different trajectories of the Han and Roman Empires, and of the different goals of their rulers, it becomes necessary to distinguish what we mean by "empire" for these ancient states. While the term is commonly employed for the Qin, Han, and Rome, "empire" is also used to describe a variety of historical states as well as contemporary empires that transcend the boundary of the state—economic, corporate, or media empires, to name but a few. As the term has been used to describe so many diverse entities, it has come to encapsulate a number of different characteristics, making definition difficult. It is tempting to classify these different "empires" under what Kathleen Morrison has described as the "pornography definition": "I can't say what they are, but I know one when I see one,"[55] yet for the empires of the ancient world, some common ground can be found on which to base a comparative analysis. The early empires of Rome and China provided "long-lasting reference points for later empire-builders,"[56] and while their governing institutions differed greatly, they share a number of characteristics with each other, as well as with later empires in world history. Jane Burbank and Frederick Cooper have argued that, while empires are not all alike, there are several properties that are common to all. First, empires incorporate "diverse peoples into the polity while sustaining or making distinctions among them."[57] This lack of homogeneity amongst the population is one of the defining characteristics of an empire,[58] and sets it in contrast to nation-states, which define themselves according to the self-rule of a, mostly homogenous, group of people.[59] Empires are also expansionist, or, at least, have a "memory of power extended over space"[60] and they develop through interactions with others—either with newly incorporated peoples with different cultural norms, or with other empires at their borders: the "intersection of empires provoked competition, imitation, and innovation."[61] Empires also create, adopt, and transmit "various repertoires of rule"[62]—the different strategies employed by the rulers as they incorporate these disparate groups of people, and seek to create their own imperial identity.

In the case of the Qin, Han, and Rome, these empires were unlike what had come before. This is made explicit in the Chinese case, while in Rome the transition to empire was completed under the pretext of a revival of tradition. This is most visible in the adoption of new titles by the early ruler: the First Emperor's adoption of the title *huangdi* 皇帝 "August Celestial Deity" ranked him above his former title of "King" *wang* 王, and marked his reign and accomplishments as something new and glorious. Augustus, in adding the title *imperator* to his newly chosen name, demonstrated his authority to command, both outside and in the city of Rome. According to Robin D. S. Yates, the imperial design of the Qin placed the emperor at the centre of a cosmographic and cosmologic system, which helped to develop the association of empire in China "with the person of the emperor, his activities, and his patrilineal ancestral line."[63] While the Chinese had a long history of inherited power, the creation of a lineage of Caesars was a new development in Rome, beginning with Caesar's adoption of Octavian (the future Augustus), and further solidified by the use of "Caesar" as a surname, and ultimately a fundamental part of the imperial title.[64]

In both of these cases, while the empire was ruled by an emperor (though the title "emperor" was not in use in Rome in the period under discussion), he was supported by, and often in conflict with, elites at his court, and in addition to attempts made to consolidate authority over newly incorporated territories, the emperors often also struggled to consolidate their authority at court. Whether or not overt attempts towards cultural homogeneity were made, in these early empires, there was a general tendency towards the adoption of an imperial culture throughout the empire.[65] In Rome, this imperial culture was defined according to the *mos maiorum* of the *populus Romanus*, the citizens of Rome, in contrast to the noncitizen subjects.[66] Imperial culture spread through the bestowal of citizenship on groups within the empire, but also through the emulation of the capital elites by the provincial elites.[67] In the Qin and Han empires, imperial culture was created, in part, by the patterning of the empire on the cosmos, in accordance with the cycle of five phases, and this imperial culture was written onto the laws, lands, and bodies of the people.[68] However, imperial culture was not unchanging, and in the process of creating an imperial ideology, these empires adopted much from outside of the rulers' own cultural backgrounds and incorporated ideas and beliefs from the disparate populations under their control.

While both the Han and Rome share these features of empire, they also diverge in a number of fundamental ways. It is by no means my contention that these societies or their systems of governance were identical, simply that there are sufficient grounds, in terms of their basic identities as empires, to warrant comparison. In terms of their political and administrative structures, not to mention their cultural systems, the two polities are substantially different. As we have seen earlier in this chapter, they differ in their basic political constitutions: the early Chinese had a long history of hereditary monarchy, and while elaborate administrative systems grew with the expansion of states in the periods prior to the formation of the first empire, there was no real question of who had ultimate authority, nor was there direct participation by the people in the decisions of government.[69] In Rome the idea of popular participation was fundamental to the legitimacy of the government, as was the principle that power should not be held by any one man for a lengthy period of time. The role of the people, and of the ruler's relationship to the people, stands as one of the main differences between the two societies: in Rome, political and religious action was always public, and it was necessary for the elite to present themselves to the people; in the Qin and Han, the emperor did not have a public role in front of the masses, and, unlike his Roman counterpart, his performance of the most important religious ceremonies was in front of a very limited audience. In the discussions that follow of the role of the emperor in religious ceremonies and institutions, this difference will be of fundamental importance.

Despite these two very different histories, as part of their creation of imperial ideology, in both empires, the rulers and historians invoked a golden age of the past—for Augustus, this was the heyday of the Roman Republic, while under Emperor Wu, a connection was made with the legendary sage-kings of antiquity, particularly the time of the Yellow Thearch 黃帝. The insistence that the new imperial order was based on a glorious historical precedent influenced the ways in which the rulers spoke about their regimes and their practices: for Augustus, this meant a "return" to traditional Roman *mores* and the "revival" of ancient religious festivals, and for Emperor Wu, a wholesale expansion of imperial cult that spanned the empire, modelled, in part, on his understanding of the actions of the sage kings of antiquity. In both cases, as we will see, elements of these "golden-age" narratives were created during the early empires, in order to lend support to contemporary practices. In both societies, literary culture and written records played a large role in how these "golden ages" were remembered, and the writers of the period contributed to the shaping of each ruler's reforms to religious institutions.

3
State Cult in Early China and Rome

At first glance, it seems there is very little to compare between the religious traditions of early China and Rome, and, as discussed in the Introduction, there are many dangers in attempting to force such a comparison. This chapter will therefore not attempt to compare the religions of early China and Rome in terms of their systems of belief, or to offer a comprehensive overview of the various religious practices in early China and Rome; rather it offers an overview of the religious institutions that were of most importance to the state and particularly those that were closely connected to ruling authority. As a result, the religious practices and experiences of the common people are not considered. The people, broadly defined, were certainly participants in many of these cults and had many other religious practices which we will not consider here.

Of central interest in both societies was how the spirits could be entreated to enrich the good of the state. Roman religion was clearly articulated as maintaining the *pax deorum*, so a variety of sacrifices were made to nourish the spirits, thank them for their assistance, or to expiate a slight. Temples were vowed to gods if they would assist a general in battle, and then constructed following a victory. In this way, not only did the people benefit from the protection of the gods in the form of a strong state, but they also benefited from the tangible benefits that came from new neighbourhood temples: improved infrastructure, sacrificial ceremonies, and the construction of a civic identity.[1] While not as explicitly concerned with the general good, the religious practices of early Chinese rulers also served to benefit the people. As Poo Mu-chou has argued, and discussed in the following section, early Chinese religion was concerned with "personal welfare"—the benefit that religious rites could bring to the individual.[2] However, in the case of imperial worship, what was good for the sovereign was good for the people. Perhaps best viewed as a form of trickle-down blessing, the sacrifices offered by the sovereign in early China were performed for the benefit of the sovereign, but it was to the sovereigns benefit to have a prosperous, peaceful empire. Likewise, if ill omens, such as droughts, earthquakes, or pestilences, were sent from

Imperial Cults. Rebecca Robinson, Oxford University Press. © Oxford University Press 2023.
DOI: 10.1093/oso/9780197666043.003.0003

Heaven, the emperor would need to offer expiatory sacrifices. A healthy population makes for a happy sovereign.

Characteristics of Imperial Cult in Early China

Imperial cult in early China followed loose outlines rather than strict rules. The topic of where and when the emperor should worship was the subject of a major debate in the post–Emperor Wu years, and it was only during the reign of Emperor Cheng 成帝 (r. 33–7 BCE) that the structure of imperial worship began to settle into a more concrete form which remained in place throughout the Eastern Han.[3] Prior to reforms in the Eastern Han, religion in the pre- and early-Han period was a moving target, both literally and figuratively, as the imperial sacrifices sometimes caused the emperor to travel to sacred sites across his realm, and what was included in the corpus of state sacrifices changed frequently, with new cults being added and others disbanded. Sarah Queen and John Major have described imperially sponsored religion in the early Western Han as "confused and somewhat chaotic,"[4] as there was no real structure to cult practice in this time. The term "imperial" (or official) cult refers in this monograph not only to the worship of deities who were literally "out of this world," as many of the spirits to whom the Qin and Han emperors paid tribute were immortals who were believed to inhabit the same terrestrial plane. "Imperial cult" is defined as any cult patronized by the emperor or worshipped on his instruction.[5] These cults changed somewhat with each emperor, and while some were maintained after the death of an individual emperor, others were abandoned. Poo Mu-chou has noted the flexibility of imperial cult during this period: "[w]hat distinguished an 'official' from an 'unofficial' cult was not the deities worshipped, but whether or not it was supported by the court."[6] The worship of imperial cult changed with each ruler, depending on their own personal interest in the extrahuman world. Emperor Wu, as the ruler who displayed the most interest in cult, built his programme of worship on earlier foundations, while also adding his own innovations. The imperially sponsored cult was not the exclusive prerogative of the emperor—while the *feng* sacrifice could only be performed by the emperor, the cults under his sponsorship were maintained by sacrificial officials, and many others pursued immortality and other cults on the advice of religious experts. The state by no means had a monopoly over either religion or sacrificial practice, though it did at times attempt to moderate sacrifices and ancestral worship through sumptuary regulations.[7] However, Emperor

Wu's personal interest in religion meant that imperial cult was a topic of renewed discussion, and his decisions as to where and when to offer sacrifice had an impact on the structure of power at the Han court. Emperor Wu's cult programme, as well as earlier cult practice, are described by Sima Qian in the "Treatise on the *feng* and *shan* Sacrifices," and it is in this chapter that Sima Qian reconstructs the history of state-sponsored cult from antiquity to his own time, attempting to assemble the earlier, incoherent practices into a cohesive linear history.

Sima Qian's investigation of historical cults may have been a part of his duties as the Grand Scribe, as he advised Emperor Wu in shaping his own religious practices. Sima Qian, and his father before him, were among those responsible for advising the emperor on how to perform the sacrifices of state, necessitating a knowledge of how previous rulers had performed these rites. As many of the most important sacrifices were of such antiquity that records of them were lost, or may have never existed, the sacrificial procedures had to be created or recreated by scholars at court. While some of these reconstructions, particularly those of the Qin-era *feng* and *shan* sacrifices, may have been an invention of Sima Qian, we must not entirely discount them as a work of fiction.[8] The pre-Qin information contained in Sima Qian's chapter is valuable to us not because it gives us a completely accurate picture of sacrifices made by rulers and kings in the ancient periods, which it does not, but because it demonstrates what the scholars, officials, and emperors of the Han thought about pre-Qin sacrifice. While the *Shiji* narrative proceeds chronologically, it primarily focuses on three important types of sacrifices, or cult activity, that were deemed most important to the imperial cult by Sima Qian. These three, the sacrificial tours, worship of the High Gods at Yong, and the *feng* and *shan* sacrifices, were also the three areas that most interested Emperor Wu. Many of the details in the history of the *feng* and *shan* sacrifices are considered by many, myself included, to have been largely an invention of Sima Qian, and these will be dealt with in detail in Chapter 7. Here, we will briefly examine the histories of the inspection tours and the sacrifices at Yong up to the time of Emperor Wu.

The system of sacrifices from antiquity that Sima Qian held in highest regard was that of Shun. Following the "Shun Dian" 舜典 chapter in the *Documents* (*shu* 書),[9] Sima Qian writes that Shun observed the movement of the cosmic bodies using a jewelled-astronomical instrument (*xuanji* 璿璣). He made special offerings to the Six Honoured Ones (*liu zong* 六宗), the mountains and rivers, and various other groups of spirits.[10] By announcing auspicious days of the sun and moon, he supervised the Regional Lords of the four directions. Shun also embarked on an inspection tour (*xun shou* 巡守) once every five years. On these tours, he sacrificed to the mountains and rivers, and in each location he observed the regional lords and ensured that in All under Heaven, the seasons, months, days, pitch-pipes, measures, and rites were harmonized.[11] Shun was succeeded by Yu 禹, and others who continued to maintain this schedule of sacrifices and tours, but over time, subsequent rulers became increasingly bereft of morals, and the rituals of these rulers became progressively marked by licentious ingenuity rather than sacrificial decorum, until they were replaced by another ruling house.

Sima Qian sees the continuation of Shun's sacrificial system in the rulers of the early Western Zhou, established by the Duke of Zhou 周公, the regent of the young King Cheng 周成王 (r. ca. 1042–1021 BCE). During this time, "the way of the king was in great harmony, rituals were regulated and music was composed" 王道大洽，制禮作樂.[12] The sacrifices were used by the king to communicate with heaven, and all within the four seas contributed, according to their offices, to the sacrificial program. The Son of Heaven sacrificed to the great mountains and rivers and brought peace to the hundred spirits. While the Son of Heaven sacrificed to all of the great mountains and rivers within All under Heaven, the regional lords only sacrificed to those that were within their domains. Individuals knew their position within the hierarchy of the state, and only sacrificed according to their office—commoners, for example, could only sacrifice to their grandfather, while those of higher rank could sacrifice to increasing numbers of ancestral and extrahuman spirits.[13] It is implied that the Western Zhou rulers travelled throughout their empire to sacrifice to the great mountains, continuing the tradition of the tours of the rulers of antiquity, while regional lords' sacrificial practices remained within their territories.[14]

The First Emperor of Qin continued the tradition of inspection tours, embarking on five such tours during his reign. On each of these tours, he sacrificed to the great mountains and rivers, as well as to the Eight Lords.[15] These tours, as Charles Sanft has demonstrated, were politically motivated, demonstrating the grandeur of the First Emperor to his subjects as he travelled across the land with his entourage,[16] but, the First Emperor also believed them to be of great spiritual importance.[17] When he offered sacrifice at the great mountains, the First Emperor also left behind inscribed tablets, now lost to us, but the texts of which have been recorded in his *Shiji*.[18] Martin

Kern has suggested that the Qin inspection tours "might have created the very tradition that he [the First Emperor] purported to revive," and that the act of erecting these inscriptions demonstrated his completion of this purportedly ancient ritual.[19] These texts proclaim the great achievements of the First Emperor in creating a unified empire and an everlasting dynasty. They praise his achievement in bringing peace to the formerly warring states and celebrate the order and abundance that is enjoyed by all in his new state.[20] By the time of the Qin, at least, the idea of the inspection tours as being a part of the traditions of the ancient sages was well established. The ruler's tours gave him the opportunity to see the lands under his rule and to ensure that his instructions were being followed. For the rulers who had recently conquered or incorporated new lands, they also served as a means to mark their territory.

While the Zhou king in the east held nominal ritual authority over the regional lords during the Spring and Autumn and Warring States periods, much of the pre-Han material in the "Treatise on the *feng* and *shan* Sacrifices" focuses on the state of Qin. It is possible that no other records were available to Sima Qian, due to the destruction of the records of the Warring States at the founding of the Qin empire, but as the Han built on the sacrificial system established by the Qin state and empire, it is also possible that this was an editorial decision.[21] Of particular importance to Sima Qian and the Han emperors was the cult established at Yong 雍 shortly after the founding of the Qin state. An altar, the "Western Altar" *xizhi* 西畤 was established by Lord Xiang of Qin 秦襄公 (r. 777–766 BCE) to the west of his capital in the newly founded Qin territory.[22] At this altar, Lord Xiang sacrificed a burnt offering consisting of one bay colt, one yellow ox, and one goat to the White Emperor (*baidi* 白帝).[23] The altar was subsequently moved to the Yong region and renamed the "Altar of Fu" *fuzhi* 鄜畤 during the reign of Lord Wen 秦文公 (r. 765–716 BCE), who received omens suggesting that the region between the Qian 汧 and Wei 渭 rivers was a more auspicious location.[24] Here, Lord Wen performed a sacrifice of the type *jiao* to the White Emperor, which consisted of three sacrificial animals, a bay colt, yellow ox, and a ram 騮駒黃牛羝羊, as were offered under Lord Xiang.[25] The *jiao* was a method of sacrifice, rather than a sacrifice to one particular spirit.[26] It was a blood sacrifice, where the offerings were later burnt, used when making offerings to heavenly spirits, as opposed to sacrifices made to earth which were subsequently buried. In this way, the fumes could travel to heaven where they would nourish the spirits. The sacrificial offering could consist at minimum of an ox, but more commonly a complement of three sacrificial animals, an ox, a sheep, and a pig, were sacrificed and burnt.²⁷

Under Lord De 秦德公 (r. 677–676 BCE), with the transfer of the capital to Yong, the sacrifices in the region became plentiful.²⁸ The altar to the White Emperor was joined by an altar to the Green Emperor (*qingdi* 青帝) south of the Wei River under Lord Mu 秦穆公 (r. 659–621 BCE), and altars to the Yellow (*huangdi* 黃帝)²⁹ and Red/Fire (*yandi* 炎帝) Emperors were established by Lord Ling 秦靈公 (r. 424–415 BCE).³⁰ These four altars remained at Yong into the Han, and it seems that they received regular sacrifices from a staff of sacrificial officials, and occasionally from the Qin lords themselves. However, neither the First nor Second Emperors was recorded to have sacrificed to the emperors at Yong in person, though they continued to employ sacrificial officials to carry out these sacrifices, and Qin Er Shi sacrificed to other spirits at the site in 209 BCE.³¹ The altars at Yong were maintained as they were until the time of Han Gaozu.

Despite declaring the founding of a new dynasty on principles different from those of the Qin, Han Gaozu maintained most Qin institutions, including the sacrificial programs, going so far as to employ the former Qin advisors, notably Shusun Tong 叔孫痛 (d. ca. 188 BCE), a Qin sacrificial official, and Zhang Cang 張蒼 (253–152 BCE), who was an expert in calendrical science and the pitch-pipes. These officials revived the sacrifices of the Qin that had been neglected due to the civil war, and Gaozu declared that the sacrifices to the High Gods [at Yong] the mountains, rivers, and the various spirits would each have their [sacrificial] time according to the ancient customs 今上帝之祭及山川諸神當祠者，各以其時禮祠之如故.³²

Gaozu placed his primary focus on securing his position and his new empire, rather than on imperial cult.³³ He did, however, make one important intervention in imperial cult, when he travelled to see the site at Yong. Having understood that there were supposed to be five emperors, Gaozu wondered why there were only altars for four. As none of his officials was able to give him a satisfactory answer, he came to the reasonable conclusion that it was up to him to complete the set by erecting an altar to the Black Emperor (*heidi* 黑帝) in the north.³⁴ After the addition of this fifth altar, the five altars to the five emperors, the High Gods (*Shangdi* 上帝)³⁵ were established, and sacrifices were regularly performed, once every three years.³⁶

Emperor Wen made few changes to the system of imperial cult, but ensured that all of the sacrifices, including those to be offered by the regional lords, were offered at the correct times, and he increased the sacrificial offerings to the High Gods at Yong, as well as to the Yellow, Han, and Qiao rivers.[37] He briefly entertained the idea of making some substantial reforms to the state's cult, but ultimately decided against it, we are told, because he discovered one of his advisors to be falsifying omens.[38] Prior to this discovery, he personally offered sacrifice to the High Gods at Yong, and established the new Weiyang altar 渭陽, north of the Wei River, to the High Gods, where he performed the *jiao* sacrifice in subsequent years. Emperor Wen's advisors informed him that in ancient times the Son of Heaven personally offered sacrifice to the High Gods, but according to the histories, this is the first time that an emperor personally performed the sacrifice.[39]

Although Emperor Wen later lost interest in pursuing the spirits, and, perhaps, in pursuing immortality, the state sacrifices were not neglected after he stopped performing them in person. It was, in fact, unusual for an emperor to perform these sacrifices themselves, and they were normally performed by sacrificial officials. At Yong, there were permanent sacrificial officials to oversee the operation, a Director of Sacrifices (*Taizhu ling* 太祝領) and a Grand Butcher (*Taizai*) 太宰, each with their own assistant(s).[40] Each of the five altars at Yong had one designated official (*wei* 尉) who was responsible for the sacrifices to that shrine.[41] These officials were under the supervision of the Superintendent of Ceremonial (*Taichang* 太常), one of the Nine Ministers (*jiu qing* 九卿), the highest officials of the Han court. The office of the Superintendent of Ceremonial was responsible for all state rituals: for determining the correct ritual performances, for announcing the protocols in advance, and for assisting the emperor while he performed the ceremonies.[42] The Superintendent of Ceremonial supervised a large staff which comprised not only ritual officials, such as those at Yong, as well as other offices connected to music, portents, astronomy and calendrics, and the examination system, and included Sima Qian's own office of Grand Scribe. The histories do not describe in great detail the exact number of officials under the Superintendent of Ceremonial, only the most important positions, and we are led to believe that the number of employees fluctuated depending on the needs of the state. As the sacrificial program expanded and contracted over the course of the early Han, it is reasonable to assume that so too did the office of the Superintendent of Ceremonial. These officials were responsible for maintaining altars, for securing or caring for sacrificial animals, and for performing sacrifices to the spirits, or assisting the emperor when he chose to do so personally.[43]

Roman Religious Institutions

State religion in Rome was far more institutionalized than that of the systems of the Qin and Han. As we have seen, the main functions of Roman religion were to forge civic identity and to ensure that the *pax deorum* was maintained. The men and women who were responsible for maintaining this peace and for organizing the many religious sacrifices and festivals were the priests and priestesses. These men and women were organized into priestly colleges, the origins of which were traditionally ascribed to the reign of Numa (trad. r. 715–673 BCE).[44] By the late Republic, there were three major colleges of priests, the *pontifices, augures,* and *quindecimviri sacris faciundis.* Under Augustus, the college of *epulones* became a major college, increasing their number to four, and the *Arvales fratres* were "revived."[45] In addition to the major colleges, there were other priesthoods dedicated to particular gods, which were not always filled, as well as the Vestal Virgins, who guarded the sacred fire.[46] These groups fell under the jurisdiction of the pontifical college. Priests held their office for life, and a place in one of the priestly colleges was coveted by both patricians and plebians alike. In the early Republic priests were only co-opted from the patrician class, but the *lex Ogulnia* of ca. 300 BCE gave the plebs access to the priestly colleges, and from that time forward the colleges remained divided between the patricians and plebians.[47]

In his speech before the Senate concerning the Response of the Haruspices in 56 BCE, Cicero provided a description of the historical roles of each of the colleges. Invoking the traditions and sagacity of Roman ancestors, he wrote:

> In their [the ancestors'] view, all prescribed and liturgical ceremonies depended upon the Pontificate, and all regulations determining auspicious action upon augury; they thought that the ancient prophecies of the oracle of Apollo were comprised in the books of the seers, and all interpretations of prodigies in the lore of the Etruscans.
>
> *Qui statas sollemnesque caerimonias pontificatu, rerum bene gerundarum auctoritates augurio, fatorum veteres praedictiones Apollinis vatum libris, portentorum explanationes Etruscorum disciplina contineri putaverunt.*[48]

The Pontifical College was acknowledged to be the most prominent of the priestly colleges, and in addition to the *pontifices* themselves, the college supervised several other religious groups and functionaries. The college was chaired by the *pontifex maximus*, who was elected by an assembly for much of the late republican period;[49] after Augustus' death, the position of *pontifex maximus* became effectively hereditary, passed down from *princeps* to *princeps*.[50] Prior to this change, however, the role of *pontifex maximus* was a highly coveted and influential position.[51] The *pontifex maximus* traditionally lived in the *domus publica*, near the *regia*, in the Forum. This house was located near the house of the Vestal Virgins, and served as the archive for the pontifical texts, as well as the calendar.[52] Under the *pontifex maximus*' supervision were the regular *pontifices* (whose numbers increased from nine to sixteen over the course of the Republic),[53] the Rex and Regina Sacrorum, the Pontifices Minores (three), the Flamines (three major and twelve minor), and six Vestal Virgins.[54] While many of these subordinate offices were often left vacant during both the Republic and Principate, the college of *pontifices* was charged with ensuring that the rites were not neglected.[55] The college was responsible for ensuring that the correct rites were carried out for consecrations, burials, and other festivals, and for ensuring the correct behaviour of people at festivals. Until the first century BCE, they were concerned with the development of both sacred and civil law,[56] and their role in relation to the Senate was primarily advisory. As possessors of specialized knowledge, in the form of the records of the *pontifices* which were stored at the *domus publica*, they were able to advise the Senate on disputes over religious affairs and instruct magistrates in the correct performance of ritual. According to Mary Beard, co-optation into the college immediately bestowed the status of religious expert upon the priest: "he *knew* things about religion that other men did not know and gained from that knowledge considerable authority (*auctoritas*)."[57] While it is not known if there were secrets into which *pontifices* were initiated, they likely had access to various writings that were off limits to those outside of the college,[58] and Plutarch suggests that the *augures*, at least, were bearers of secrets which must be protected until death.[59] Rather than being possessors of secret knowledge, it is possible that the *auctoritas* of the *pontifices* derived from their role as senatorial consultants: the priests were able to have private discussions and render judgements (based on pontifical texts and precedent) that would have appeared opaque to outsiders. When a question was raised in the Senate concerning religious matters, the Senate could refer the question to the *pontifices*, who would prepare a decision. The Senate could then choose to act based on this decision, but, while the college of *pontifices* spoke with a unified voice, each member (presuming he was also a member of the Senate) could vote according to his own proclivity, for there was a recognized division between judgement on religious issues, and the judgement of the law.[60] Knowledge of the actions of the *pontifices* was not confined solely to the Senatorial elite; in the early Republic, the *pontifex maximus* kept a *tabula dealbata* in front of his house, which "informed the public about his measures and doings."[61] While this practice was later discontinued, the publication of various *tabulae* as monographs took place in the mid-first century, and these *annales* were accessible to the public.[62]

While the *pontifices* were concerned with questions of sacred law and served as an advisory board to the Senate, the College of Augurs was able to directly intervene in the functioning of the state. The *augures* were considered to be secondary to the *pontifices*, although membership in this college gave the individual priest much more political power than the other colleges,[63] and only death could remove an augur from office. Cicero wrote that the *augures* were the "interpreter and assistant of Jupiter the Best and Greatest," and that they were charged with taking the auspices "in order that he may obtain from them frequent assistance for the Republic."[64] Indeed, an augur could disrupt an assembly by reporting ill omens, indicating that the assembly was proceeding without the approval of the gods.[65] *Augures* also had the power to designate a piece of land as a *templum*, a location which linked heaven and earth, and from which a magistrate could take the auspices.[66] The *augures* also served to advise the Senate on questions relating to the auspices, though, like the *pontifices*, the final decision on how to act rested with the Senate, and, of course, many of the *augures* were themselves Senators.[67] The *augures*, too, likely had access to a set of secret texts, which only they could consult. Despite his already long and successful career, Cicero did not attain a position in the college until 53 BCE (he had attained the consulship in 63), and so he indicates in his address to the *pontifices* on the question of his house that what he understands from Augural practice is derived from what he has seen and heard, rather than from any consultation of their sacred books; indeed, he even expresses doubt as to their existence.[68]

Far less is known about the two other major colleges during the Republic, the *quindecimviri sacris faciundis*, and the *septemviri epulones*. However, over the course of the late Republic and early Principate, their importance and prestige increased. The *quindecimviri sacris faciundis*, the college of fifteen men responsible for supervision of the sacred rites, were primarily responsible for the consultation of the Sibylline books when requested by the

Senate. During the reign of Augustus, they became responsible for the organization of the *ludi saeculares*, discussed in detail in Chapter 7. The college was said to have been created under the reign of Tarquinius Superbus, when he obtained the books from the Sibylline Oracle. Originally established as a college of two men (the *duumviri*), the college was expanded in the fourth century BCE to ten (*decemviri sacris faciundis*), and later grew to fifteen.[69] Like the *pontifices* and *augures*, after the *lex Ogulnia* of 300 BCE, half the college of the *quindecimviri* was to be composed of plebeians.[70] Although membership in this college was considered to be less prestigious than membership in the pontifical or augural colleges,[71] its prestige increased over time, and, as we will see in Chapters 4 and 5, it was of fundamental importance to the recentering of power under Augustus.

The *septemviri epulones*, originally the *tresviri epulones*, had been founded by a plebiscite in 196 BCE.[72] The college was expanded to seven men, likely under Sulla, and a further three were added by Caesar in 44 BCE, to reward his followers, bringing their number up to ten.[73] The *epulones*, "feast organisers," were responsible for the organization of the dinners and public banquets that followed sacrifices, festivals, and games. Cicero writes that the *epulones* were founded by the *pontifices*, who delegated the responsibility of organizing feasts to them, and they took their name from the great "Sacrificial Banquet of the Games," the *ludorum epulare sacrificium*.[74] This particular feast was attended by members of the Senate, who gathered on the Capitoline; according to Aulus Gellius, this was an important opportunity for the senators to bond with each other, and form alliances.[75] Membership in this college had little prestige until the time of Augustus; no high-ranking members are seen until the mid-first century BCE.[76] As the college gained in prestige, it may have forsaken some of its responsibilities: Ogilvie suggests that the administrative arrangements of organizing feasts were eventually re-delegated to "underlings, probably public slaves."[77]

A final college, though never listed as one of the major colleges, the Arval Brothers, was elevated to a high status under the Principate, though they had likely existed in some form during the Republic.[78] According to Ronald Syme, the "*Arvales* were revived, and all but invented"[79] by Augustus in 29 BCE.[80] Membership of the college was fixed at twelve, and this number would only be exceeded by the appointment of an imperial heir.[81] Unlike the other colleges, where it was unusual for a priest to hold a dual membership, the majority of the Arval Brothers were members of the other priestly colleges.[82]

The men who comprised the Arval Brothers were "drawn from the most prominent members of the senate" and primarily carried out sacrifices and ceremonies regarding the *princeps* and his family.[83] Comprised of members from the most powerful and prominent families, the college was thus both a group through which political consensus could be reached, as well as an honour bestowed by the *princeps*.[84]

While priests were generally selected from the social elite, new priests had to be voted in by an assembly consisting of seventeen of the thirty-five voting tribes.[85] While there were no written rules to the effect, it was standard practice during the Republic that no individual would hold more than one priesthood. This was to change under Julius Caesar, who was a member of both the pontifical (co-opted in ca. 73 BCE, elected *pontifex maximus* in 63 BCE) and augural (47 BCE) colleges. Augustus would subsequently attain membership in each of the colleges, a precedent that was to be followed by subsequent rulers. The office of *pontifex maximus* also became linked to the *princeps* following Augustus' election to the post in 12 BCE.

Attaining a position in one of the colleges was considered a high honour: the individual priest was given a prominent place in religious festivals, feasts, and games, important in the public theatre of Roman politics. Using Pierre Bourdieu's theory that wealth can be transformed into power "only in the form of symbolic capital,"[86] Richard Gordon writes that "the sacerdotal colleges of Rome can be seen as the guardians of the alchemical transmutation of base wealth into inexhaustible prestige," and that, like the magistrates, the priests were able to accumulate social capital and maintain their high status in society, through expenditure on religious festivities.[87] Membership provided him (or, her, in the case of the Vestal Virgins) with access to carefully guarded secret knowledge as well as an opportunity to participate in conversations about public policy outside of the more overt structures of political authority. While membership in a college meant "the lifelong right to participate prominently in the processions at *ludi* and in public banquets,"[88] it also gave the priest a lifelong right to participate in discussions of importance to the state that were not (or could not be) conducted within the Senate. As Jörg Rüpke has argued,

> Membership [in colleges] did not entail only the obligation to participate in a few cult activities; it was also associated with lavish meals and celebrations in members' private houses, and opportunities to discuss politically sensitive subjects, personal affairs, and the like. *The colleges were*

circles of communication within the political elite, and their significance as informal venues for the establishment of consensus among senators should not be underestimated.[89]

The colleges all shared a similar role: as groups of religious experts, they were primarily seen as advisors to the Senate and magistrates, who would ultimately determine the correct course of action, or perform the requisite sacrifices. The *pontifices*, *augures*, and *quindecimviri*, each had their own texts, which contained the "accumulation of the Romans' religious observations,"[90] and could only be consulted by members of that college; their recommendations were often made on the basis of, or after discussion of, one of these texts.[91] Membership in any one of the colleges was coveted by men who sought power in Rome, and while this was surely due in part to the prominent role that priests played in the theatre of public festivals at Rome, it may also have been related to the importance of the priestly colleges as consultative bodies. While reconstructing the lists of priests is a challenging endeavour, we can see that there were sometimes empty seats in each college and particularly after the deaths and proscriptions during the civil war, the colleges were nearly emptied of their members.[92] The co-optation of priests was a highly politicized affair, and the membership in priestly colleges, as we will see, often reflects political trends.

The Roman priests had great influence in society, as the mediators between gods and men and the possessors of special knowledge. In maintaining the *pax deorum*, one of their prime tasks was to ensure that the temples to the gods were maintained and that the gods themselves received proper sacrifices. Many of the gods had their own designated priests, the *flamines maiores* and *minors* (major and minor). The three *flamines maiores* in particular, "enjoyed the highest prestige within the pontifical college,"[93] and were responsible for looking after Jupiter, Mars, and Quirinus, respectively.[94] Attached to these high priesthoods, however, were numerous prohibitions, particularly for the priest of Jupiter, the *flamen Dialis*. Such prohibitions effectively prohibited the *flamen* from holding office, and as a result, this priesthood, and others, were frequently left vacant.[95] While the vacancies of the important priesthoods were not considered ideal, they were tolerated—during the late Republic, the priesthood of the *flamen Dialis* was vacant for over seventy years—but as long as the rites for which the priests were responsible were maintained, it seems the *pax deorum* was not upset.[96] These sacrifices, such as the sacrifice of a castrated ram to Jupiter on the

Ides of every month, were performed by other members of the Pontifical College.[97]

Roman religious festivals and sacrifices were, for the most part, public events, and the number of festival days increased over the course of the Republic. Religious rituals took place in front of temples and were attended by the community as well as magistrates and priests. Sacrifices generally included an animal sacrifice, the type, sex, and age depending on the status of the offerants and the god, as well as various grains, fruits, and drinks.[98] These were carried in procession to the altar, where the sacrifice took place. After the sacrifice, while some of the victuals were given to the god, either burnt, buried, or submerged in water, the remainder of the sacrificial animal was prepared for a banquet, attended by the officiants and elite. Non-elite members of society were generally excluded from these banquets, though they may have been able to obtain a share by purchasing it from a butcher.[99] The sacrifices were offered to gods for the protection of the Roman people, and while the Roman people may not have participated directly in the rites or in the banquets, they would have known that these rites were being conducted in their honour.[100] *Ludi*, on the other hand, were religious spectacle entertainments that had broad appeal. Comprised of sacrifices, games, theatrical performances, and feasting, the *ludi* were not only a way to commemorate religious festivals but for ambitious politicians to earn the hearts (and votes) of the people. While state funds were provided for the *ludi*, it became increasingly common for magistrates to spend large sums of their own money to make the festivals one to remember.[101]

Conclusion

Although it is impossible to find much common ground between the various religious traditions of early China and Rome, the pursuit of religion by the rulers, or ruling class, for the benefit of the state and its people gives us some grounds for comparison. This chapter has outlined the areas of state-sponsored cult that were of interest to the ruling authorities, and through which they attempted to contact the gods and accrue benefits for the people. As we have seen, the religious institutions of the Roman Republic, in the form of the priestly colleges, were much more formalized than the institutions of the pre-Han states, though state religious infrastructure did exist through the office of the Superintendent of Ceremonial. While this distinction is

48 IMPERIAL CULTS

certainly valid, we must also consider that our impression of these religious institutions has been shaped by our sources. The Roman sources, concerned with elite competition and the rise of men through Rome's elite institutions, tell us much about the institutionalized form of the priestly colleges, as well as their connection to politics. The *Shiji*, on the other hand, is primarily concerned with painting a broad history of the various cults that were worshiped by rulers of antiquity and less interested in providing detailed information about the bureaucratic structure of government, which Sima Qian may have imagined familiar to his readers. The following chapters will turn to look at the changes made to these religious institutions by Emperor Wu and Augustus, and they will follow this distinction, following Emperor Wu as he travels throughout the empire to connect with powerful spirits and Augustus as he works inside the priestly colleges in order to dominate imperial cult.

4
Reshaping Religious Institutions

Although the religious systems of early China and Rome bear little resemblance to each other, some grounds for comparison can be found if we look at the relationship between the state and its religious institutions and the role of religion in bringing prosperity to the state. Rather than comparing the different religious institutions, we will look at how each ruler worked within existing structures to refocus imperial cult around themselves. The system of priestly colleges and sacrifices was more institutionalized in Rome; the Qin and early Han religious institutions, while not highly formalized, were not entirely without structure. Rather than creating entirely new institutions, the rulers reshaped the existing structures, shifting the focus of cult onto themselves and their allies. In this chapter, we will explore how Augustus and Emperor Wu strengthened their own positions at the centre of religious activity by restructuring their religious institutions and recruiting new men into their ranks. In Chapter 5 we will see how these new men helped to expand each ruler's political influence: for Emperor Wu, this expansion takes place across the empire, while Augustus' efforts were largely concentrated in the city of Rome.

In both cases, the most significant change that took place in the restructuring of religious institutions was that the rulers each took a more active role in religious practices than their predecessors. As we have seen, the early Han emperors, while maintaining the state sacrifices, did not take an active role in their performance or attempt to pursue new spirits. In Rome, the priestly colleges had lost many members during the civil war, and the most important priesthoods were frequently left empty. While this seems not to have impacted the scheduled offering of sacrifices, it demonstrates that, prior to Augustus, active involvement in the state's religious institutions was not a pressing concern for the city's leading men. As each ruler became more involved in their religious institutions, they recruited men who could assist them. In the Han case, this involved recruiting religious experts from across the empire who claimed to have access to powerful spirits, including the

Imperial Cults. Rebecca Robinson, Oxford University Press. © Oxford University Press 2023.
DOI: 10.1093/oso/9780197666043.003.0004

immortal sages. In Rome, Augustus incorporated his supporters and allies into religious institutions, offering them the prestige that came along with co-optation into a college while simultaneously ensuring that his allies were always present during priestly gatherings.

Our understandings of the transformations to religious institutions are both shaped and frustrated by our sources. The main source for the incorporation of new men into Emperor Wu's cult is the *Shiji*, and while it provides much information about the changes, Sima Qian was strongly opposed to many of the emperor's decisions and particularly objected to the religious experts he recruited. The Roman sources for the members of priestly colleges are largely fragmentary but have been reconstructed by scholars. These reconstructions can be read in conjunction with the histories and biographies to reveal Augustus' efforts to not only become a member in each of the colleges, but to promote his supporters to important roles.

New Men in Han China: The *Fangshi*

Sima Qian's "Treatise on the *feng* and *shan* Sacrifices" is usually read as a critique of Emperor Wu's expansion of imperial cult. Indeed, the sacrificial tours, the lavish sacrifices, the construction of palaces and shrines, and the employment of thousands of people in conjunction with sacrificial practices accounted for a significant portion of the government's budget. Combined with Emperor Wu's expenditure on warfare and colonization of the North-West, by the end of his reign, Han finances were greatly reduced, and it is not surprising that many later writers placed the blame on Emperor Wu's vain pursuit of immortality, as he spent vast sums of money to chase down spirits and immortals across the empire. The development of the Qin and early Han sacrificial system was closely linked to new ideas of empire and emperorship, and with the potential divinization of the emperor himself.[1] Emperor Wu continued the trend started in the Qin but expended more energy on elevating the status of the emperor than any previous ruler. Sima Qian was not entirely opposed to the Qin-Han imperial system, nor necessarily to the expansion of cult throughout the empire; what he objected to was the way in which the emperor carried it out, and particularly, to the people he chose to employ.

The primary goal of Emperor Wu's sacrificial programme was to allow the emperor to "personally contact as many divine powers as possible in order to obtain their power,"[2] so that he could himself attain immortality and demonstrate his unparalleled command of spiritual affairs across the empire. The emperor's pursuit of immortality was closely connected to his imperial ideals. In order to attain immortality, he needed to demonstrate that he reigned supreme over All under Heaven, and that he had close contact with the various spirits across his domain. The Son of Heaven was, according to ancient ritual texts, supposed to sacrifice to the spirits of Heaven and Earth, while the regional lords sacrificed to the mountains and rivers in their domains.[3] Quite early on, we see the idea that spirits should only receive sacrifice from the rulers of their domains, and that sacrificing to a regional spirit was equivalent to claiming authority over that territory.[4] By sacrificing to spirits across the empire, Emperor Wu elevated himself above all other men, and indeed, perhaps to the level of a spirit himself, while at the same time claiming sovereignty over those spirits' territories.[5] In order to access these various spirits, many of whom were associated with other cultural traditions, Emperor Wu chose to employ men who claimed to have knowledge of these spirits and the immortals. These men are classified by Sima Qian as *fangshi* "Masters of Methods," and it is clear from the outset that he did not approve of their influence over the emperor.

The *fangshi* were men who were specialists in a variety of different technical arts, *fang shu* 方術, including divination, numbers and numerology, alchemy, and communication with immortals.[6] The *Shiji* narrative of Emperor Wu's expansion of cult is largely preoccupied with the role of the *fangshi* in advising the emperor in his pursuit of immortality. It is clear that the historian finds them to be contemptible: he draws attention to their extraordinary claims, to their failures, and to their deceptions, leading the reader to believe that the emperor was so desperate to attain immortality that he was willing to listen to the outrageous claims of men who sought only to improve their own position. While it was true that at least one of these men was caught in outright deception of the emperor and others proved incapable of delivering on their promises,[7] what perhaps frustrated Sima Qian the most was the promotion of men from outside the traditional court elite to becoming some of the emperor's closest advisors. Sima Qian and the office of the Superintendent of Ceremonial were supposed to be responsible for the empire's sacrificial programme, but the advice of the *fangshi* was often privileged over their traditional knowledge, and the court officials were then required to implement the sacrifices devised by the *fangshi*. This in itself would have surely created a hostile attitude towards these new men.

Sima Qian names fourteen *fangshi* advisors to the emperor, though he also notes that many, many more sought the emperor's ear.[8] The majority of the *fangshi* came from the east, particularly the former state of Qi. Qi had long had a reputation for its specialists in technical arts, and, due to its location on the east coast, it served as a natural point of contact between the fabled immortals of the eastern isles and those who sought them. Some of the others came from newly incorporated regions, but all of the men that Sima Qian designates as *fangshi* came from outside of the capital region. While most of the *fangshi* were engaged to help the emperor pursue immortality and offer sacrifices to various spirits, some were also engaged in using their skills to assist the emperor in other ways: Luan Da was brought into the emperor's service in part because of his claim that he would be able to repair the breach of the banks of the Yellow River, which had caused a devastating flood in 132 BCE,[9] while Ding Furen 丁夫人 and Yu Chu 虞初 were charged with uttering curses against the Da Yuan 大宛 and Xiongnu, in order to secure Han victory in the campaigns against them.

As can be seen from Table 4.1, rather than simply encouraging the emperor to pursue the immortals, the *fangshi* were responsible for the establishment of several new cults to various spirits, including Sovereign Earth and Great Unity, discussed further in Chapter 7. Some were also responsible for advising the emperor on the *feng* and *shan* sacrifices, which were considered to be the most important sacrifices of antiquity, sacrifices that could only be performed by a sage ruler who had received the sanction of heaven.[10] For their services to the emperor, these *fangshi* received substantial rewards, and while they were able to ingratiate themselves with the emperor, the literati at court were less enamoured with them. The sacrifices to these new spirits required the emperor to travel across the empire, and to incorporate spiritually important locations into commanderies under the control of the imperial court. The incorporation of these sites was, as I will argue in the next chapter, an important component in extending Han imperial control throughout the empire.

Priestly Colleges in Augustan Rome

Much has been said about the Augustan "revival" of religion in the transition period, primarily because of the rhetoric of the revival of tradition that was employed by Augustus and ancient scholars. Suetonius' biography of

Table 4.1 The *fangshi* under Emperor Wu[a]

Name	Place of Origin[b]	Notable Activities	Official Position, Titles, and Awards Received
Li Shaojun 李少君[c]	Zhongshan 中山	• Established shrine to god of the furnace	
Kuan Shu 寬舒[d]	Qi 齊	• Advised on shrines to Sovereign Earth and Great Unity • Recommended regular performance of rites to *Taizhi tan*	• Official concerned with religious matters (*ci guan* 祠官)
Miu Ji 謬忌[e]	Wei 魏	• Proposed inauguration of cult to Great Unity, with the High Gods as subordinate assistants.	
Shaoweng 少翁[f]	Qi 齊	• Claims to have seen spirit of Wu's deceased consort Li Furen 李夫人 • Fakes discovery of immortal text by feeding it to a sacrificial cow	• Title: Wencheng jiangjun 文成建軍 • Rewarded with gifts and privileged treatment.
Youshui Fagen 游水發根[g]	Chu 楚	• Informed Emperor Wu of a shamaness who could cure illness	
Luan Da 欒大[h]	Qi 齊	• Claimed to be able to produce gold, produce an elixir of immortality, secure a meeting with immortals, and seal the breached banks of the Yellow River	• Title: Wuli jiangjun 五利將軍 • Awarded four seals (*tianshi* 天士, *dishi* 地士, *datong* 大通, *jiangjun* 將軍) • Ennobled as Marquis of Letong 樂通候. • Married imperial princess, Wei Zhang Gongzhu 衛長公主
(Shamaness) Jin (巫)錦[i]	Wei 魏	• Discovered tripod at Fenyin while sacrificing to Sovereign Earth.	
Gongsun Qing 公孫卿[j]	Qi 齊	• Advised Wu to perform *feng* and *shan* sacrifices • Advised construction of special halls at Chang'an, Ganquan, and on the Tong Tian Tai 通天臺 • Assisted in creation of new Han calendar	• Appointed: o Gentleman *lang* 郎 o Counsellor of the Palace *Zhong dafu* 中大夫 o Grand Counsellor of the Palace *Taizhong dafu* 太中大夫
Ding Gong 丁公[k]	Qi 齊	• Took part in consultations on *feng* and *shan* sacrifices	

(*continued*)

Table 4.1 Continued

Name	Place of Origin[b]	Notable Activities	Official Position, Titles, and Awards Received
Wang Shuo 王朔	Unknown	• Specialist on watching the vapours *wang qi* 望氣 • Gave opinion on comet that was seen after Emperor Wu performed the *feng* and *shan* sacrifices in 110 BCE.	
Gongyu Dai 公玉帶[m]	Qi 齊	• Advised on how to build a Ming tang 明堂 • Advised on rites that the Yellow Thearch had performed to attain immortality.	
Yong Zhi 勇之[n]	Yue 越	• Described the longevity techniques of the Yue people • Advised on the construction of the Jianzhang Palace 建章	
Ding Furen 丁夫人[o]	Yue 越	• With Yu Chu, spoke curses against the Da Yuan 大宛 and Xiongnu.	
Yu Chu 虞初[p]	Luoyang 洛陽	• With Ding Furen, spoke curses against the Da Yuan and Xiongnu. • Listed as author of esoteric text *Yu Chu Zhou shuo* 虞初周說	• Gentleman in Attendance *Shilang* 侍郎 • Title: Huangju shizhe 黃車使者

[a] See also the table and descriptions of *fangshi* in Yang Hua 楊華, "Qin Han diguo de shenquan tongyi: chutu jianbo yu 'Fengshan shu', 'Jiaosi zhi,' de duibi kaocha" 秦漢帝國的神權統一：出土簡帛與《封禪書》、《郊祀志》的對比考察, *Lishi Yanjiu* 5 (2011): 20. References are given to the first appearance of the individuals in the *Shiji* and Hanshu chapters, as well as to Michael Loewe's *A Biographical Dictionary of the Qin, Former Han, and Xin Periods, 221 BC–AD 24* (Leiden: Brill, 2000), which compiles information on all of these figures.

[b] Sima Qian generally lists the place of origin of the *fangshi* according to the former Warring States. This table retains those categorizations.

[c] *Shiji* 28.1385; *Hanshu* 25A.1216; Loewe, *A Biographical Dictionary*, 227.

[d] *Shiji* 28.1386; *Hanshu* 25A.1217; Loewe, *A Biographical Dictionary*, 213.

[e] *Shiji* 28.1386; *Hanshu* 25A.1218; 25B.1248; 1257; Loewe, *A Biographical Dictionary*, 439.

[f] *Shiji* 28.1387; *Hanshu* 25A.1219; Loewe, *A Biographical Dictionary*, 467.

[g] *Shiji* 28.1388; *Hanshu* 25A.1220; Loewe, *A Biographical Dictionary*, 658.

[h] *Shiji* 28.1389; *Hanshu* 25A.1222; Loewe, *A Biographical Dictionary*, 429–30.

[i] *Shiji* 28.1392; *Hanshu* 25A.1225; Loewe, *A Biographical Dictionary*, 195.

[j] *Shiji* 28.1393; *Hanshu* 25A.1227; Loewe, *A Biographical Dictionary*, 129.

[k] *Shiji* 28.1397; *Hanshu* 25A.1233; Loewe, *A Biographical Dictionary*, 62.

[l] *Shiji* 28.1399; *Hanshu* 25A.1236; Loewe, *A Biographical Dictionary*, 553.

[m] *Shiji* 28.1401; *Hanshu* 25B.1243; Loewe, *A Biographical Dictionary*, 131.

[n] *Shiji* 28.1402; *Hanshu* 25B.1241; Loewe, *A Biographical Dictionary*, 658

[o] *Shiji* 28.1402; *Hanshu* 25B.1246; Loewe, *A Biographical Dictionary*, 62.

[p] *Shiji* 28.1402; *Hanshu* 25B.1246; Loewe, *A Biographical Dictionary*, 659.

Augustus, in particular, emphasizes this theme of revival, detailing the numerous changes made during rule of the *princeps*. The emphasis is likely due to the fact that Augustus himself emphasized this during his reign, making it a central part of his rule. According to Suetonius, he collected and edited prophetic texts, fixed the calendar, and changed the name of the month Sextilis to Augustus, he increased the number and salary of priests and Vestal Virgins, and he revived numerous ancient cults, rites, and festivals, including the *ludi saeculares*.[11] In addition to concerning himself with religious affairs, "Next to the immortal gods he honoured the memory of the leaders who had raised the estate of the Roman people from obscurity to greatness," not only emphasizing the (purportedly) ancient roots of the religious traditions he had revived, but also placing himself in that line of the great leaders of Rome.[12] In his autobiographical *Res Gestae*, Augustus himself places emphasis on the religious honours that he held in his lifetime, placing his membership in all of the priestly colleges on par with his status of *princeps senatus*.[13] Writing in the third century CE when the emperorship had been more firmly established, Dio Cassius attributes the supreme power of the ruler, in part, to his occupation of all of the priestly colleges, and position as *pontifex maximus*, which gave him "supreme authority over all matters both profane and sacred," along with the ability to appoint new priests.[14] Indeed, Augustus was the first Roman citizen to hold a priesthood in each of the colleges, though Sulla and Caesar also both attempted to accumulate priesthoods.[15] Following the death of Augustus, *princepes* would hold office in each of the colleges, along with the position of *pontifex maximus*, though it was not until the reign of Titus (r. 79–81 CE) that a *princeps* was automatically co-opted into *omnia collegia*.[16]

Augustus' domination of religious affairs in Rome was a long process, carried out over the course of his long life. While he had succeeding in attaining a priesthood in each of the colleges by 29 BCE, he was not the leading member of each until the death of Lepidus in 12 BCE.[17] While the priestly colleges were not hierarchical, with the exception of the position of *pontifex maximus*, the annual lists of the colleges were usually "arranged in order of entrance to that college,"[18] and so it was only by outliving his peers that Augustus rose to become the senior member of each college.[19]

In this instance, Augustus did keep with tradition, and it was only after his death that his successors violated the standard progression through the priesthoods and claimed the position of *pontifex maximus* as hereditary right.[20] As we can see from his handling of the case of Lepidus, Augustus was clearly very careful to avoid making dramatic changes in the well-established priestly colleges, just as he avoided enacting radical change in other areas. While he did appoint some men to the colleges, during the period of civil war, he did not initially alter the structure of the colleges, nor outright change their method of co-optation, as Sulla had done.[21] Rather, he maintained the status quo of the Pontifical and Augural colleges, even declining the "priesthood of Lepidus," the position of *pontifex maximus*, when it was offered to him by the people.[22] Not only did Augustus become a member of each of the colleges himself but he also filled the colleges with men who were loyal to him, ensuring, through the prestige of the colleges and their close connection to him, that they would have the opportunity for further political success. The colleges were themselves important forums for elite discussion and friendship, meaning that the prestige of belonging to a college extended far beyond religious affairs.[23]

As a member of each college, Augustus could participate in all of the colleges' discussions and influence decisions. It was clearly important to him that he be a member of each of the colleges not simply for the prestige that came with it, but so as to be able to ensure that the religious activities that were undertaken by all of the colleges were supportive of his own goals. As membership in the colleges was considered to be very prestigious, it should come as no surprise that during the Principate admission to the college was almost always predicated on having a close personal relationship with the *princeps*. It is no great revelation to note that political careers in Rome were frequently the result of patronage, but during this period, it became increasingly apparent that there was now only one patron.[24]

The Augustan "revival" of neglected religious traditions was, in many respects, truly a revival, but because so much of ancient tradition had been lost, there was much room for innovation. The increase in the number of priests, the elevation of the Epulones, and the revival of the Arval Brothers were all part of a larger programme to re-centre political and religious authority around Augustus.[25] Rather than attempt to enact change in the most well-established colleges, the pontifical and augural colleges, the most important modifications were made in less-contested arenas, the colleges of the *quindecimviri*, *epulones*, and *Arvals*.

Augustus began by increasing enrolment in the *quindecimviri*. Registration in the college had not been maintained in the late Republic, and with the deaths of Dolabella and Cassius Longinus (in 43 and 42 BCE, respectively), the college was emptied of members. While it is not always possible to tell if the lacunae in the membership lists of the colleges is simply due to poor record keeping during a period of civil war, it is clear that at the very least the record keeping of the colleges improved dramatically after Augustus joined, and that their ranks were filled. The college of the fifteen had long been considered to be the least prestigious of the major colleges and its members had a far less prominent place in society. They were only consulted by the Senate in connection with extraordinary events, which may explain why membership was not diligently maintained. Augustus effectively had carte blanche to fill the college with his friends and colleagues and to transform this lesser major college into an important organization. Unsurprisingly, his son-in-law, and likely heir apparent, Marcus Agrippa, joined the college shortly after Augustus himself.

Given the fragmentary nature of evidence from this period, it is impossible to reconstruct the careers of all of the men who held priesthoods during this period. However, for those priests for whom we do have some evidence, it is clear that their co-optation was related to their connection to Augustus. The *fasti* lists of the college of *quindecimviri* in 17 BCE well illustrate this point, as this was the college that saw the greatest expansion, and for which we have a reliable list of members for the year 17.[26] We can see two phases of co-optation: the first following the Treaty of Misenum in 39 BCE, and the second throughout the early- to mid-twenties. Of the twenty-one *quindecimviri* in 17 BCE, the numbers inflated to support the *ludi saeculares* of that year, nine were co-opted ca. 39 BCE. After the wars of the 40s and 30s, the colleges had been emptied of their members and the college of *quindecimviri*, one of the less influential colleges, was particularly empty. Following the treaty, the members of the second triumvirate, Augustus, Antony, and Lepidus, appointed their supporters to the priesthoods, and the ranks of the *quindecimviri* were increased. The men who were co-opted in this period were, for the most part, military supporters of Augustus and Antony, many of whom are otherwise unknown, suggesting that their co-optation into the college was based on their military alliances rather than any familial or political connections.

Following his victory in the battle of Actium, Augustus continued to co-opt priests into the colleges. The second stage of co-optation into the *quindecimviri* in the 20s is thus dominated by personal allies of Augustus, either military supporters, relatives, or otherwise. It is impossible to fully reconstruct the lives of the priests, but at least six of the ten new priests added to the college in the twenties owed their position to their relationship with

Augustus or Agrippa, themselves also members of the college.[27] In so doing, Augustus ensured that in any debate, he would have allies in the college, and people who could watch over his agenda when he was outside of Rome. As we will see in Chapter 5, the college of *quindecimviri*, previously a college of low stature compared to the *pontifices* or *augures*, became significantly more important during the Principate.

Through joining each priestly college and influencing to a great degree the new appointments, in his revival of the colleges, Augustus, where possible, appointed men who were loyal directly to him. The priestly colleges, formerly the domain of elite families, who often considered membership to be effectively hereditary, were now open to new men, as long as they proved themselves loyal to the *princeps*. The effects of this repopulation of the priestly colleges will be seen in the next chapter.

Conclusion

While working within their existing religious systems, Augustus and Emperor Wu took a much more active role in religion than their predecessors. While this attention to religion was to some extent a reflective of the religious interest of the First Emperor, Emperor Wen, and Julius Caesar, the extent to which Emperor Wu and Augustus inserted themselves into and reshaped their religious institutions was unprecedented.[28] Emperor Wu, while maintaining the state institutions for sacrifice, exerted his own will by recruiting new mantic experts into his imperial staff. These men, largely from outside the capital region, were disliked by the traditional court elite who saw them as charlatans and as a threat to their own influence. Although many of the *fangshi* may have truly desired only to deceive the emperor for profit, Sima Qian's account of them is biased by his disagreement with them over the correct shape of imperial cult, as well as by the fact that he felt his own position to be threatened by the influence of these new men.[29] What his account fails to consider, however, is that despite the deception of these *fangshi*, and despite the vast sums expended by Emperor Wu in his pursuit of immortality, their advice aligned with the emperor's desire to create a unified empire and to sacrifice to spirits in areas where he traditionally had little practical authority. The territorial expansion of imperial cult is the subject of the next chapter. Augustus, like Emperor Wu, took an active role in reshaping his state's religious systems. Because the Roman religious institutions were much more formalized than those of the Han, he was constrained to a certain extent by tradition. He used this rhetoric of tradition to his advantage by reviving the priestly colleges that had been emptied out during the civil war. Although some of this revival may have been more accurately described as an invention, couched in the language of tradition as it was, it was deemed correct and acceptable to the Roman elite. The new members of these colleges were carefully chosen allies of Augustus, men who hoped to have a successful political career under his patronage. We shall see in the next chapter the political ramifications of the revival of the priestly colleges under Augustus. Although he filled the colleges with his allies, Augustus continued to oversee the state's religious institutions, despite not claiming the highest priesthood. Breaking with tradition, and thereby establishing a new one, he became a member of all of the colleges, ensuring that there would be no room for religious debate without him. In the following chapter, we will explore the importance of the colleges in the political life of Rome, and how Augustus' reconstitution of the colleges contributed to his own political agenda.

5
Expanding Influence

Incorporating new men into their respective religious institutions helped the two rulers solidify their position at the helm of state religious activities. In the process of doing so, they also expanded their reach, using state-sponsored religious activity to accrue more personal authority. In the Han, Emperor Wu travelled across the empire to offer sacrifices to important spirits and sacred locations; by so doing, he was also laying claim to their territory. As a result of his expansion of cult some sacred locations, namely famous mountains, came under the direct control of the Han court. In Rome, the previously less-important college of *quindecimviri* came to have greater importance in the political life of Rome. The men who Augustus co-opted into the priestly colleges assisted him in his governing of Rome and in his reforms to Roman state religion.

The expansion of authority through religion took place primarily outside the capital in the Han and primarily within the capital at Rome. Before we dive into this material, a few words must be said about this distinction. The "Treatise on the *feng* and *shan* Sacrifices" is concerned with the history of state-sponsored pursuit of extrahuman cult, and does not go into detail on imperial ancestral worship which took place at ancestral temples located, during the early Han, near the imperial mausolea.[1] While we would now perhaps lump these activities together as acts of religion or ritual, at the time they were considered to be very different. The sacrifices described in the "Treatise on the *feng* and *shan* Sacrifices" occur almost entirely outside of the capital at Chang'an, which tells us that in the pre- and early-imperial periods, rulers who wanted to sacrifice to powerful spirits had to travel to those spirits. As we will see in the Conclusion, the ritual reform in the late Western Han reversed this, requiring instead that the spirits come to the capital to receive sacrifice.[2] In Rome, on the other hand, the expansion of Augustus' influence through religion took place within the capital. This is of course not to say that Augustus did not seek to expand his influence outside of the city of Rome—he certainly did—but that he did not use the traditional state religious institutions to do so. Nor can we say that Roman religious cults did not spread outside the city of Rome—they did as well—but that the priests of Rome had no jurisdiction in the provinces.³

Expanding Influence outside the Han Capital

The changes in personnel in the Han and Augustus' collection of priesthoods gave both rulers the ability to make further changes and expand their reach into religious institutions and sacred territories. Emperor Wu's worship of the Five Sacred Peaks (*wu yue* 五嶽) had both a significant impact on his own time, as well as into later imperial China. While mountains and rivers had been important sites of worship from earliest times, it was not until the reign of Emperor Wu that a fixed pantheon of Five Sacred Peaks was established.⁴ Prior to his reign, kings and emperors had worshipped various mountains and rivers in the pre-Qin period; each state had their own set of mountains that they worshipped, within their own territory. During the Warring States period, the idea emerged that there were nine mountains, corresponding to the nine provinces (*jiu zhou* 九州) described in ancient texts. Yet the texts which describe this schema are not consistent in which mountains they include, which Yang Hua suggests may imply that these texts are imposing a later concept onto Zhou-era histories.⁵ With the creation of the Qin empire, the First Emperor expanded his worship of mountains to include those outside of the territory of the former state of Qin. To the seven mountains in the Guanzhong area (Mt. Hua 華山, Mt Bo 薄山 [a.k.a. Mt. Shuai 衰山], Mt. Yue 岳山, Mt. Qi 岐山, Mt. Wu 吳岳, Crane Mound 鴻塚, and Mt. Du 瀆山 [Mt. Wen 汶山 in Shu]) that the Qin had offered sacrifice the First Emperor added five more in the east (Mt. Song 嵩高, Mt. Hengg⁶ 恆山, Mt. Tai 泰山, Kuaiji 會稽, and Mt. Xiang湘山).⁷ This "set" of twelve mountains, together with designated rivers across the empire, constituted a fairly fixed set of state sacrifices to be performed to mountains and rivers. However, the Qin system was not strictly regulated, and there is evidence that commoners continued to sacrifice at these mountains, rather than it being the exclusive right of the state.⁸ In his description of the Qin sacrificial system, Sima Qian notes that previously, spirits of faraway regions were worshipped by the local populations, and that these did not fall under the emperor's sacrificial domain.⁹ This may be a criticism of the decisions of the First Emperor and Emperor Wu to personally offer sacrifice, but it also reflects that ideas about the worship of great mountains and rivers was, under the Qin and Han, changing dramatically.

During the early years of the Han, it was left to the regional lords or kings to perform sacrifices to the great mountains and rivers within their domains. However, it is clear from the outset of the Han that there was a desire to bring these sites of worship under imperial control. During the reign of Emperor Wen, the kingdoms of Qi and Huainan were temporarily abolished, and Emperor Wen attempted to bring the rites to these mountains and rivers back under the auspices of the imperial court, ordering imperially appointed sacrificial officials to ensure that the rites were carried out according to tradition.[10] This was warranted, according to the "Regulations of the King" *wang zhi* 王制 chapter of the *Liji*:

> Where any of the spirits of the hills and rivers had been unattended to, it was held to be an act of irreverence, and the irreverent ruler was deprived of a part of his territory.

> 山川神祇，有不舉者，為不敬；不敬者，君削以地[11]

While the Qin worship of mountains had a predominantly western bias, Emperor Wu determined to refine the worship of great mountains to reflect the geography of empire more closely, traditional accounts of mountain worship, and contemporary correlative thinking. Under his reign, the Five Sacred Peaks were determined to be Mt. Song 嵩高, Mt. Hua 華山, Mt. Tai 泰山, Mt. Heng 衡山, and Mt. Hengg 恆山. There are likely several reasons for this decision. First, the choice of five mountains, each representing a different region of the empire, corresponded with contemporary five phases ideology, which, as Mark Edward Lewis notes, may have created a "cosmic mandala of the four directions, with the nodal points marked by the Five Sacred Peaks."[12] At the same time as the choice of these five mountains aligned with contemporary cosmology, it also evoked the legendary sage rulers of China's past. The legendary emperor Shun, to whom much of the foundations of Chinese civilization were attributed, was said himself to have gone on inspection tours, offering sacrifices to five mountains. While the *Documents* does not record any of the mountains except for Mt. Tai, it notes that each of the mountains corresponded with one of the cardinal directions and the centre. Sima Qian, helpfully, annotates his quotation of the *Documents* by including the names of the mountains that came to be worshiped under Emperor Wu.[13]

Each of the five mountains was east of the capital at Chang'an and at the time of Emperor Wu's reign, only two of these peaks, Mt. Song in the centre, and Mt. Hua, the furthest west, were under control of the capital, while the other three, Mt. Tai, in the east, Mt. Heng, in the south, and Mt. Hengg, in the north, were part of the kingdoms of Jibei 濟北, Hengshan 衡山, and Changshan 常山, respectively. For the emperor, it was important for all five of the peaks to be within his domain, as they reportedly had been during the time of the Yellow Thearch and Shun, and this quickly became clear to many of the regional lords. With remarkable foresight, in 122 BCE, the King of Jibei, having heard rumour that the emperor was considering performing the *feng* sacrifice, submitted a memorial to the throne presenting Mt. Tai and its surrounding cities, which were located within his kingdom, to the emperor as a gift. The emperor accepted this gift and bestowed upon him another district in compensation.[14] Other rulers had less foresight, and the emperor had to resort to other means. Mt. Heng, in the kingdom of Hengshan, was incorporated into the empire with the abolition of the kingdom in 122 BCE, due to the revolt of the king.[15] Mt. Hengg was located in the kingdom of Changshan, and on the pretext of resolving a messy succession in the kingdom—caused, we are told, by a queen with loose morals—the Kingdom of Changshan was abolished, its territory divided, and the two claimants to the throne were each given their own domains.[16] While we have few details about these events, the identical *Shiji* and *Hanshu* passages are explicit that these territorial claims were made to further the emperor's sacrificial program:

After this, the Five Sacred Peaks were all within the commanderies of the Son of Heaven.

然後五嶽皆在天子之郡。[17]

These five peaks had formerly, according to legend, been sacred to the Yellow Thearch, who frequently visited them and sacrificed to them before he achieved immortality. Rather than simply resolve the succession struggle, or outright replace the king with another member of the Liu clan, Emperor Wu chose to divide the kingdom of Changshan, and keep for himself the territory surrounding Mt. Hengg. Liu Kuan 劉寬, the King of Jibei, may have suffered a similar fate had he not made the donation of Mt. Tai to the emperor, though he and his kingdom would only barely outlive the reign of Emperor Wu.[18] In 85 BCE, having had an affair with his step-mother and cursing the emperor during a sacrifice, he committed suicide, and Emperor Zhao reincorporated his land into the empire as Bei'an commandery.[19] We have little information about the specifics of sacrifices at the mountains other than at Mt. Tai, the emperor did visit them on several occasions, and sacrifices to the mountains were performed by imperially employed sacrificial officials (see Figure 5.1).

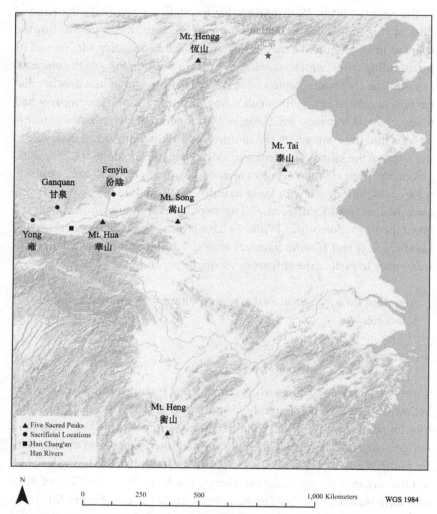

Figure 5.1 Important sacrificial locations and the Five Sacred Peaks during Emperor Wu's reign[a]

[a] Map created by Janice Ngiam. Rivers represent Han-era courses. Sources: 中國歷史地圖集 Zhongguo lishi ditu ji The historical atlas of China. (Shanghai: Ti tu chu ban she: Xin hua shu dian Shanghai fa xing suo fa xing, 1982). ESRI, USGS, NOAA.

The establishment of the Five Sacred Peaks, and their incorporation into commanderies under Han central authority, was not the only form of spiritual imperialism that took place under Emperor Wu. In addition to the mountains, Emperor Wu frequently offered sacrifices at Yong, the site of sacrifice to High Gods that the Han had inherited from the Qin, as well as to newly established sacrificial locations to Great Unity at Ganquan 甘泉 and to Sovereign Earth at Fenyin 汾陰. He also made journeys to the east coast, to attempt to find the immortals of Penglai. The tours to the various sacred locations in the empire increased as Emperor Wu continued to age and searched more desperately for the secret to immortality. He sought to personally contact more spirits, and to access more spiritual locations, adopting spiritual sites and deities from other regional cultures.

One of the most important sacrificial locations that was established under Emperor Wu was in the northwest, where the emperor established the altar to Great Unity at Ganquan. Ganquan Mountain was located 100 km to the northwest of Chang'an. The first Han palace was built at the site by Emperor Wu in 119 BCE, on the recommendation of the *fangshi* Shaoweng 少翁,[20] but the location had formerly been important during the Qin dynasty as the southern terminus of the Zhidao 直到, the Qin Direct Road, which was built on the orders of the First Emperor in 212 BCE. The road was to open a passage to the north, with a northern terminus at Jiuyuan (near Baotou 包頭, Inner Mongolia).[21] While the road was not completed,[22] it was an important part of the Qin campaigns against the Xiongnu, and Ganquan remained an important site on the border of the Han Empire.[23]

While Emperor Wu had visited Ganquan on several occasions prior to 113 BCE, it was only after this point when it became an important part of his cult.[24] This was largely due to the fact that he had been informed by Gongsun Qing that the Yellow Thearch came into contact with the spirits there, at Mingting 明庭 which he identified as Ganquan.[25] On the Winter Solstice, the first day (*xinsi* 辛巳) of the eleventh month of the 6th year of Yuanding (24 December 113 BCE), the emperor performed the first sacrifice to Great Unity at Ganquan, and renewed it in 107, 100, and 88 BCE, though he visited the site on at least seven other occasions (111, 105, 97, 94, 91, 89, and 87 BCE).[26] In 105 BCE, again on the advice of Gongsun Qing, Emperor Wu began holding court at Ganquan, and decreed that residences must be maintained for the Regional Lords at the site (a similar requirement would be made at Mt. Tai), and on this occasion, he received the "accounts" from the regional lords (受計于甘泉).²⁷ Court was held for the regional lords again in 97 and 87 BCE. In 94 BCE, Emperor Wu travelled to Ganquan to banquet guests from foreign countries, though the *Hanshu* does not specify precisely from where: 饗外國客,²⁸ and this trend would be continued by Emperor Xuan 漢宣帝 (r. 73–49 BCE), who on two occasions even required that the Xiongnu Shanyu himself come to pay court.²⁹

This final point is important, though it is not emphasized by the *Hanshu*. Ganquan was a site that was sacred to the Xiongnu; it was a mountainous region where they worshipped heaven,³⁰ and Emperor Wu's adoption of Ganquan as a place sacred to the Han can thus be seen as an attempt to take over this rich spiritual location. Given the Han's knowledge of the Xiongnu and their customs,³¹ it is likely that Emperor Wu and his advisors knew of the spiritual power of Ganquan; however, nowhere in the rhetoric that is preserved is this point discussed. Rather than seeing the use of Ganquan solely as an attack against the Xiongnu, it is more likely that Emperor Wu and his advisors made use of every location that they believed was suitable to communicate with heaven in his pursuit of immortality, though the increasing importance of the Ganquan site also indicates the importance which Emperor Wu placed on the conquest of the western regions. While it would appear that Emperor Wu did not achieve immortality there, Ganquan was an important symbol of imperial unity: not only did it represent Emperor Wu's triumphs against the Xiongnu and provide him with a location closer to the ongoing campaigns, but it was also a meeting point for all of the nobles; a sacred location where the emperor could call them all together, and where no one was in doubt as to who was truly the ruler of All under Heaven.

In addition to the journeys on land, Emperor Wu also sent out many men to search for the immortal islands of Penglai in the eastern sea. Emperor Wu was not the first ruler to send *fangshi* into the eastern sea to find the immortal isles; the First Emperor sent numerous failed excursions into the eastern sea to seek immortals and elixirs of immortality. Sima Qian invites us to see the *fangshi* who embarked on these voyages as profit-seekers, for each time they returned to shore they claimed that they had almost accessed the islands, and that they simply required more time and resources.³² However, some scholars have interpreted these voyages outside of their religious context, arguing that the missions were also exploratory, and sought to extend the emperor's reach into the maritime regions.³³ As no records of these voyages exist, this must remain speculative, but it is consistent with both emperors' programmes to expand their imperial influence as well as to reach more spirits.

As the imperial cult expanded, it became impossible for the emperor to perform all of the sacrifices himself. Indeed, this did not seem to be a problem at all—the sacrificial system was designed so that officiants could offer sacrifice on the emperor's behalf, and they ensured that all of the proper steps were taken in sacrificing to the spirits. As we have seen, each of the important sacrificial locations were staffed by officials who were responsible for the maintenance and upkeep of the ritual locations, as well as performing the necessary rituals, large and small. Indeed, it was not until the reign of Emperor Wu that the emperor personally regularly officiated the important sacrifices.[34] In years when the emperor himself visited the sacrificial location, presumably these officiants would have acted as assistants, not only facilitating the emperor's performance of a sacrifice, but also ensuring that it was performed correctly. These sacrificial officials were under the supervision of the Superintendent of Ceremonial,[35] who was also responsible for the supervision of the Grand Scribe, the Grand Diviner (*taibu* 太卜), and the erudites (*boshi* 博士).[36] The rituals performed throughout the empire were connected to the centre, under the supervision of this high-ranking official.[37] The establishment of sacrificial officials at important locations throughout the empire, some of which had been recently appropriated from kingdoms, contributed to the development of imperially promulgated networks, along with the infrastructure that went with it. While most of our information about these sacrificial networks are allusions in the histories, on several occasions they mention the existence of sacrificial officials at important cult locations, and, in the case of Emperor Wen, we know that the emperor ordered the Director of Sacrifices to ensure that the sacrifices to the mountains and rivers were carried out properly, in kingdoms that had been temporarily abolished.[38] Officials were likely sent out to inspect sacrifices and to ensure that the local officials were maintaining the sites.[39] After Emperor Wu sacrificed at Mt. Song, he established a town of three hundred households to maintain the sacrifices.[40] When the mountains and rivers were outside of the jurisdiction of the Han court, the kings or lords of that domain were responsible for making the sacrifice, but there could be imperial repercussions for failure to do so. What this sacrificial oversight looked like on the ground, we do not know. However, it likely would have encouraged compliance with the wishes of the imperial court, at least insofar as observations of ritual propriety were concerned. Failure to correctly follow ritual prescriptions could, at times, be very dangerous for the emperor's inferiors. In 112 BCE, one hundred and six nobles were purged of their titles and their domains for failing to correctly observe ritual propriety when presenting the emperor with contributions for his sacrificial programme. The nobles had sent gold instead of wine for offerings in the ancestral temple, and while this was a common practice, it went against ritual prescriptions, providing the opportunity for their removal.[41] The purge was likely political, as it had been common for nobles to pay their dues in cash rather than in kind, it reinforced the court's willingness to use ritual prescriptions to further political aims. By staffing spiritually important locations with imperially appointed sacrificial officials, the Han *imperium* was granting itself the prerogative to ensure that sacrifices were being performed according to the imperial court's wishes.

The locations where the emperor sacrificed were important, not only for their spiritual significance. Many of the emperor's tours went to the eastern regions, regions that had long maintained semi-autonomy from the Han court. As the emperor travelled not only with his sacrificial advisors, but with much of the court, these sites became loci of imperial power themselves. As Tian Tian has argued,

> As the important cult sites such as Yong, Ganquan, and Mt. Tai often served as centers of political and administrative activities, this dispersal of cult sites over a very wide area might well have diluted the importance of the imperial capital. Probably the decision to combine political progresses with cultic activities at key sites was aimed at building a "control network" throughout the empire.[42]

Unlike the consolidation of religious authority under Augustus, which was largely confined to the city of Rome, Emperor Wu's religious authority, and his corresponding political authority, extended across the empire. This territorial expansion of cult, and with it the movement of the political centre across the empire is natural given that the Han empire did not expand outward from a single city, as the Roman empire had.[43] Lewis has described the Han cities as "transitory phenomena built of perishable substances"[44] unlike the Roman capital, which Augustus "found . . . built of brick and left [it] in marble,"[45] and while the Han capital was the centre of the empire, during the reign of Emperor Wu, the emperor and his officials spent much of their time outside of the capital. While the Han capital was in the west at Chang'an, Han authority travelled with the emperor across the realm, and "the Han house came to justify its rule through its ability to transcend all local ties and limitations."[46] One of the ways in which they were able to do so, was through this expansion of religious authority.

Priestly and Political Power in Rome

As we have seen in Chapter 4, in reviving the college of *quindecimviri* during the Principate, Augustus filled the empty seats with his supporters. While he also added some supporters to the *augures* and *pontifices* when positions became available, he was able to make more substantial changes to the College of Fifteen, for several reasons. First, as the Pontifical and Augural colleges were considered to be the most important colleges, and the most prestigious, their numbers had not been allowed to decline to the same extent as the *quindecimviri*. Second, as the college of *quindecimviri* was not considered to be particularly prestigious, there may have been less objection to the inclusion of these supporters of Augustus, many of whom were *novi homines*, into filling these seats. However, in addition to filling the ranks of the college, Augustus also transformed it into the most influential priestly college: the *quindecimviri* organized and presided over the *ludi saeculares*, and the members of this college ultimately came to occupy the highest ranks of the *cursus honorum* more frequently than the members of other colleges.

The *ludi saeculares* themselves will be discussed further in Chapter 7; here I would like to raise the question as to why this lesser college was given the task of performing such an important ceremony of state. The simple answer is obvious: while Lepidus still held the position of *pontifex maximus*, the actions of the pontifical college had to be restricted as much as possible. Indeed, G. W. Bowersock has remarked that the Pontifical College, and particularly its leader, were embarrassingly absent from the games,[47] which were led by Augustus and Agrippa in their roles as *quindecimviri*, and as holders of tribunician power. Lepidus, in exile from 36 until his death in 13/12 BCE, had not been stripped of his title of Pontifex Maximus, out of respect for the office. Bowersock has convincingly argued that Augustus' hesitation to take the title was not due, as others, notably Syme, have argued, to the fact that he did not particularly care about the position (having already been named *princeps senatus*), but rather because he believed the "priesthood was simply too important to tamper with."[48] Bowersock goes on to argue that achieving the position of *pontifex maximus* was the high point of Augustus' career, and it is his inaugural procession as *pontifex maximus* in 12 BCE that is depicted on the Ara Pacis. He writes that it "was in the majesty of the pontificate that Augustus presented himself as the conqueror who brought peace."[49] However, it was as a holder of tribunician power and as a *magister* of the *quindecimviri* that he inaugurated the new *saeculum*.[50]

This suggests that the symbolism of the *pontifex maximus* was actually more important than the duties of the office. The priesthood *was* too important to tamper with, as it was held by the highest religious official in Rome, and to do so would be to disrespect not only the traditions of the Roman Republic but also perhaps the gods themselves. While there was certainly no conception in the minds of the Romans that the priests were divinely appointed, Augustus had to maintain the façade of Republican institutions. In order to do so while simultaneously transforming the Republic into something unrecognizable by the ancestors, Augustus needed to shift the focus of religion away from the *pontifices* and away from their worship of Jupiter. For this, he employed the *quindecimviri*, and through the language of a revival of tradition, he quietly reshaped religion, political influence, and popular support in the first decades of his rule.

This is not to suggest that the pontifical college or its duties were neglected. On the contrary, the college maintained its usual schedule of sacrifices, and the ritual role of *pontifex maximus* was filled by the oldest member of the college, Calvinus. Calvinus, in his sixties at the time of the reforms to the colleges, was close to Augustus and had been enrolled in the Pontifical College prior to 44 BCE.[51] As acting *pontifex maximus*, he would have ensured that the correct sacrifices to Jupiter were taking place in the absence of a *flamen Dialis*, as well as maintaining the regular activities of the Pontifical College. Additionally, he was instrumental in assisting Augustus in establishing the Arval Brothers and was one of the founding members of that minor college.[52] However, the Pontifical college was prevented from making any major changes, such as fixing the calendar, and it was rendered politically quite impotent. Indeed, after 44 BCE, the Senate only consulted the college on issues concerning political matters on four occasions, none of which occurred during the Augustan period.[53] The impotence of the college was deliberately maintained by Augustus, who, despite being a member of the college himself, refused to let the college undertake any major acts while Lepidus was still at its head.[54] The position of *flamen Dialis*, which was to be filled by the Pontifex Maximus, was left vacant until Augustus replaced Lepidus. His decision to revive the *flaminate* after the office had been vacant for over seventy years drew parallels between Augustus and Numa, the second king of

Rome, who had established the priesthood in the first place.[55] The parallels between Augustus and Numa was one that the princeps chose to highlight, in order to create precedence for this succession: as Numa succeeded the founder of Rome, Romulus, so Augustus succeeded the founder of the new order, Caesar.[56]

The impotence of the pontifical college was not restricted to exclusively religious affairs: a survey of the consular lists from the Treaty of Misenum, when the college of *quindecimviri* was revived, to the death of Lepidus reveals that members of the pontifical college did not dominate the consular lists in the early years of the Principate.[57] While only 48.6 per cent of consuls between 39 to 13 BCE concurrently held priesthoods, the highest college of priests made a poor showing in the consular lists. In fact, the priests of the *quindecimviri* far outnumbered their colleagues in the Pontifical College in the highest magistracy (see Table 5.1). Twenty-one per cent of the consuls in this period belonged to the college of *quindecimviri*, while only 4 per cent held membership in what was perhaps no longer the most prestigious college. In the years in which Augustus held the office of *pontifex maximus* (12 BCE to 14 CE), this dominance decreased, with 5 per cent of the consulships being held by *pontifices* and 11 per cent belonging to the *quindecimviri*. While the percentage of priests who held consulships in the two periods remained fairly constant (48.6 per cent versus 40.7 per cent) the distribution changed dramatically, seeing the newly restored colleges gain much more importance in the political sphere.

Table 5.1 Consulships held by Priests[a]

	Pontifices	Augures	Quindecimviri	Epulones	Arvales[b]	Priests out of Total Number of Consuls[c]
39–13 BCE	3 (4%)	11 (14.9%)	16 (21.6%)	3 (4%)	3 (4%)	36/74 (48.6%)
12 BCE–14 CE	4 (5%)	7 (8.75%)	9 (11%)	9 (11.3%)	4 (5%)	33/81 (40.7%)

[a] These numbers do not include members of the imperial family (Augustus, Tiberius, Germanicus, or Gaius) who were members of multiple colleges. They have also been excluded from the total number of consuls.

[b] As this college only came into existence in ca. 29 BCE, I have only included members who held consulships after that date. An additional two men held consulships prior to the formation of (and their co-optation into) the Arvals. See Scheid, *Romulus et ses frères*, 690–703 on the dating of the formation of the Arvals.

[c] Including suffect consuls, but excluding the imperial family.

While it is true that the highest magistrates of the Roman Republic were drawn from the same social group as the priests, that is, the elites, this was far from a cohesive group, and competition was rife, both in the case of elections and in discussions in the Senate.[58]

Here is where the secondary role of the priestly colleges comes into importance: while the colleges all had their assigned duties, and the priests were entitled to participate in public festivities in priestly dress,[59] they also had the opportunity to meet as a group, on the orders of the Senate to discuss a question, to take care of priestly business, or simply to banquet together.[60] It was on these occasions that the colleges could discuss, informally, affairs of state, and perhaps reach consensus on certain issues. While Augustus would have been entitled to participate in the meetings of all of the colleges, influence seems to have been wielded through the *quindecimviri*, comprised in large part of long-time supporters of Augustus. Like the Arval Brothers (and *epulones*), the *quindecimviri* was composed of nobles from different groups in order to "weld the senatorial elite into a homogenous bloc"[61] in order to achieve a unity of ideology which could be enacted by the *princeps* and his consuls.

In a recent study of the consulship under Augustus, Frédéric Hurlet has shown that although there were no "fundamental institutional modifications of the consulship under Augustus,"[62] there was a marked change in the way in which the office was employed. Augustus was to use his tribunician power to govern civil affairs, and while the consuls retained their imperium, they used this power "in a spirit of perfect collaboration with the *princeps*."[63] During the period of civil wars, many of the consulships had been assigned, as part of treaty and alliance negotiations, but beginning in 28 BCE, the consulship was again determined by an election, albeit with a very different character. Rather than being a competition between aristocrats that took place entirely in front of the people, the competition was now arbitrated "above all by the *princeps*."[64] While Augustus did have the right to intervene in the choice of consul, as well as the ability to apply informal pressure, the elections themselves still took place in front of the assemblies, and as such, maintained the façade of a fair and competitive election.[65] That over 20 per cent of the consuls between 39 and 13 BCE were also members of the *quindecimviri* (while only 4 per cent of the consuls were *pontifices*) suggests that this college rose in stature, not only in religious affairs, but also in prestige and in affairs of state. While there was by no means a monopoly of power within the college, by selecting consuls from this college, the *quindecimviri* may have functioned as a sort of unofficial advisory body, populated by long-term supporters of Augustus, where politics could be discussed. When Augustus was not present in Rome, which was a frequent occurrence during the early Principate, care of the state was left in the hands of Marcus Agrippa, the second member to join the revived *quindecimviri*, and Augustus' most trusted advisor.[66]

While extant sources do not permit us to recreate the day-to-day activities of the college of *quindecimviri*, one of their most important functions during both the Republic and the early Empire was to consult the Sibylline books. These texts, said to have been obtained at the beginning of the Republic were consulted with some frequency, over fifty times between the fifth and second centuries BCE.[67] As the "original books," which had supposedly been purchased by Tarquinius, had been destroyed in a fire in 83 BCE, the Senate appointed a commission in 76 BCE to collect a new set of oracles, which the *quindecimviri* were charged with editing, to ensure that all of the oracles were authentic.[68] We do not know how the college actually used the oracles, but there is indication that Senate may have encouraged the *quindecimviri* to find a particular solution from the books:[69] as the oracles themselves could often be interpreted in various ways, it was the task of the *quindecimviri* to find a suitable response within the texts, and to provide the Senate with a decision as to what rites should be performed to resolve the situation.[70] During the Principate, the *quindecimviri* were once again charged with editing the Sibylline books, in 18 BCE, as, according to Dio, the verses had become "indistinct through lapse of time."[71] In 12 BCE, the books were transferred, on the authority of the new Pontifex Maximus, Augustus, to the Temple of Apollo, which was connected to his house.[72] At the same time, Augustus collected and destroyed all publicly held prophetic writings, ensuring that the Sibylline books were the sole collection of prophetic writings held in Rome, and that they could only be consulted by the *quindecimviri*, a college of which he was the senior member.[73]

The elevation of the *quindecimviri* took place in several stages. The emptying out of the colleges in the 40s provided Augustus with the opportunity to rebuild it almost from scratch, initially in conjunction with Antony after the Treaty of Misenum, but later on his own terms. Having a college filled with his supporters proved to be useful, and the men who became members were rewarded for their support in more ways than simply obtaining a priesthood. In return, they supported Augustus as he prepared to host the *ludi saeculares*, effectively declaring the beginning of a new, Augustan, age.

Conclusion

As Emperor Wu travelled across his empire, taking over important spiritual locations and establishing sacrifices, he incorporated these into the sacrifices overseen by the government, perhaps even leaving sacrificial officials to maintain the altars.[74] In this way he ensured not only that the spirits he offered sacrifice to would not be neglected, but that an imperial presence would remain in those locations after he had moved on to other areas. Similarly, by ensuring that political power was wielded by his allies and that the most important religious discussions took place within the newly revived colleges, Augustus maintained a presence within the colleges and Rome, even if he was unable to be present personally. Most importantly, by recruiting new men into religious institutions, they were able to ensure that they were able to dictate how their state-sponsored cults would be used in shaping imperial ideology and in communicating their position to the people of their empires. The publicity of religious authority and the narratives of imperial ceremony will be the subject of the next two chapters.

6
Communicating Imperial Authority

We have so far considered the contestation of religious authority only within the spheres of elite power. The elites, of course, were not the only people who mattered. Support from the people was necessary in both early China and Rome.[1] The Roman elite had long courted popular support, as they relied on the masses to vote in elections, serve in the army, and participate in displays of social prestige. While not as directly courted in early China, it was the duty of the ruler to ensure the livelihood of the common people and to avoid overburdening them with tax and labour services, or overly harsh punishments. The short-lived Qin empire was brought to an end by the spread of popular rebellions against the overly demanding and punitive government, and so it is somewhat surprising that there was no recorded popular resistance to Emperor Wu's expensive sacrifices, which later courtiers claimed were so lavish that they drained the state's finances.[2] Likewise, there was not only much resistance to one-man rule in Rome, but the recent civil wars had taken their toll on the people and the city. In this chapter, we will explore the question of how the two rulers were able to broadcast their position as supreme authority over religion and state, without antagonizing or overburdening the population. As in the previous chapter, Augustus' activity largely takes place within the city of Rome, while Emperor Wu's will take him across the empire. Both rulers inserted themselves into their respective religious landscapes, showing their authority to the people and securing their cooperation via the bestowal of awards and honours. In Rome, this took the form of public building: both the construction of temples and monuments to the gods, creating an urban landscape that was unified in its architectural style and emblematic of the Augustan vision and extended to the construction of neighbourhood shrines.[3] In the Han, the emperor went on a series of inspection tours, travelling and sacrificing across the empire; during these tours he granted amnesties and awards to the residents of the areas he travelled through, to alleviate the burden of an imperial visit and spread the prosperity of his reign.

Different strategies were required to publicize the new religious programmes and to attain the support or compliance of the elite and commoners. In this chapter, we will consider the rulers' public building and inspection tours, along with the sacrificial ceremonies discussed in detail in Chapter 7, as media events, intended to broadcast each ruler's dominance in all religious affairs, as well as their supreme position in matters of state. Before turning to the respective cases, we will first examine how these "media" can be used to encourage support and compliance.

Public Display as Media

The ways in which the message of imperial authority was promulgated through rituals and ceremonies will be discussed in Chapter 7. In those rituals and ceremonies, the rulers communicated their authority to men and gods through the language of spectacle. However, these rituals and ceremonies were not the only means through which the rulers broadcast their authority; they also engaged in large-scale symbolic displays: in Rome through public building and in China through imperial processions.

In his study of Balinese imperial rites, Clifford Geertz has argued that imperial power was not static: it was "an argument, made over and over again in the insistent vocabulary of ritual."[4] Through the performance of continual rituals and the creation of a symbolic order, the theatre state "construct[ed] a state by constructing a king."[5] Performance of rituals reminded the Balinese "that worldly status has a cosmic base, [and] that hierarchy is the governing principle of the universe."[6] Status was articulated and solidified through rituals. While the divine kingship and theatre state of nineteenth century Bali bears little resemblance to the early Han or to Rome, some of Geertz's insights about the use of ritual in constructing imperial power can help us think through the ceremonies in the ancient world. In both Han and Rome, the performance of imperial rituals simultaneously articulated and reinforced the imperial regime, and, with the performance of the new "revived" rituals in Han and Rome, they provided the emperor's own commentary on the shape of imperial power. Geertz's study focused explicitly on the performance of rituals, but his description of the necessity of rearticulating the argument of imperial power over and over again can be applied to more fields than clearly defined rituals of state. We will examine some of these rituals in Chapter 7; in this chapter I would like to suggest that the argument of imperial power was also made in the realm of urban architecture in Rome and through the bestowal of gifts that accompanied inspection tours in the Western Han.

Umberto Eco, the Italian semiotician better remembered for his mystery novels, argued that architecture, rather than being solely functional, had important symbolic functions and communicative power.[7] The messages conveyed by different architectural features may change over time, and cannot always be controlled by the architect, but the forms of objects can, to a certain extent, modify the attitudes and behaviours of those who interact with them. Eco takes as an example the symbolic difference between an ordinary chair and a throne; certainly the function of these two objects is the same: to sit down upon. But while one may simply sit in a chair, only certain individuals may sit on a throne, and they must sit in a certain way: with regalness, usually marked by a rigid and uncomfortable position.[8] Thus the function of the throne as a seat is ultimately its secondary function, its primary function being to denote regalness and power, which causes (usually) the sitter to modify their behaviour (their way of sitting).[9] The communicative power of architectural objects, he argues, requires that the architect take into consideration social factors when designing her building or city. The architect must not only be concerned with the primary function of her design (a temple where sacrifices are offered to a god), but the symbolic messages that will be communicated to the users of that edifice (the priests, the worshippers, the passers-by). Likewise, the first- and second-order functions of the inspection tours in the Han should be considered. The purpose of the tours was to allow the emperor to inspect his empire and to offer sacrifices at important locations along the way. The sacrifices that served as the purpose of these tours, as we shall see in Chapter 7, were not public affairs, but rather closed events which only a privileged few were permitted to witness. The imperial processions that went on the tours, however, would have been visible to those who lived in the regions through which they passed. As such, the secondary function of the processions was communicative and efforts were made to shape the message that was delivered.[10] Like the regalness of the throne that causes the sitter to position themselves rigidly, as we shall see in this chapter, the inspection tours also induced a modification of behaviour in the regional officials.

Michael Suk-young Chwe has argued for the importance of the production of common knowledge in establishing support for, or maintaining, a regime. Rituals, particularly public rituals, are "social practices that generate common knowledge."[11] A public ritual is thus "not just about the transmission of meaning from a central source to each member of an audience; it is also about letting audience members know what other audience members know."[12] His definition of ritual is very broad, encompassing "public ceremonies, rallies, and media events."[13] In *Rational Ritual*, he uses examples from premodern history, as well as from near-contemporary times, including royal progresses, the French Revolution, and Super Bowl advertising campaigns.[14] The book explores how common knowledge is generated and how common knowledge can, and has been, used to enact societal change or maintain the status quo.

Chwe's argument is that each individual is more likely to support, or submit to, a particular authority, or engage in open rebellion, if they know that many others are doing the same, and knowledge of other people's support is communicated through these public rituals.[15] Writing about royal progresses, Chwe, expanding Geertz's 1983 arguments on ritual, writes that "progresses are mainly a technical means of increasing the total audience, because only so many people can stand in one place; common knowledge is extended because each onlooker knows that others in the path of the progress have seen or will see the same thing."[16] By witnessing these royal progresses, and witnessing others witness them, public support, or acceptance, is built for a regime. Particularly if these progresses take place without disruption, they can help create not only common knowledge of a regime, but common knowledge of the widespread *acceptance* of a regime.

In what follows, I propose that we look at the public building of Augustus and the inspection tours of Emperor Wu in these terms. While neither category is precisely ritual or media event, these actions had the effect of articulating imperial authority, by conveying common knowledge, and by eliciting support for the two rulers. In both cases, the rulers certainly attempted to shape the messages they conveyed, but, as with any form of public communication, the message was ultimately interpreted by those who received it.

Rebuilding Rome

One of the most oft-quoted statements attributed to Augustus is that he found the city "built of brick and left it in marble."[17] Dio records the statement slightly differently, that Augustus claimed to have left the city in marble, after finding it built of clay, which he states was in reference to the stability of the empire rather than simply the city's edifices.[18] Regardless of the context of the statement, it is indisputable that Augustus' building program drastically reshaped the city, both by building new temples, monuments, and public structures, and rebuilding those that had fallen into disrepair. The rebuilding of Rome was, in fact, one of his proudest achievements, demonstrated by the inclusion of a lengthy list of the buildings which he had built or restored in his *Res Gestae*, occasionally informing the reader exactly how much he had spent.[19]

According to the *Res Gestae*, acting on a decree from the senate in 28 BCE, Augustus restored eighty-two temples.[20] As with his other reforms, Augustus couched the rebuilding in the language of restoration and claimed to be following the will of the Senate. It was certainly true that Rome's temples were in need of restoration and that Augustus, with his vast financial resources, was the logical choice to carry out the expensive rebuilding. However, the Senate's decree effectively gave a monopoly on monumental construction to the new imperial family. While the city of Rome had formerly been a canvas on which the elite could demonstrate their achievements in war by dedicating temples and public buildings, Rome's magnificent structures would now only be associated with one family, signalling the end to yet another field of elite competition.[21]

The rebuilding of the city's temples was itself celebratory in nature. In his seminal study on the Augustan image programme, Paul Zanker writes that "these marble temples were not simply a stately setting for newly revived rituals, but were in themselves an expression of the new mood of self-confidence."[22] The temples restored by Augustus all employed the same aesthetic: a classical style with Roman characteristics, which served to unify the appearance of the city.[23] These temples endured and dominated the cityscape well into the future. Only two new state temples were built in the following fifty years,[24] suggesting that Augustus truly had the final word in defining the architecture of the city. The temples of the city were unified not only by architectural style, but by theme—all of the new state temples, and some of the restored temples, that were built by Augustus or immediately following his death, "refer directly or indirectly to the emperor," commemorating the *princeps'* victories, the virtues he promoted, and the divinity of the new royal family.[25] In one of Augustus' more audacious moves, he constructed a new temple to Apollo on his own land. Following a lightning strike in 36 BCE on the property, Augustus deemed it an auspicious location for the temple and subsequently dedicated the land to the public.[26] The temple itself, dedicated in 28 BCE, was connected to his own house, not only emphasizing the connection between Augustus and his patron god, but giving him unrestricted access to the temple, and the sacred texts that were stored therein.[27]

Augustus' rebuilding of Rome's great temples, an honour bestowed on him by the Senate and couched, like so many of his other projects, in the language of tradition, made the *princeps* the sole authority over the gods in Rome. These new and restored temples demonstrated his close connection with the gods, from whom he received auspicious signs and protection,[28] as well as his authority to speak to their needs. As a member of each of the priestly colleges, Augustus was a part of every important decision regarding the practice of religion at Rome; as the architect of its greatest temples, he sought to visibly demonstrate his central position in the realm of Roman religion.[29]

Augustus' celebrated his rebuilding of Rome's great temples in the *Res Gestae* and further accolades were given by contemporary authors and generations of historians of Rome. Less remarked upon, however, is the attention that he and his colleagues paid to patronizing and rebuilding small, local shrines within the city. Before he became *princeps*, together with Marcus Agrippa, Augustus began supporting religious sites, including rebuilding neighbourhood shrines.[30] While it is likely that these actions were taken in order to ensure the support of the population before he overcame his political rivals,[31] this early support of local shrines would pave the way for the unification of the network of *comptia*, the crossroads, and the transformation of the individual cults of the *lares compitalia* into the cult of the *lares augusti*.

The *lares compitalia* were deities of the crossroads. *Lares*, more broadly, were "thought of as very ancient deities, who were ubiquitous in the home, on the farm, and at the street corner in a town."[32] These deities were "gods of place," protector spirits who looked after their designated territory, be it a individual home or farm, or a region bounded by crossroads.[33] The *lares* were ubiquitous in Rome, not only having their own temples (there were two: the first restored by Augustus *in summa sacra via*, and the second on the Campus Martius), but shrines in each home, for each neighbourhood, and at crossroads.[34] Crossroads shrines were numerous and visible religious sites both within and without the city of Rome, and they were important to all classes of the population. As Harriet Flower has argued, "the compital shrine was a place of worship where the largest cross section of Roman society could (at least potentially) perform common ritual actions, regardless of social status, ethnicity, or gender, simply on the basis of living locally."[35] The crossroads, and their associated shrines, formed a network throughout the urban sprawl of Rome: "Rome was conceived of as a vast network of *comptia*, a network that brought people together in and beyond the street and neighbourhood (vicus)."[36]

The worship of the *lares compitali* took place at the Compitalia festival, an annual winter festival that was celebrated by all Romans, including the lowest classes, and which was an important festival for defining Roman identity. During the Augustan period, the festival, and the worship of the *lares*, became closely associated with the *princeps*, through his introduction of the cult of the *lares augusti* in 7 BCE.[37] It is not clear to us from the sources the reasons for the introduction of this new cult, but it was almost certainly connected to the redistricting of the city into *vici* which also took place in 7 BCE.[38] During this process, Augustus appointed new *vicimagistri*, local magistrates who were responsible for maintaining the compital shrines and for organizing the compitalia in their district. This, often done out of their own pocket, brought the *vicimagistri* honour and support within their communities, and when the cult of the *lares augusti* was introduced, they enthusiastically supported it, sponsoring dedications of *lares* within their *vici*.[39] The creation of the cult of the *lares augusti* wove Augustus and his legacy throughout the city of Rome by inscribing his name at each of the crossroads, the points of connection and intersection that traversed the city. Furthermore, the creation of the *lares augusti* "integrated the neighbourhoods' religion into the wider contexts of state religion" while maintaining "the traditional practices of compital cult."[40] Augustus' building and rebuilding of monumental temples was one grand way in which he left his mark on the city, but he also tapped into the popularity and pervasiveness of the *lares* cult, inserting his name into the crossroads of the city and into the tradition of the ancient protective deities of Rome.

The communicative media that we have discussed have been based primarily in the city of Rome. While this was indeed the primary focus of Augustus' religious reforms, a few words should be said about the ways in which Roman imperial authority was communicated beyond the city of Rome. There were many difficulties in exporting Roman religion from both practical—the gods had to give consent to be moved—to legal—the priests had no jurisdiction outside Rome.[41] While it was difficult to export Roman cults, the image of the ruler was less difficult to export. Augustus repeatedly refused divine honours at Rome during his lifetime, but allowed for the worship of the *divi Augustus* in the provinces. The worship of the living Roman ruler in the east became an important cult connecting the Roman provinces to the capital and, perhaps more importantly, was an important venue where local elites could demonstrate their own position. The cult to the living emperor was often initiated by governors, rather than being mandated by the Senate or emperors, and it served as a means of connecting local Hellenistic tradition with the new political realities at Rome.[42] In this way, the cult of the ruler in the Roman east was a way for the local subjects to "represent themselves to the ruling power"[43] and articulate their own position within the empire, by incorporating the emperor into their own religious traditions. Knowledge of the changes in ruling authority at Rome were also spread through the empire through the use of coins. The designs on coins were constantly changing and reflected changing political concerns at Rome. Towards the end of the Republic, designs increasingly portrayed elite men and their achievements, becoming yet another sphere of elite competition, one which would ultimately be dominated by the *princeps*.[44] Coins were significant communicative media because of their familiarity and ease of circulation. New coins were minted primarily to pay soldiers and the civil service, men who were actively involved in the day-to-day service of the state, and in the case of soldiers, who travelled to different parts of the empire.[45] The changing iconography on coins would have been clear to these civil servants and soldiers, who, while likely more interested in the intrinsic value of the coin, would have recognized the message being transmitted through the carefully curated images.[46] While coinage was only occasionally connected to state cult, it served as an important medium for the production of common knowledge and the transmission of that knowledge throughout the empire.

Inspection Tours and Publicity in the Han

Augustus' primary concern was in extending his influence in the city of Rome, amongst both the elite and commoners, as this is where politics were primarily contested. In the Han, imperial authority was not disputed at the capital, but did not fully extend into the outer reaches of the empire. For that reason, Emperor Wu pursued cult across the empire and into newly subdued territories. As we have seen, the emperor incorporated important spiritual locations into his empire, and attempted to personally contact as many spirits as possible, recruiting mantic experts from regions outside of the capital to serve as his aides. The locations where the emperor sacrificed were important, but not only for their spiritual significance. Many of the emperor's tours went to the eastern regions, regions that had long maintained semiautonomy from the Han court, or in the northwest, the site of frequent wars with the nomadic federations. Imperial authority extended into these spiritual locations by incorporating local sacrifices and rituals into state sacrifices, and the appointment of religious officials to supervise those sacrifices. Due to his interest in pursuing the spirits, for the inseparable goals of strengthening the state and achieving immortality, it was not enough to establish this network of sacrificial officials; the emperor wanted to personally travel and offer sacrifice himself. And in so doing, he also revived the ancient ritual inspection tours, tours around the empire taken by the sage rulers of antiquity, in order to personally examine their territory and ensure that it was being properly governed.[47] Imperial inspection tours began again under the First Emperor and during the Qin and Han the inspection tours became linked to the sacrifices at the various sacred locations in the empire, connecting the system of inspection tours of the ancient sage rulers and Western Zhou kings with the new political culture of the Qin and Han.[48] These imperial tours reached their apex under Emperor Wu. He went on over thirty inspection tours in his 53-year reign, and scholars agree that they helped to enforce imperial regulations and standards throughout the empire, as well as to promote the image of the emperor in far-flung regions.[49] While the emperor would not have been directly visible to the population, the tours were large, consisting of soldiers, guards, officials, and assistants/servants to the emperor, and often carried with them numerous sacrificial objects and rare animals. These large processions would likely have made manifest the emperor's power and grandeur as he travelled around the empire.

Unfortunately, there are no records that tell us in detail what an inspection tour might have looked like, and so the image must be pieced together from various inferences in the texts. The rulers of the pre-Qin period levied troops to accompany them on inspection tours, as the roads were full of perils, and we know that the First Emperor also travelled with his army.[50] Not only was there the very real possibility of an attack on the imperial convoy, as happened to the First Emperor in 218 BCE, but the roads and mountain passes were sometimes blocked by bandits.[51] The emperors were also travelling across varied and difficult territory, summiting mountains and visiting rivers, and they would have required manpower to build or repair roads and bridges that led them across perilous paths. One of the prime arguments during Emperor Cheng's reign in favour of consolidating the sacrifices in the capital at Chang'an was the difficulties in reaching the various sacrificial locations, and the implication that ritual objects were often lost in the journey.[52]

Emperor Wu's tours did not follow a fixed itinerary. His inspection tours sometimes corresponded to the schedule he had set for himself for imperial sacrifices, for example, to perform the sacrifice to Great Unity once every three years, but this schedule was often disrupted. Often, the emperor performed sacrifices when passing through sacred locations, whether on an inspection tour or otherwise.[53] At the beginning of Emperor Wu's reign, the imperial tours primarily went to Yong or Ganquan, sites to which roads had long been established, but, as he pursued immortality with more fervour, the tours went to locations that were increasingly far from the capital. Between 113 and his death in 87 BCE, there are only three years in which the emperor did not undertake some kind of tour, and he often spent months at a time on the road.[54] Prior to 113 BCE, the *Hanshu* biography only records visits to Yong and Ganquan, whereas after 113 BCE, the tours took him to a variety of sites.[55] While Yong, Ganquan, and Mt. Tai remained the three most frequently visited locations, the emperor also toured through the east, stopping at sites where he believed, on the advice of the *fangshi*, that he might meet the immortals.

Sima Qian suggests that the primary reason for undertaking the inspection tours was the emperor's quest for immortality. And indeed, the emperor's inspection tours increased in frequency after 113 BCE, the year that Gongsun Qing became his most trusted advisor. Qing informed the emperor that the immortals would only reveal themselves if he personally sought them, and this certainly contributed to the frequency with which the emperor travelled to the east in the years leading up to his death. The tours were thus directly connected with the emperor's quest for immortality, but in travelling across the empire to access sacred sites, the emperor also publicized his ability to access these spirits as well as his authority all across the empire. Through these tours he was also able to inspect the land and its people, and bestow rewards on the population, which may have contributed to the stability of the empire.

This argument is not new, nor were the Qin and Han emperors the first or last to pursue this strategy. He Pingli has argued that Emperor Wu's *feng* and *shan* sacrifices were part of large-scale publicity campaigns,[56] and Charles Sanft has argued that the First Emperor's imperial tours promoted the idea of the emperor throughout the empire, even to those who had not personally seen him or the tours.⁵⁷ While we have no evidence for how the commoners reacted to the processions of Emperor Wu, at least among the elites the tours served to inform them of his rule, and of his elevated position. Not only did the inspection tours transport the emperor and his very large entourage across the land, but they also required the regional lords and kings to travel to him.⁵⁸ The important sacrifices were marked not solely as ritual occasions, where the emperor communed with the spirits, but also as important political occasions, where the emperor met with the regional lords and kings. Politics and religion were not separate; the regional lords met the emperor on these important spiritual moments, and were reminded of their position, both figuratively and literally, within the empire.

I suspect that the impression of the common people, as explained by Sanft in his discussion of the First Emperor's inspection tours, were ultimately less important to imperial unity than that of the regional lords. However, this is not to suggest that the common people were not important: indeed, as the Han well knew from the history of the Qin, the commoners could be instrumental in determining the legitimacy of a dynasty. What I suggest is that the commoners were less concerned with dynastic legitimacy, with imperial pageantry, than they were, like the emperor, with their own personal welfare. The emperor was himself concerned with this: in addition to the amnesties and exemptions that were given to the people, on at least one occasion, the emperor sent out envoys to investigate the conditions of the commanderies, and had them report any officials who had been exploiting the population.⁵⁹ Indeed, given the flow of communication in the ancient world, it is likely that, with some exceptions, commoners were probably not particularly concerned with, or aware of, high level politics at court. The question remains, then, how these exceptionally expensive imperial tours could have inspired the complicity of the commoners.

While we have no data for the number of men, animals, and goods that were transported across the Han with the emperor, it is apparent that these tours were exceedingly costly, both in terms of manpower and finances. These costs, ultimately, were borne by the people themselves, as they were the ones who provided the labour and taxes that were used to finance the emperor's tours. However, rather than seeing popular opinion turn against an onerous governmental program (as the people did against the First Emperor's successor), there is evidence to suggest that the commanderies *desired* an imperial visit. The *Shiji* notes that after once again increasing the number of sacrifices and imperial tours on the advice of Gongsun Qing in 113 BCE,

Thereupon the commanderies and kingdoms each opened their gates and improved their roads, repaired and administered the palace guest-houses at the named mountains where the sacrifices to the spirits took place, and hoped for an imperial visit.

於是郡國各除道，繕治宮觀名山神祠所，以望幸矣。[60]

This passage raises a number of important questions and provides us with some insight as to how the Han sacrificial system and the imperial visits proceeded. It is clear that the commanderies and kingdoms maintained lodgings for the emperor, and perhaps for other important guests, but it is also clear that imperial visits were not as regular as the ritual texts might lead one to believe.[61] Given the irregularity with which the emperor performed the important sacrifices in person, this should not be surprising. Hope for an imperial visit was also impetus to improve infrastructure within a commandery or a kingdom, and this, presumably, contributed also to ease of trade and travel between the commanderies and kingdoms of the empire. However, this alone does not explain why a commandery or kingdom would so hope for an imperial visit.

The answer likely lies in the very unsystematic distribution of rewards that followed successful sacrifices, omens, of both the favourable and unfavourable variety, and imperial tours themselves. The proclamation of amnesties was not an innovation of Emperor Wu,[62] but their occurrence increased dramatically under his long rule. On some occasions, amnesties were granted for the entire empire, on others, only for regions through which the emperor passed.[63] Sometimes these amnesties were accompanied by gifts of rank or material objects, and on some occasions certain groups of the population were singled out for reward. Another reward was the designation of a period of several days of "universal drinking," a celebration which allowed commoners and officials to gather together to feast and drink.[64] Over the course of Emperor Wu's reign, a total of sixteen amnesties[65] were granted to All under Heaven, along with five five-day periods of universal drinking.[66] In addition to the amnesties granted to the entire empire, in the decade in which Emperor Wu travelled the most (109–100), on three occasions amnesties were granted specifically to the areas he passed through. When the amnesties were given to All under Heaven, the areas through which Emperor Wu travelled sometimes received additional tax exemptions, material gifts, or gifts of rank.[67] Because many of the sacrifices that the emperor performed were done in secret, or at least out of the sight of the common people, the commoners would know that with each imperial tour came rewards, which presumably offset the expenses incurred by a region which hosted the emperor. While the imperial tours were certainly costly and a major strain on the court's finances, attempts were made to alleviate the burden on the people whose regions were most affected by the tours, and to offer sufficient rewards so as to stave off any popular rebellions.

Conclusion

While neither strictly speaking ritual or media events, the public building in Rome and the inspection tours with their associated rewards and amnesties in China had powerful communicative functions in spreading the message of imperial authority. The creation of the *lares augusti* and the transformation of the city of Rome into a city with unified architectural motifs created an urban landscape where Augustus was omnipresent. Architecture, unlike art, is a medium which is usually perceived passively; the *flaneur* walking through a city perceives it distractedly, but also collectively, knowing that other city-dwellers inhabit the same spaces and see the same structures.[68] The unified architectural programme in Rome and the abundance of local shrines which shared a name with the *princeps*, combined with the period of relative peace and prosperity, made, for the Roman *populus*, the sole rule of Augustus a natural and beneficial affair. The imperial tours in the Han communicated Emperor Wu's reign in a very different way, but to similar effect. While we do not have any evidence for the ways in which people viewed the tours—did they line the streets to see the convoy pass, or were they confined to a safe distance?—we do know that they would have been aware of their impact. The tours would not have been perceived in the background, like Augustus' shrines and temples, but may have nonetheless had long-lasting impact on people's lives. Not only were the tours accompanied by amnesties and gifts, but they would have, in some cases, been accompanied by improved infrastructure.

The acceptance of these public communications—the approval by the Senate for construction and the enthusiastic adoption of the new cult of the *lares augusti* in Rome and the acceptance of gifts along with the lack of disruptions to the imperial tours in the Han—signals a tacit approval of the new orders. Chwe describes the decision to rebel against a regime as a "coordination problem" a problem where people will only participate if they know that a significant number of other people will also participate.[69] Communicating the message of mass participation is thus key to a successful protest. Likewise, acceptance of a regime can be inferred from the lack of coordinated protest. Had the inhabitants of Rome not been willing, even excited, to have Augustus as their *princeps* in perpetuity, they might have rejected the cult of the *lares* or disfigured the new marble temples. The people of the Han, too, might have rejected their government's exactions of taxes and labour by attacking or otherwise disrupting the emperor's tours, despite the temporary relief that followed them. As the public construction, both the grand temples and local shrines, was intended to spread the message of Augustus' benevolence, so too were the amnesties and gifts bestowed by Emperor Wu intended to demonstrate the emperor's generosity and exalted position in the eyes of Heaven.

The construction in Rome and the inspection tours in the Han had large-scale communicative functions, which made the new position of each emperor visible to the people, elite and commoners alike.[70] The benefits accrued by the people were restricted to Roman urbanites and to residents of the territories through which the imperial tours passed, but they nonetheless created widespread awareness, and perhaps tacit acceptance, in the areas that were of most concern to each ruler. The messages that were spread were likely somewhat unspecific, and open to much interpretation. The power of ritual to articulate and negotiate authority and to produce common knowledge is not limited to this large scale. As we will see in the following chapter, both rulers carefully crafted their religious ceremonies and sacrifices to define their imperial authority.

7
Redefining Ceremony

We have seen how the two rulers took an active role in reshaping religious institutions, and how the images of these sagely rulers were broadcast throughout their empires. This chapter will concern itself with what the practice of imperial cult actually looked like under Emperor Wu and Augustus: what new sacrifices and ceremonies they established, how they performed them, and what message the rulers conveyed through them. The sacrifices established, revived, or reformed by the emperors were multivalent performances: offerings to the spirits, demonstrations of cultural or imperial unity, and performances in front of gods and men. The sacrifices established, revived, or reformed by the emperors reflected their times, as viewed by the rulers: an age of peace and prosperity, an age of a ruler who had received the highest blessings of the spirits.

This chapter focuses on the major sacrifices and ceremonies that took place during the Han and Principate, respectively. Particularly in the Han, there were a multitude of smaller sacrifices and offerings, exploratory ventures to find traces of the immortals, and establishments of shrines to individual spirits for specific purposes. While these smaller sacrifices certainly contributed to the expansion of cult into the far corners of the empire, they had overall a less significant impact on the overall shape of Han imperial cult than the large-scale sacrifices, which fell under the supervision of the Director of Sacrifices. In the Han, we will focus on the formalization of the three most important sacrifices of the state: to the cults of the High Gods, to Great Unity, and to Sovereign Earth. The first of these was an old cult, established, as we have seen, in the Qin, while the second two were cults created by Emperor Wu, in order to formalize the worship of the supreme deities of Heaven and Earth, respectively. In Rome, we will see how Augustus "revived" ceremonies that, it was claimed, had fallen into disuse. The new ceremonies were a mixture of tradition and innovation, updating the ceremonies to fit Augustus' vision for the state. The final part of the chapter will turn to compare the two most significant ceremonies performed during these two reigns: the *feng* and *shan* sacrifices of Emperor Wu and the *ludi*

90 IMPERIAL CULTS

saeculares of Augustus. These ceremonies announced the dawning of two new ages: of Augustus and Emperor Wu, and celebrated the achievements of the two rulers in uniting their empires and attaining the blessing of the gods. In the creation of the new ceremonies and sacrifices, both rulers laid claim to tradition, performing rituals that had been neglected or overlooked by previous rulers. At the same time, they created ceremonies that demonstrated their position at the centre of their new vision of empire.

Establishing New Sacrifices in the Han

The sacrifices established by the present emperor are: those to Great Unity, Sovereign Earth, and the *jiao* sacrifice [to the High Gods] which is performed personally by the emperor every three years, the *feng* and *shan* to establish the house of Han; the *feng* is renewed every five years. [He also established] the five [sacrifices recommended by] Miu Ji: [those to] the Great Unity and Three Unities, the Dark Ram, the Horse Traveller, and the Red Star, and those sacrifices [recommended by] Kuan Shu, which are performed by officials according to the correct seasons. These six [groups of] sacrifices are all under the supervision of the Director of Sacrifices.

今天子所興祠，太一、后土，三年親郊祠，建漢家封禪，五年一修封。薄忌太一及三一、冥羊、馬行、赤星，五，寬舒之祠官以歲時致禮。凡六祠，皆太祝領之。¹

Sima Qian's summary of the additions made to imperial cult dramatically oversimplifies the many changes that he traces throughout the "Treatise on the *feng* and *shan* Sacrifices." Perhaps the summary was intended to impose some order on the disorderly expansion of state sacrifices: the emperor did not always follow the sacrificial schedule that was created for him, for example he sometimes personally performed the *jiao* every three years, sometimes not. Additionally, Sima Qian's summary glosses over the fact that some of these sacrifices were changed, moved, or possibly disbanded. For some of these sacrifices, those to the Three Unities (*sanyi* 三一), the Dark Ram, Horse Traveller, and the Red Star, the historian has only recorded one instance each. We are left wondering whether or not these sacrifices were performed on other occasions during Emperor Wu's reign, or after.² While it is possible that Sima Qian simply did not record performances of these sacrifices after the first, given that he records the times that the emperor performed the other sacrifices, to the Great Unity, to Sovereign Earth, to the High Gods, and the *feng* and *shan* sacrifices, it is more likely that some of these sacrifices were abandoned. This section will focus on the most significant of Emperor Wu's sacrifices and the changes he made, namely, the *jiao* sacrifice to the High Gods at Yong, and the establishment of sacrifices to the cults of Great Unity and Sovereign Earth. In making his changes, Emperor Wu built upon earlier tradition, but also sought to develop new sacrifices that could access the most powerful spirits in the land, and that would reflect his vision of a strong and unified empire.

As we have seen in Chapter 3, the *jiao* sacrifice to the High Gods was already well established in the early Han, and from the short-lived establishment of a shrine to the High Gods during Emperor Wen's reign at the Wei river, we can see that worship of the High Gods was not tied exclusively to Yong. Sima Qian's summary suggests that Emperor Wu created the *jiao* sacrifice to the High Gods, but it would be more accurate to say that he institutionalized it, formalizing the sacrifice at Yong, ensuring that the sacrifices took place once per year, and establishing the precedent that the emperor would personally offer the sacrifice once every three years, though this was not always followed to the letter. The *Hanshu* annals records that the emperor personally offered sacrifice at Yong in 134, 123, 122, 113, 112, 110, 108, and 92 BCE, suggesting that the frequency with which he sacrificed there was dependent on his ability to travel.[3] However, from the numerous sacrifices he personally offered at Yong, it is clear that the emperor considered it an important cult, and he maintained sacrifices there even after he established shrines to the High Gods at Ganquan, in support of the cult of Great Unity. In the years when he did not personally offer sacrifices, staff under the supervision of the Superintendent of Ceremonial offered them on his behalf. This experimentation, or an attempt to cover all the bases, is characteristic of Emperor Wu's cult practice: he preferred to offer too many, or even redundant sacrifices to ensure that no spirits were neglected or offended as he pursued others and dramatically expanded the pantheon.

While expanding imperial cult across the empire, Emperor Wu also incorporated and formalized the worship of a variety of spirits who had previously not been worshipped, or only held a minor place in the Qin and Han pantheon. The *feng* and *shan* sacrifices, discussed at the end of this chapter, were considered to be the most important sacrifices that the emperor performed, but the most significant innovation was the formalization of the cults of

Great Unity and Sovereign Earth, deities of heaven and earth, respectively. These were not entirely new cults, but their formalization and incorporation into Emperor Wu's programme of worship demonstrated his personal ability to access the most powerful spirits and spiritually powerful locations in his empire.

The entity Great Unity (*Taiyi* 太一),[4] is difficult to define. The first formal sacrifice to Great Unity is mentioned in the *Shiji* "Treatise on the *feng* and *shan* Sacrifices," during the reign of Emperor Wu,[5] but Great Unity is also referred to in Warring States era texts, though only in passing and without mention of an associated sacrifice.[6] Great Unity appears with more frequency in Han-era literature, but there is no consensus in the early texts as to what kind of entity Great Unity actually was. Li Ling has shown that in early China Great Unity was not only a spirit to be sacrificed to, but also closely connected to astronomy, technical arts, and early Daoist ontological concepts.[7] These various ideas of Great Unity, including the "sense of astral body, spirit, and ultimate thing," were circulating in pre-Han China, and were not mutually exclusive categories.[8] Rather, the Great Unity that was sacrificed to in the early Han, ultimately above all other spirits, was at once astral body, spirit, and the ultimate unity. As we consider each of these constituent parts, it is important to remember that the definition of Great Unity that coalesced for a period in Emperor Wu's sacrificial program contained all of these identities.[9] In the *Shiji*, Great Unity is identified as residing in the brightest star in the Pole Star 天極 asterism, the fulcrum around which the stars revolve.[10] In some excavated manuscripts, Great Unity is identified with the Dao itself,[11] suggesting that Great Unity was representative of the entirety of the cosmos. It is not surprising, then, that Emperor Wu decided to formalize worship of this deity and elevate it to the highest position within his cult program.

The first appearance of Great Unity as a distinct object of worship appears in the "Treatise on the *feng* and *shan* Sacrifices." In 121 BCE, the *fangshi* from Bo, Miu Ji, informed the emperor that in ancient times, the Son of Heaven had sacrificed to Great Unity, and that such worship should be restored. Miu Ji described it as "the most revered spirit in Heaven" and that its "assistants were the High Gods" 天神貴者太一，太一佐曰五帝.[12] The emperor thereupon ordered that a shrine to Great Unity be built to the southeast of Chang'an, where sacrifices would be held each Spring and Autumn, over a period of seven days.[13] Following the establishment of the Great Unity altar, other *fangshi* encouraged the emperor to sacrifice to a variety of other spirits, claiming that they also had been performed in ancient times, and all of these sacrifices were offered at the site of Miu Ji's Great Unity shrine.[14] At this stage, it seems that the emperor was experimenting widely, and that the worship of Great Unity began simply to see if it was efficacious.[15] He appears at this time not to have followed Miu Ji's claim that Great Unity was the supreme spirit in heaven, and that the five should be moved, and worship of the High Gods continued at Yong.

It was only while the emperor was preparing to perform the *jiao* sacrifice to the High Gods at Yong in the autumn of 112 BCE that the emperor began to question the traditional sacrifice held there. A man, who remains unnamed in our sources, approached the emperor and informed him that he, too, thought that the High Gods were merely the assistants of Great Unity, and that the emperor should instead be personally performing the *jiao* sacrifice to Great Unity: 五帝，太一之佐也，宜立太一而上親郊之.[16] The emperor carried out the traditional sacrifice at Yong, but after doing so, he travelled to the palace at Ganquan and ordered that a new altar to Great Unity be built, following the plan of the altar previously established by Miu Ji's near Chang'an. The emperor performed the *jiao* sacrifice to Great Unity on the winter solstice of 112 BCE, the first day of the eleventh month, mere months after sacrificing to the High Gods at Yong.

This new altar to Great Unity was an elaborate structure, consisting of three levels, with the altar to Great Unity at the top. At the base, surrounding the Great Unity altar, the emperor ordered altars built to the High Gods. They were oriented, as at Yong, according to their related cardinal directions, with the altar of the Yellow Emperor, traditionally in the centre, placed to the southwest. When the sacrifice was performed, Great Unity was offered a full complement of sacrificial animals, and added to this were sweet wine, preserved jujubes, and dried meat; a yak was killed, and served with the ritual implements for the *lao* [牢 sacrificial animals]: 而加醴棗脯之屬，殺一貍牛以為俎豆牢具.[17] The High Gods, now demoted at Ganquan to the role of assistants to Great Unity, were individually only given sweet wine as an offering, though perhaps they were expected to share in the carnal offerings given to Great Unity. The establishment of this sacrifice to Great Unity at Ganquan was an important moment in the transformation of cult under Emperor Wu. He not only established this sacrifice to the highest celestial spirit, and its accompanying earthly spirit, Sovereign Earth, he restructured the hierarchy of spirits by making the High Gods subordinate to Great Unity. Along with this restructuring of these important sacrifices, as well as the expansion of the rites under the supervision of the Superintendent of Ceremonial, he also expanded the Office of Music to take greater part in the sacrifices, composing songs to be performed at the sacrifices:

> When Emperor Wu determined the rites for the *jiao* and *si* sacrifices, he performed the sacrifice to Great Unity at Ganquan, thus giving it the [supreme] place of the *qian* trigram; He sacrificed to the Sovereign Earth at Fenyin, on the square mound in the middle of a swamp. He charged the Office of Music with selecting songs to be chanted every night, from among the music of [the former Warring States of] Zhao, Dai, Qin, and Chu. He appointed Li Yannian as the Commandant of Harmonies, and often recommended Sima Xiangru and many others to compose Songs and Rhapsodies. They discussed the characteristics of the pitch pipes, to harmonize them with the melodies of the eight [instrumental] notes, in order to compose the nineteen songs. On the *xin* day of the first month, the emperor performed the sacrifice atop the round mound at Ganquan, he had seventy boys and girls perform the songs together, and there were sacrifices from dusk to dawn. In the evening, there was a heavenly light that appeared like a shooting star above the sacrificial altar, the Son of Heaven himself offered prayers from the bamboo palace, and the hundred sacrificial officials and hundreds of people were all filled with awe.

> 至武帝定郊祀之禮，祠太一於甘泉，就乾位也，祭后土於汾陰，澤中方丘也。乃立樂府，采詩夜誦，有趙、代、秦、楚之謳。以李延年為協律都尉，多舉司馬相如等數十人造為詩賦，略論律呂，以合八音之調，作十九章之歌。以正月上辛用事甘泉圜丘，使童男女七十人俱歌，昏祠至明。夜常有神光如流星止集于祠壇，天子自竹宮而望拜，百官侍祠者數百人皆肅然動心焉。[18]

Not only did the emperor institute a new sacrifice which modified the hierarchy of gods, unifying the High Gods of the five directions under the Great Unity, but he also charged the Office of Music with unifying the music of the former Warring States. As he took over the spirits of the formerly independent states, so too he took over their music.[19] This passage is significant, too, as it is one of the rare occasions that we get a glimpse of the performances that accompanied the sacrifice, that is, the choral performance, as well as the reaction of the spectators. Far from being private, solemn ceremonies, these sacrifices involved multiple actors and catered to all of the senses. We will return to this at the end of the chapter.

The sacrifice was taken to be a great success: sacrificial officials reported that at the time of the sacrifice, "a beautiful light appeared, and on the following day, yellow vapours arose towards the heavens" 是夜有美光，及晝，黃氣上屬天. Following this great success, the officials, including Sima Qian, encouraged the emperor to make the altar and its sacrifices permanent, which he did, placing it under the jurisdiction of the Director of Sacrifices, who ensured that the sacrifices were performed every autumn. The emperor himself was to make the journey and offer sacrifices every three years.[20]

The demotion of the High Gods, at least at the Ganquan altar, to being the assistants to Great Unity, and the physical location of their altars, below and encircling the Great Unity altar, served to not only demonstrate the supremacy of Great Unity over all other celestial spirits, but also symbolically elevated Emperor Wu above all other rulers. While he continued to personally offer sacrifices to the High Gods, Emperor Wu was the first emperor to sacrifice to the higher power, surpassing the First Emperor of Qin and previous Han emperors.[21]

The sacrifices to Great Unity were also closely connected to Emperor Wu's territorial aspirations: his desire to expand the Han empire and to take over spiritually important locations. As we have seen, Ganquan had been an important military base for the wars against the Xiongnu, and, indeed, had been a site where the Xiongnu themselves worshipped heaven.[22] Perhaps the recent conquest of the Xiongnu and access to this sacred location itself prompted the renewed interest in the cult of Great Unity, and what Great Unity could offer the empire. Emperor Wu made an announcement to Great Unity about his upcoming campaigns against the Southern Yue and offered prayers for the soldiers, suggesting that he believed there was a connection between the expansion of his cult and the expansion of his empire, and that this deity could assist him in his military campaigns.[23]

The cult of Great Unity, after it was established at Ganquan, became the most important of the state sacrifices under the jurisdiction of the Director of Sacrifices.[24] Almost as important was the sacrifice to Sovereign Earth (*Houtu* 后土) a sacrifice to earth that complemented the sacrifice to the heavenly spirits. The sacrifice to Sovereign Earth was established almost a year prior to the creation of the Great Unity shrine at Ganquan. Sovereign Earth was not a deity invented by the emperor, but, as with the cult to Great Unity, he standardized its worship. As Great Unity was the supreme heavenly deity, so Sovereign Earth was an earthly deity, its counterpart.[25]

It was also after performing the sacrifice to the heavenly High Gods at Yong (*Yuanding* 4th year 113 BCE) that the Emperor questioned his officials as to why there was no complementary sacrifice to earth. Kuan Shu, who was then a sacrificial official (*ci guan* 祠官), discussed the topics with other officials, including Sima Tan, and presented a plan to the emperor for establishing a sacrifice to Sovereign Earth. Together they came up with a basic outline for the sacrifices: that five altars should be created on a round hill in a swamp and that the sacrificial animals should be buried rather than burned, as was traditional for sacrifices to earthly spirits, but they allowed the emperor latitude in determining where the altars should be established. For this sacrifice, the emperor chose the site of Fenyin, east of the capital of Chang'an, overlooking the Yellow River.[26] This site had previously been considered as a potential sacrificial location during the reign of Emperor Wen, but the *Shiji* does not tell us which particular sacrifice was being considered during this time, and the site was never developed. Emperor Wen's advisor, Xinyuan Ping, later proven to be a fraud, informed the emperor that the conditions were right for him to discover the lost cauldrons of Zhou, and that golden emanations in the sky above Fenyin indicated that this would be the location where the cauldrons might be found. Xinyuan Ping's deceit was discovered, he was executed (along with three sets of relatives), and Emperor Wen abandoned his plans to further expand the Han sacrificial program, or to attempt the *feng* and *shan* sacrifices.[27] Later, however, the site was determined under Emperor Wu to be suitable for the sacrifices to Sovereign Earth, and a shrine was duly established. This sacrifice became one of the most important in the Han canon,[28] but the emperor only visited this site to perform the sacrifice on four subsequent occasions, in 107, 105, 103, and 100 BCE, usually following a sacrifice to Great Unity at Ganquan. As with the other sacrificial locations, staff were employed to maintain the sacrifices.

In the sixth month of 113 BCE,[29] the shamaness Jin[30] was performing a sacrifice to Sovereign Earth at Fenyin, and there discovered an "object shaped like a hook sticking up out of the ground," and unearthed a large cauldron inscribed only with a pattern.[31] Scholars and commentators now believe that this cauldron was, in fact, the one planted by Xinyuan Ping to be "discovered" during the reign of Emperor Wen. It was taken at the time, however, as an authentic and highly auspicious omen, though Emperor Wu was suspicious as to why the omen had appeared at that particular time, as recent years had seen frequent floods and poor harvests.³² Interpretation of the cauldron was much debated, but ultimately the emperor was swayed by the argument of the *fangshi* Gongsun Qing, who told the emperor that this auspicious omen identified him as the successor to the Yellow Thearch, and encouraged him to perform the *feng* and *shan* sacrifices. The discovery of the cauldron at Fenyin also indicated that the site was appropriate for the Sovereign Earth sacrifice, and that for correctly determining that this important sacrifice was missing from his cult, the earth rewarded the emperor with a most auspicious omen. It was this omen, perhaps that revived the emperor's interest in the cult of the Great Unity, and compelled him to move the location of the altar to Ganquan.³³

The cult to Sovereign Earth was a counterbalance to the celestial Great Unity.³⁴ In the Great Unity cult at Ganquan, Emperor Wu sacrificed to the most important celestial deity—the fulcrum around which the universe rotated. In Sovereign Earth, he instituted a sacrifice to the earth itself, declaring his own sovereignty on earth, and further demonstrating the unity of all of the earth under heaven.

To summarize, Sima Qian credits Emperor Wu with the establishment of a number of imperially sponsored cults, and, writing from the first century BCE, he may have expected these cults to continue to be important in later reigns. Some of the cults established in this period were not maintained, and it is true that Emperor Wu did fervently pursue immortality, and did, sometimes, act on the advice of questionable advisors. However, the major cults that he did establish, particularly to Great Unity and Sovereign Earth, reflect Emperor Wu's vision of his empire, and his place within it. While some of these "new" cults were not entirely new, Emperor Wu designed their sacrifices so that they would emphasize the glory of the Han and emperor who ruled it.

Reviving Festivals in Augustan Rome

In his *laudatio* of Augustus' achievements, Suetonius makes special remark of the importance of Augustus' revival of religion in restoring Rome to glory. He congratulates Augustus for his membership in each of the priestly colleges and commends him for waiting until the death of Lepidus to assume the position of *pontifex maximus*, a position which many believed was his by right. As we have seen in Chapter 5, he filled the diminished priestly colleges, bringing their numbers up to their full complement, and increasing the importance of the lesser colleges. In addition to these achievements, Suetonius records that he revived certain ancient ceremonies:

> He also revived some of the ancient rites which had gradually fallen into disuse, such as the Augury of Safety, the office of Flamen Dialis, the ceremonies of the Lupercalia, the Secular Games, and the festival of the Compitalia. At the Lupercalia he forbade beardless youths to join in the running, and at the Secular Games he would not allow young people of either sex to attend any entertainment by night except in company with some adult relative. He provided that the Lares of the Crossroads should be crowned twice a year, with spring and summer flowers.
>
> *Nonnulla etiam ex antiquis caerimoniis paulatim abolita restituit, ut Salutis augurium, Diale flamonium, sacrum Lupercale, ludos Saeculares et Compitalicios. Lupercalibus vetuit currere inberbes, item Saecularibus ludis iuvenes utriusque sexus prohibuit ullum nocturnum spectaculum frequentare nisi cum aliquo maiore natu propinquorum. Compitales Lares ornari bis anno instituit vernis floribus et aestivis.*[35]

However, with the exception of the office of the Flamen Dialis many of these ceremonies were not actually in real need of revival. The Augury of Safety had been performed as recently as 63 BCE, though that augury had produced a negative result, and after Augustus' revival in 29 BCE, it once again fell into disuse until 49 CE.[36] The Lupercalia had famously last been performed in 44 BCE, and were well remembered for the scandalous behaviour of the elites. The *ludi saeculares* were due to be performed soon, but had hardly fallen into disuse, while the festival of the Compitalia was performed annually without fail. What, then, is the meaning of Suetonius' claim that he revived these ceremonies?

Individually, each of these "revived" ceremonies helped to reshape aspects of the city of Rome and its inhabitants to align with Augustus' vision. Particularly when presented in this way by Suetonius, they collectively painted a picture of Augustus as a sage ruler: one who had attained the highest praise from the gods and who would, through reviving ancient religious practices, restore Rome to her former glory. The *lares augusti* we have seen in Chapter 6, and the *ludi saeculares* will be discussed at the end of this chapter. In this section, we will look in more detail at what was revived or reshaped in the "ancient ceremonies" of the Augury of Safety (*augurium salutis*), the Lupercalia, and the festival of the Compitalia.

We know little about the Augury of Safety, save that it was an augury that was performed by the new consuls before taking office, which inquired "whether the god permits them [the augurs] to ask for prosperity for the people."[37] A positive augury allowed them to then offer a prayer to Salus for the safety of the Roman people.[38] This augury, however, could only be taken during a period when Rome was not currently at or preparing for war, and was therefore, as Dio notes, seldom taken, as it was difficult to find a day when no Roman armies were in the field, nor were there any civil disturbances in Rome.[39] Dio's comments were made during his discussion of the notable augury taken in 63 BCE, during the consulship of Cicero, which proved to be a failure. Cicero, in his *De Divinatore*, recorded that the augur responsible, Appius Claudius Pulcher, "declared that because the augury of safety was unpropitious a grievous and violent civil war was at hand."[40] While the Augury of Safety had indeed fallen into disuse, as we shall see, the Augustan revival in 29 BCE did not establish a precedent for annual observations, but it did subtly reshape the meaning of the augury, and the way that the Senate thought about war and peace in Rome.

Rosalinde Kearsley notes that for Augustus, 29 BCE was a very good year.[41] This was due to two events: the decree of the Senate to close the gates of Janus[42] and the taking of the *augurium salutis*, this time, we are led to believe, successfully.[43] Dio states that these twin honours pleased Augustus more than all the other decrees of the Senate.[44] Augustus was not at that time in Rome, and therefore would not have taken the augury himself, but the implication in Dio and Suetonius is that the revival of the augury was at his instigation.[45] These two events, one of which, the closing of the gates of Janus, was proudly recorded by Augustus in his *Res Gestae*,[46] were only possible due to the period of peace at Rome, but Dio reminds us that these two events took place despite the fact that there were still several Roman armies in the field. Kearsley argues that the Augury of Safety was revived by Augustus as part of his strategy to attain sole rulership in Rome, and that the "Senate's action in sanctioning the ceremony meant that it endorsed his campaigns as the only significant ones for the well-being of the State," and that by so doing, this decree also served to diminish the significance of the campaigns currently being undertaken.[47] This certainly did much to promote Augustus' position as *princeps*, and further implied that the peace that Augustus brought to the city of Rome was sanctioned by the gods, despite the ongoing campaigns in other parts of the empire. Perhaps, then, the closing of the gates of Janus and the taking of the Augury of Safety now implied that peace at Rome, and the end of civil war and factional infighting, was of greater significance than wars being conducted against non-Romans. This would present Augustus' successful Augury of Safety in direct contrast to the failed Augury of Safety in 63 BCE, when, although there were no Roman armies in the field, there were significant political rivalries and conspiracies at Rome. The Augury of Safety proclaimed Augustus not only as a bringer of peace, but as the only individual capable of ending factional rivalry at Rome. He was thus the only person capable of instigating the ancient ceremony of inquiry, and then perform prayers for the prosperity of the Roman people.

While the Augury of Safety was "revived" by Augustus after 34 years of disuse (though one could also consider the performance in 63 BCE itself a revival, after a much longer period of time), it again quickly fell into disuse. After 29 BCE, it seems that the augury was not taken again until 49 CE, when Claudius determined that it "should be reintroduced and continued for the future."[48] The sources are silent on the subject; no reference is made to later Auguries of Safety on the other occasions when Augustus closed the gates of Janus. Perhaps it was no longer necessary for the *princeps* to ask permission to offer prayers for the prosperity of the people.

The Augury of Safety contributed to the image of Augustus as the sole ruler of Rome, but Augustus was always careful to avoid comparison with both the monarchical aspirations of his adoptive father and the decadent licentiousness of the late Republic. His so-called revival of the Lupercalia demonstrates his attempt to use this popular festival to define his position in contrast to his predecessors. The festival traditionally took place in February, and generally involved the elite men of Rome running naked through the streets, whipping women with goat hides, supposedly to promote fertility or ease childbirth.[49] Much has been written about the depravity of the Lupercalia as well as its popularity both before and after the Principate. Indeed, the festival persisted well into the fifth century CE when Pope Gelasius I (492–496 CE) attempted to ban it, because of its celebration of "nakedness, sex, bawdy violence, voluntary or forced flagellation, riotous disorder and drunkenness, as well as antique pagan superstitions."[50] These concerns, except for the pagan superstitions, were shared by Augustus and he attempted to make the festival less licentious and more in keeping with the values of modesty that he was attempting to instil in the population. However, precisely because of its antiquity and that it allowed for the loosening of morals, it was a popular festival. The Lupercalia was also a festival which Keith Hopkins has argued, "helped Romans identify themselves as Romans," and Roman nobles boasted about their participation in the Lupercalia, and even went so far as to give their children names reminiscent of the festival.[51]

The Lupercalia was particularly significant not only for its antiquity and popularity, but due to a notable recent episode. In 44 BCE, the Lupercalia was the occasion when Mark Antony, naked, oiled, and drunk, (*nudus, unctus, ebrius*), mounted the Rostra and offered a diadem to the dictator in perpetuity, Caesar, in an attempt to have him accept the kingship. Caesar wisely refused,[52] but in the early Principate, the image of the refused diadem, as well as that of the senatorial elite running oiled and naked through the streets would have been indelibly etched into the minds of the population.[53] How, then could Augustus allow this festival to continue while simultaneously distancing himself from both the image of licentiousness and the image of kingship, which he was himself pursuing in all but name? First, he tried to make the festival less indecent, by forbidding beardless youths from participating[54] and possibly requiring that participants wear loincloths.[55] These changes were in alignment with Augustus' broader moral programme, which sought to promote traditional familial structures and to encourage childbirth, at least among the Roman elite. It further restricted unmarried individuals from participating in certain festivals that were considered morally corrupting, as will be discussed further below. Second, he perhaps attempted to remove the association with kingship, and with his adoptive father, by reviving the role played by the *flamen Dialis* in the festival. Ovid notes that the *flamen Dialis* presided over the rites,[56] a line which has vexed scholars, as the *flamen Dialis* was prohibited from touching or even naming goats and dogs, the primary sacrificial animals in the Lupercalia.[57] Holleman has argued that the role of the *flamen Dialis* in the revived festival was intended to remove the Lupercalia's association with divine kingship, and with Caesar, allowing the popular festival to proceed under Augustus who continued to divorce himself from the image of Caesar being presented a crown.[58] This change may have also reminded spectators that, unlike Caesar, Augustus had not been appointed *flamen Dialis*, although Caesar had only remained in that priesthood until 81 BCE and would therefore not have participated in the Lupercalia in that role.[59] We do not know how long this chaste version of the Lupercalia persisted, only that by the time of the fifth century CE it had once again become a bawdy celebration. However, Suetonius' inclusion of the festival in his accolades of Augustus suggest that the reshaping of this festival was an important factor in Augustus' program of religious revival.

In similar fashion, the Festival of the Compitalia was not revived by Augustus, but rather subtly reshaped. The festival was named for the *comptia*, the shrines at the crossroads, and the worship of their associated *lares*.[60] *Ludi* were incorporated into the festival at some point during the Republic but were banned by the senate in 64 BCE. The festival without *ludi* continued annually without disruption, and it was only the games which were truly restored by Augustus.[61] Dionysius of Halicarnassus traced the establishment of the festival to the sixth king of Rome, Servius Tullius, and comments that the celebration of this festival continued on until his own time.[62] It was a festival which was celebrated by all Romans, but was particularly beloved by, and came to be associated with, freedmen and slaves.[63] The Compitalia was a moveable feast, celebrated in late December or early January, always after the Saturnalia.[64] The date of the celebration was announced by the praetor nine days in advance of the festival, who called "the Roman people, the Quirites," to celebrate the Compitalia, and further proclaimed that no business was to be undertaken during the festival period.[65] The festival was thus one for all Romans; a rare occasion when everyone, including farmers, freedmen, and slaves, could enjoy a break from work and celebrate with their fellow Romans.[66] As Harriet Flower has argued, the festival was also a time when people demonstrated their social status and, perhaps, when local magistrates, the *vicimagistri*, performed some kind of population count.[67] Woollen dolls and balls, representing free persons and enslaved, respectively, were hung, originally at the *compital* shrines and later on the doors of households.[68] These effigies were perhaps intended to be offered to the *lares* in lieu of the rumoured human sacrifices that were associated with the festival in Tarquin Superbus' time, but also served as a visual representation of the population in each *vici* and the status of members therein.[69] Flower notes that not only was this a way in which the population could be visually represented, it was also an opportunity for individuals to demonstrate their status: formerly enslaved men and women could demonstrate their freed status by hanging a woollen doll instead of a ball.[70] Through the festival of the Compitalia, Romans, both in Rome and other Italian cities, were able to mark both their community and their boundaries, and the festival was thus central to the performance of Roman identity.[71]

It was this meaning of the festival that was the focus of Augustus' reform. He "patronized the festival and fostered a renewed local celebration of civic identity,"[72] a civic identity which was now closely associated with the *princeps*. This was a gradual change, which began with Augustus' patronage of local shrines throughout the city beginning in the 30s, and must be seen as a significant contribution to the so-called revival of Roman religion alongside the building of monumental shrines and temples in Rome.[73] As we have seen in Chapter 6, Augustus' division of the city into fourteen administrative regions, with the further subdivision into *vici* and the introduction of the *lares augusti* in 7 BCE, united the localized worship of *lares* into one large celebration. While the Compitalia had previously been a series of celebrations worshipping local *lares*, the "revived" Compitalia was now a series of local celebrations unified in their worship of the *lares augusti*.

We do not know the specifics of the changes made to the Compitalia under Augustus, other than the provision that the *lares* were to be crowned with flowers twice per year,[74] and it is clear from the sources that the festival of the Compitalia was a robust annual celebration which had by no means fallen into disuse. What then are we to make of Suetonius' statement that the Compitalia, along with the *ludi saeculares*, the Lupercalia, and the Augury of Safety were revived by Augustus? Perhaps it is simply that Augustus left such a profound mark on the meaning of each of these festivals that Suetonius and his contemporaries that they took Augustus at his word when he wrote that he "restored many traditions of our ancestors which were then falling into disuse."[75]

Epoch-Making Sacrifices: The *Feng* and *Shan* Sacrifices and the *Ludi Saeculares*

Two legendary religious ceremonies represent the apex of Augustus' and Emperor Wu's reigns and religious reforms.[76] These are the *feng* and *shan* sacrifices in the Han and the *ludi saeculares* in Rome. Both events clearly portrayed both rulers' vision of their position within state religion, and further demonstrated the role of religion in shaping the sociopolitical order. The two ceremonies appear at a first glance to be almost entirely different from each other: the *ludi saeculares* were multiday public games and sacrifices, to which the entire population of Rome was invited to participate, while the *feng* and *shan* sacrifices were much smaller affairs, consisting primarily of semi-private sacrifices performed solemnly by the emperor to heaven and earth, respectively. However, when we look at the place each ceremony occupied in society, the deliberate invention of tradition in both Rome and China, and the performance of the ceremonies in front of audiences, albeit of very different sizes, the *feng* and *shan* sacrifices and *ludi saeculares* present us many points for comparison. As the ceremonies were, for the rulers, the culmination of their religious transformation of empire, so too, the ceremonies bring together the various threads of this monograph, and this case study will show how religious ceremony was used to fully enact imperial authority in both the Han and Roman empires.

In Rome and the Han, both of the ceremonies were considered to be of highest antiquity, and the performance of the ceremonies was only possible when certain conditions had been met. In Rome, the *ludi saeculares*, the Saecular Games, could only be performed once per *saeculum*, a period defined by Censorinus as *spatium vitae humanae longissimum partu et morte definitum* "A *saeculum* is the lifespan of the longest lived individual of a given generation," approximately 100 or 110 years.[77] There was also a messianic element to the *saeculum*; Richard Beacham has argued that "the concept of a *saeculum* was linked with the notion of divine intervention in the form of a heaven-sent hero who would bring great victories and lasting peace marking the beginning of a new age."[78] The implication being that in each age, there could only be one such man worthy enough to usher in a new era. In the Han, while there was no set cycle during which the sacrifices were to be performed, there were certain conditions that had to be met before the ruler could consider offering these most supreme sacrifices. Specifically, the ruler had to rule over a united territory, and had to receive omens from Heaven that demonstrated that he had received the Mandate of Heaven, which would then sanction the performance.[79] As in Rome, the *feng* and *shan* sacrifices were exceptional, and could only be performed by an extraordinary ruler.[80]

The *feng* and *shan* sacrifices were understood to be the most significant of the sacrifices performed by ancient rulers, yet little was known of them, and scholars throughout imperial Chinese history, and today, continue to debate their meaning and origin. Even after Emperor Wu's celebrated performance of the *feng* and *shan* sacrifices, they remained elusive to later historians. Only six men are recorded in imperial Chinese history as having carried out these sacrifices: the First Emperor (Qin Shi Huang), Han Emperor Wu, Emperor Guangwu 和光武 (r. 25–57 CE) of the Eastern Han, Tang Gaozong 唐高宗 (r. 649–683 CE), Tang Xuanzong 唐玄宗 (r. 712–756 CE), and Song Renzong 宋仁宗 (r. 1022–1063 CE).[81] It was understood by scholars of imperial China that the *feng* and *shan* sacrifices could only be performed by a ruler who had received the Mandate of Heaven, demonstrating his legitimacy, while simultaneously announcing to heaven and earth that the ruler had "unified the empire and brought peace to the world" thus fulfilling his mandate.[82]

While the Warring States and Han scholars claimed great antiquity for the sacrifices, asserting that they had been performed by the Yellow Thearch and many other sage rulers, little was known of their origins, or how they should be performed. According to Mark Edward Lewis, for the Han scholars this enigma of the sacrifices pointed to their antiquity, rather than to their novelty.[83] In part this mystery was due to the form of the sacrifice—at its heart, the ritual required that the emperor personally and privately offer sacrifice at the summit of Mt. Tai, and bury a text.[84] Emperor Wu's decision to perform the sacrifices opened up a debate about the nature of the sacrifices and how they should be performed. This debate is recorded in the *Shiji*.[85]

At the time when Sima Qian wrote, while legend stated that seventy-two rulers had performed the sacrifices, only the names of twelve rulers had been recorded, and there was no information about how they had actually performed the sacrifices.[86] Of the twelve rulers listed by Guan Zhong 管仲 (720–645 BCE), as related by Sima Qian, only the last, King Cheng of Zhou, is a historical figure, and, according to the text, the last to perform a legitimate *feng* sacrifice.[87] In the *Shiji* narrative, Guan Zhong dissuaded the ruler of his own time, Duke Huan of Qi, from performing the sacrifices, on the basis that he had not received auspicious omens, and the debate over the *feng* and *shan* sacrifices ended there. In fact, by the time of Confucius, information regarding the sacrifices was entirely lost.[88] No subsequent discussions about the *feng* and *shan* sacrifices are recorded until those describing those attributed to the First Emperor, and as early as the Liang Dynasty 梁朝 (502–556 CE), scholars began to assert that the sacrifices had, in fact, been an invention of the Qin Dynasty.[89]

When the First Emperor of Qin determined to perform the sacrifices, he assembled a team of seventy *ru* scholars and erudites from Qi and Lu at the base of Mt. Tai, in order to debate the proper format of the sacrifices. However, no consensus was reached, and their "recommendations were difficult to carry out," so they were all dismissed 始皇聞此議各乖異，難施用，由此絀儒生.[90] As a result, he chose to use the *jiao*-type rituals that were performed at Yong to perform the *feng* at the summit of Mt. Tai, and the *shan* at Mt. Liangfu. At the summit of the mountain, he erected an inscribed stone, so that all would know that he had succeeded in performing the rite.[91] However, while ascending the mountain he encountered a violent storm, and had to take cover under a tree. The recently unemployed *ru* scholars used this storm to mock him, and subsequent *ru* took this to mean that his sacrifice had been unsuccessful.[92] Whether or not the First Emperor met with success in his sacrifice, his performance of the sacrifice was the only one for which the Han had any concrete evidence, and it was generally agreed during the time of Emperor Wu that it had been a genuine attempt at a *feng* sacrifice.[93]

The precedent set by the First Emperor was therefore not entirely satisfactory. First, the sacrifice he performed was not itself based on ancient practice, the *ru* who advised him had been unable to reconstruct this. Second, there was speculation that his sacrifice was unsuccessful and thus should not necessarily be taken as a model to follow. Emperor Wu, while constrained by some elements of the sacrifice, and the need to prove that he had auspicious omens, had ample room to create his own version of the sacrifice.

As with the *feng* and *shan* sacrifices, the *ludi saeculares* were considered to be a ceremony of some antiquity, which few rulers would have the honour of presiding over. While the games likely began as a ceremony to quell the people's fear after a series of frightening prodigies,[94] subsequent performances of the games, including those of Augustus, transformed them into a celebration of both the past and future glory of Rome. Due to their infrequency, as well as the vague definition of a *saeculum*, in the first century BCE it was generally agreed that games were due to be held, but there was little consensus as to exactly when. During the first century BCE, the *saeculum* was due to be renewed, and there were attempts made prior to the reign of Augustus to initiate the new *saeculum* and thus declare the man who inaugurated it to be the "hero" of the new age. In 88 BCE, several omens appeared, including a prolonged "shrill and dismal note" as if sounded by a trumpet in the "cloudless and clear air," which the Etruscan haruspices, after being consulted by the Senate, interpreted as being indicative of the "advent of a new age."[95] This discussion in Plutarch suggests that Sulla had considered inaugurating the *saeculum* himself.[96] Other contenders included Cicero, who suggested that Pompey might fill the role of the new man (in tandem with Cicero), and the Consul of 71 BCE, P. Cornelius Lentulus Sura, tried to claim the title for himself.[97]

There is also evidence to suggest that Julius Caesar had begun to think of staging the *ludi saeculares*, but due to the civil war, and his untimely assassination, was unable to do so.[98] Games were due in either 49 or 46 BCE (given that the previous games had taken place in either 149 or 146), and a series of portents in the year before Caesar's death may have encouraged speculation about the dawning of a new *saeculum*.[99] This speculation, according to Weinstock, set the foundation for the growing belief that it was, in fact, Augustus, who was to usher in the new *saeculum*.[100] For these great men, it was not simply enough to host the games and declare a new *saeculum* to have begun: in order to do so, sufficient omens were required and the Sibylline books needed to produce an oracle that indicated the beginning of a new age.[101] Like the *feng* and *shan* sacrifice, there was the need to demonstrate that the *ludi saeculares* had been divinely sanctioned.

Because the *ludi saeculares* were performed so rarely, while there were certain elements of the games that were known, there was no script for the celebration, and so at the time of Augustus, it was both necessary and possible to reconstruct these games of antiquity. The confusion over the timing and performance of the games is reflected in the discussions by the *quindecimviri* prior to the Augustan games of 17 BCE. The *quindecimviri* were tasked with determining how the games were to be conducted, and with consulting the Sibylline books to ensure that the performance of Augustus' games had been prophesied. In investigating the correct timing of the games, the College determined that the games had been performed four times prior to the reign of Augustus: in 456, 346, 236, and 126 BCE, and that it was subsequently time in 17 BCE for the games to be renewed.[102] Like many of Augustus' other reforms to imperial cult, the language employed about the *ludi saeculares* speaks about a revival of traditions which had been neglected.[103] And while the *ludi saeculares* could only be performed once per century, the ill-defined length of a saeculum provided some flexibility in determining when exactly the games should be held.[104]

Both in the Han and Rome, there was sufficient historical precedent to justify the performance of these once in a lifetime ceremonies, and these historical precedents imposed some constraints on the rulers, in terms of how and when they chose to celebrate them. However, at the time of Augustus and Emperor Wu, technical details about the performances were lacking—the priests and scholars of the time only had rough outlines of the structures of the ceremonies, allowing the rulers to fashion ceremonies in a manner consistent with their other performances of imperial cult.

Emperor Wu, advised by the *fangshi* Gongsun Qing, determined that the time was right to perform the *feng* and *shan* sacrifices. He had united the Five Sacred Peaks under his rule, he had defeated challenges to his dynasty both from within and without, and he had received numerous auspicious omens from heaven. All of his advisors, including Sima Qian who generally disagreed with the emperor's excessive sacrifices, hoped that he would perform these legendary sacrifices.[105] Like the First Emperor, Emperor Wu gathered together both *ru* and *fangshi* to determine the correct rituals to be used in the sacrifice, and, like the *ru* a century before, they were unable to provide many details, and, again, like the First Emperor, Wu dismissed them and largely relied on a tried and true sacrifice—the *jiao*. In 110 BCE, in the fourth month, on the day *Yimao* 乙卯, he ordered the *ru* to don the leather hats and silk sashes and to shoot an ox, the only parts of the sacrifice that the scholars could agree on, while he himself performed the *feng* at the eastern side of the base of Mt. Tai, using the *jiao* sacrifice as it was performed to Great Unity.[106] The emperor, along with his coachman, Zihou 子侯, ascended the mountain, where the emperor performed a second *feng* sacrifice at the summit, this time, in secret.[107] The next day, the emperor descended via the northern road, and on the *Bingchen* day, he performed the *shan* sacrifice at Mt. Suran, near Mt. Tai. He used the rites for the sacrifice to earth at Fenyin to perform the *shan*. Following the sacrifice, a number of "strange beasts and flying birds," (奇獸飛禽) including a white pheasant, were let loose, adding to the spectacular nature of the sacrifice. Also in attendance were other large and exotic animals, including elephant and rhinoceros, but these were not set free.[108] After the completion of the sacrifice, there was a bright glow at night and white clouds seemed to emerge from the sacrificial mounds. These were interpreted as favourable omens from Heaven after the successful completion of the sacrifice.

The *Shiji* account of the *feng* sacrifice is quite short and lacking in detail, and it presents the sacrifice as a very secretive affair.[109] This view has been reflected in later scholarship on the topic, which fails to note that the emperor, who indeed performed a secretive sacrifice at the summit, first performed the sacrifice at the base of the mountain, in front of his officials, and, on later occasions, the regional lords.[110] While the sacrifice at the peak may have been the most solemn part of the ceremony, when the emperor could personally communicate with the gods and receive their blessings out of the eyes of his many advisors, the sacrifices at the base of the mountain were no less significant. The emperor performed the *feng* using the same *jiao* sacrifice that was performed to Great Unity at Ganquan. We have seen how this sacrifice required the sacrifice of the three sacrificial animals, along with thick wine, jujubes, and a yak, with all of its accompanying dishes. The Great Unity sacrifice was also accompanied by musical performances by a choir of seventy young boys and girls. As there were special songs composed for the *feng* sacrifice,¹¹¹ now lost to us, it is reasonable to assume that similar choral performances accompanied the *feng* sacrifice at the base of the mountain. These performances, combined with the spectacle of the exotic birds and animals, and the elaborate yellow robes that were prepared for the emperor,¹¹² tell us that the *feng* sacrifice was anything but a quiet, secretive affair.

Following the successful completion of the sacrifices, the emperor issued two edicts. The first celebrated the success by granting gifts in the form of oxen, wine, and silk cloth to the populace, as well as remitting labour service and taxes for the regions which had been burdened by the sacrifice. A general amnesty was granted to the empire.¹¹³ The second edict spoke to the emperor's vision of the empire and his place within it:

> Of old, the Son of Heaven made one inspection tour every five years, using this to serve Mt. Tai, [and] the regional lords [all] had court residences there. Thus, We order the regional lords to each maintain a residence at the base of Mt. Tai.

> 古者天子五載一巡狩，用事泰山，諸侯有朝宿地。其令諸侯各治邸泰山下。¹¹⁴

While the *feng* sacrifice was not renewed at exactly five year intervals (just as the *jiao* sacrifice was not performed regularly every three), it was renewed five times during Emperor Wu's reign, in 106, 102, 98, 93, and 89 BCE.¹¹⁵ The regional lords were expected to convene at Mt. Tai for the performances of the *feng* sacrifice after the first, and on two occasions, in 106 and 98, the emperor also held court at the *mingtang*, where he "received the accounts" from the commanderies and kingdoms 受郡國計.¹¹⁶ Far from being a secret ceremony, the *feng* was a sacrifice which not only communicated the Emperor's exalted position to Heaven, it was also a celebration of his reign and an assertion of his supremacy to the men in attendance. That the spectators were not permitted to see the sacrifice at the summit at the top of the mountain only contributed to the emperor's authority and to his mystique, for the gathered officials and lords, having witnessed part of the ceremony, were aware that there was a clear division between the emperor and all other men.¹¹⁷

The *ludi saeculares* were likewise crafted to give further prominence to Augustus, ten years after he had chosen that title, and particularly cemented his position at the top of the religious hierarchy, despite the fact that he had not yet been named *pontifex maximus*. The games also elevated the position of Agrippa, at the time Augustus' son-in-law, and most trusted ally, as well as the college of *quindecimviri*. Like the revival of other religious institutions, the *ludi saeculares* were a mixture of ancient tradition and modern inventions.[118] The "revival" of the *ludi saeculares* was also closely linked to the revival of other religious institutions, particularly that of the college of *quindecimviri*, who were responsible for orchestrating the games.[119] As is known from the inscriptions, twenty-one *quindecimviri* were present at the games in 17 BCE: sixteen members and five *magistri*, appointed supernumerary to assist the regular members, and they were led by the main officiants of the festival, Augustus and Agrippa, both themselves members of the college.[120] During the discussions about the games, the college consulted the Sibylline books, and produced an oracle calling for the renewal of the celebration, specifying certain elements of the performance, and emphasizing the importance of the worship of Apollo in the celebration.[121] The Senate voted to hold the games on May 23, 17 BCE, to be conducted under the direction of Augustus and Agrippa, who held tribunician power.[122] At the same meeting, the Senate also issued a decree stating that due to the once-in-a-lifetime nature of the event, that the consuls of that year should ensure that columns of bronze and marble be erected, and engraved with a record of the games, in order to preserve "the memory of this great benevolence of the gods."[123] The Senate also decreed that unmarried individuals would be allowed to attend the games, in contradiction of the newly promulgated Augustan marriage laws.[124] Opened with a sacrifice of nine ewe-lambs and nine she-goats on the evening of May 31, the *ludi saeculares* went on for twelve days, which included additional sacrifices, both day and night, Latin and Greek plays, chariot racing, and the performance of songs composed for the occasion, most notably Horace's *Carmen Saeculare*.[125] Presiding over the majority of the ceremonies, Augustus and Agrippa were the most prominent men, though the inscriptions record the presence of other members of the *quindecimviri* in attendance at other parts of the festival. Augustus presented the evening sacrifices by himself, while the day-time sacrifices were presented by both Augustus and Agrippa. In addition to the festivals organized and sponsored by the College, Agrippa sponsored chariot racing on the final day, June 12th.[126]

The *ludi saeculares* were without question a celebration of the beginning of a new golden age, one which not only celebrated the power of Rome, but also "to proclaim with pomp and pageantry their own victory and the glory portended for Rome under the leadership of Augustus Caesar."[127] While the celebration was certainly a glorification of the victories of Augustus, it also demonstrated the different distribution of power under the new regime. The festival was not only a celebration of the renewal of Roman power, but also the era of peace that had been ushered in. The *ludi saeculares* were intended to represent this new era of peace, which would again be commemorated by the dedication of the *Ara Pacis* in 12 BCE, after Augustus had become *pontifex maximus*.[128] There has been some speculation as to why Augustus did not wait until he had attained that position to hold the *ludi saeculares*, and rather hosted them with Agrippa in his role as *quindecimvir*.[129] While the games had historically been the domain of the college of *quindecimviri*, the absence of the highest priest of Rome on this historic occasion would have been conspicuous. As we have seen earlier, Augustus refused to take the title of *pontifex maximus* while Lepidus was still alive, choosing even to allow some important institutions to become neglected rather than intervene in the affairs of the *pontifex maximus*.[130] In holding the games "in the embarrassing absence of the *pontifex maximus*,"[131] Augustus demonstrated that he did not need to hold the highest priestly office in order to dominate imperial religion; Augustus himself, the son of a god, was the highest religious authority in Rome, regardless of the office he held.[132]

Augustus' religious authority was also enacted through the expansion of the *ludi* to include day-time celebrations and by changing the gods to whom sacrifices were offered from previous *ludi*. The probable origins of the games in 249 BCE came about when the *decemviri* consulted the Sibylline books in response to the people being frightened by prodigies. Games were ordered, as were sacrifices to Hades and Proserpina over a period of three nights.[133] The emphasis in these early games was thus on exorcising pestilence or inauspicious prodigies, so night-time sacrifices were offered to appease the gods of the underworld.[134] In his *ludi*, Augustus held night-time sacrifices, but this time to the Moerae (fates), Ilithyiae (goddess of childbirth), and Terra Mater (mother earth), and most importantly, he also offered day-time sacrifices: to Jupiter on June 1st, Juno on June 2nd, and Apollo and Diana on June 3rd.[135] The night-time sacrifices took place on the Campus Martius, outside of the Pomerium, while the sacrifices to Jupiter and Juno took place at their Palatine temples, and the sacrifices to Apollo and Diana in front of the new Temple of Apollo, also on the Palatine.[136] Michael Lipka argues that the Campus Martius may have been considered "symbolically as Greek territory," and this division of sacrifices served to differentiate "Greek" versus "Roman" gods, redefining Apollo and Diana as Roman deities. As Diana's own temple was outside of the pomerium, she received sacrifice at her brother Apollo's, inside the pomerium.[137] The gods now worshipped at night changed the orientation of the sacrifices "away from infernal expiation towards fecundity,"[138] celebrating the strength and renewal of the Roman state. The day-time sacrifices, offered by Augustus and Agrippa, recognized the traditional gods of Rome, Jupiter and Juno, and elevated Apollo and his sister Diana to their side. Virgil proclaimed that the new *saeculum* was not only the age of Augustus, but of Apollo,[139] further reinforced by the construction of the Temple of Apollo attached to Augustus' own home.[140] In sacrificing to Jupiter, Juno, and Apollo and Diana together, Augustus associated himself not only with Apollo and Diana, but with Jupiter and Juno as well.[141]

The *ludi saeculares* were, perhaps unsurprisingly given Rome's culture of public performance, a very public event, attended by men and women from diverse socio-economic backgrounds. Unlike the *feng* and *shan* sacrifices, Roman *ludi* were entertainments enjoyed by rich and poor alike, and while Augustus had been without real rival for power for over ten years, displays of adoration from the *populus Romani* were still valuable currency.[142] In addition to communicating his new *saeculum Augustum* to the largest possible audience, the presence of a large, celebratory crowd communicated the message to the others in the crowd, as well as the political elite, that there was mass support for this new order.

Not only did the *ludi* offer the inhabitants of Rome to witness a once in a lifetime event, but the games were recorded for posterity: coins with the head of Augustus on the obverse, and a detail of a sacrifice on the reverse were issued to commemorate the games,[143] and bronze and marble columns were inscribed with records of the games.[144] The celebrations were thus inscribed in popular memory for both those who had been able to attend the games and those who had not.

The *ludi saeculares* thus had the immediate effect of demonstrating the new political order, which was itself legitimated by the mass participation of the people. Participation in the festival indicated a submission to the ruling order and participation, even as a spectator, demonstrated to others that this new order had been tacitly approved. That Augustus was able to conduct the games and inaugurate the new *saeculum* without holding the office of the *pontifex maximus* demonstrates not that he did not covet the office, but that his power was so great, and his other honours so many, that he was able to inaugurate the new *saeculum* and perform sacrifices to the most important gods without holding the office. This, perhaps, may be read as a final, and devastating, snub at the *pontifex-in-absentia*, Lepidus.

The *feng* and *shan* sacrifices of Emperor Wu and the *ludi saeculares* of Augustus were carefully scripted performances, intended to affirm and communicate the reality of the new ruling order. In both cases, modern innovations were combined with ancient traditions to create performances that demonstrated the new reality of power centred on the person of the emperor. The spectacles were, fundamentally, about demonstrating the power and glory of the reigns of Emperor Wu and Augustus. They demonstrated not only the supremacy of the ruler over the elites, but also that this supremacy had been divinely sanctioned; both the *feng* and *shan* sacrifices and the *ludi saeculares* were preceded by favourable divine omens, and the *feng* sacrifice was determined to have been successful following the appearance of further omens. While these spectacles differed in their medium, message, and audience, both were also epoch-making events, declaring to men and gods the triumph of the ruler, who had ushered in an era of unity and peace.

In both cases, Emperor Wu and Augustus were not creating imperial rituals out of nothing, but were bound to some traditions, based on what was remembered about the earlier performances of the sacrifices. As such, they were not able to completely invent the rites, and were therefore constrained by their respective ritual traditions and layers of interpretation that these sacrifices, or types of sacrifices, held.[145] Given the very different histories of both the *ludi saeculares* and the *feng* and *shan* sacrifices, as well as the differences in performance culture within each society, it is unsurprising that the two spectacles were performed with very different relationships with the people. It was necessary for Augustus to demonstrate his majesty to the entirety of the city of Rome, and the empire, with the circulation of commemorative coins, while for Emperor Wu, witnessing an imperial sacrifice was a privilege only given to those closest to the emperor, and who were part of the system of imperial power themselves.[146] The audience to whom these visions of the new order were presented, and who contributed to creating it, were thus representative of a longer history of political power in Rome and China. In Rome, consensus, or the appearance of consensus, was needed from the masses,[147] while in the Han, it was necessary to demonstrate that the emperor was supreme amongst all of the regional lords, and for both, that they had received the sanction of supernatural powers.

Conclusion

The new, or revived, ceremonies in Augustan Rome and the early Han built upon earlier traditions while simultaneously creating new ritualized messages about the shape of empire and the position of each ruler within it. These ceremonies invented new traditions for each society, inculcating new ideas about rulership while presenting them as a logical extension of the past.[148] Sima Qian's discussion of Emperor Wu's sacrificial program, which has shaped most discussion of early Han religion, presents the pursuit of spirits and addition of new sacrifices as an expensive and foolhardy pursuit of immortality for the emperor. While the sacrifices were certainly expensive, and some of the *fangshi* charlatans attempted to fool the emperor, the expansion of sacrifices and pursuit of immortality should not be seen as purely selfish exercises. For Emperor Wu, like the First Emperor and mythical Yellow Thearch before him, immortality would only be possible once the empire was united and at peace. The pursuit of immortality was clearly inseparable from the emperor's desire to expand and centralize Han authority. As we have seen, the imperial sacrifices took place at sacred locations throughout the empire, including those that had not previously been under Han control. By taking over those locations, the emperor was proclaiming both his hegemony over the land and his ability to access and commune with the highest spirits on earth and heaven. Although some of the lesser sacrifices he briefly pursued may have been invented out of thin air by the *fangshi*, the major sacrifices implemented at this time were in keeping with previous sacrificial innovation under the Qin and early Han, and, when taken in the context of the emperor's larger program of political centralization and territorial expansion, the new sacrifices were quite clearly designed for the grandeur of the empire. The *feng* and *shan* sacrifices illustrate this most clearly. As purportedly ancient sacrifices that were reinvented to offer the emperor the occasion to contact the highest spirits in heaven, they demonstrated not only his authority over his territory and its inhabitants but also the success of his sacrificial program in the eyes of heaven.

Augustus wanted to show himself as a sometimes reluctant leader of Rome which had been restored to glory after the recent civil wars. Emperor Wu sought to emphasize the fact that he was superior to all other men in the Han, but Augustus had to downplay his primacy. He therefore frequently refused honours, and often proclaimed that he was merely restoring the religious traditions of ancient Rome, which had been allowed to lapse by impious custodians. For this reason, he preferred to have himself portrayed in religious dress, as a priest rather than a senator or general.[149] By presenting himself this way, he softened his image, retreating from the image of dictator or king that Caesar had sometimes entertained. But he also reinforced his position as a member of each priestly college, and as the man in Rome who was most favoured by the gods. In reviving ancient religion, he took the opportunity to change the messages of ancient ceremonies, updating them to fit with his vision of Rome. At the *ludi saeculares* this vision was on display before all the citizens, and while he officiated the games accompanied by Agrippa and the other *quindecimviri*, it was clear to all, man and god, who held supreme authority in Rome.

8
Conclusion

Beginning with the simple observations by Sima Qian and Suetonius that both Emperor Wu and Augustus made major changes to their respective religious institutions, *Imperial Cults* has attempted to demonstrate that not only were these transformations important to the centring of authority around the person of the ruler, but also that the comparative approach can lead us to a more nuanced understanding of each society, and reveal similarities or trends in the forging of imperial authority. The "revival" of religion in Rome has long been considered an important part of the changes made by Augustus during the transition to empire, yet the changes made by Emperor Wu in the Han have largely been dismissed as the foolish quest of an emperor who was motivated only by his own desire for immortality. Confrontation with the Roman materials has forced us to take his pursuit of immortality and expansion of cult seriously, and to consider it within the larger context of ideas about empire and emperorship from early China. While the Roman historiographical tradition has taken the Augustan reforms much more seriously, debate exists for his motivations: were these reforms due to his extreme piety, or were they merely calculated political moves?[1] As the Chinese tradition contains much more substantial discussion over ideologies of rulership, it is easy to see how Emperor Wu situated his expansion within the context of sage rulers of the past; less easy is to see that Augustus' reforms, rather than being based solely on religion or politics, served to articulate his own vision of Rome and the place of religion, and the princeps, within it. This vision included active and fully staffed priestly colleges, a network of civic shrines, and the enthusiastic celebration of Rome's most important festivals, carefully structured to bring stability to the city. Of course, this is not to say that if one explanation holds true for Rome, so too for China, or vice versa, only that we can go deeper in our understandings of each society by exploring unfamiliar perspectives. At the same time, we can see similar processes at work. Religious institutions became important venues for the contestation of power, whether within the circles of elite or across a vast empire. Changes made in the realm of religion not only allowed the rulers to promote men whose interests aligned with their own, but to reshape and communicate messages of their imperial grandeur.

In expanding his cult across the empire, Emperor Wu followed in the tradition of the Qin kings, the First Emperor, and the early Han emperors. His expansion was characterized not only by his search for immortality, as has so often been noted, but by an openness to adopt new cult practices and seek out new spirits, and, in so doing, a willingness to listen to the advice of those who claimed mantic knowledge, whether they came from within the court establishment or not. Scholars both at the time and later were opposed to the fact that Emperor Wu adopted cults from a variety of different traditions, but the plurality of religious practice was, in fact, a strength. The inspection tours took the emperor from one end of the empire to the other, establishing his authority over contested or newly conquered territories, and claiming jurisdiction over any and all cults practiced by the people living within his domain. These tours not only had the emperor travel around the empire, but mobilized the nobles, who were required to witness some of his major sacrifices and congratulate him on his successes. This expansion of cult culminated in the *feng* and *shan* sacrifices, which demonstrated the achievements of the reign of Emperor Wu. Notably, the *feng* and *shan* sacrifices showed that the emperor had achieved a level of territorial unity and personal authority that was surpassed only in legend.

In Rome, the expansion of cult primarily took place within the city, rather than in the empire at large, due to the different focus of Augustus.[2] Like Emperor Wu, he began to claim authority over cult: not over individual cults, but by co-opting himself into the major priestly colleges in Rome. While the priestly colleges had no official political role, membership in the colleges brought with it prestige and influence, as well as the ability to participate in informal conversations about affairs of the state with other leading men. These reforms had been initiated by Julius Caesar, who was himself both Augur and Pontiff. Prior to Caesar, it was almost unheard of for a man to be a member of more than one college; after the reign of Augustus it became the norm for the *princeps* to be a member of each of the colleges, and the position of *pontifex maximus* became, effectively, hereditary. Under Augustus, it became increasingly common for his closest supporters to belong to more than one college, and, as we have seen, with the "revival" of religion, the traditional ranking of prestige of the colleges shifted, with men from the college of *quindecimviri* holding high office more frequently during the Principate. The men who were incorporated into these roles, while previously not totally removed from the theatre of power, were men who were personal allies of Augustus, and represented the new order, rather than the old guard. These men helped Augustus bring about the once in a lifetime *ludi saeculares*, a grand display of the new imperial order, with the *princeps* at the helm. The Roman emperor's religious authority was diffuse, but ever present. There was no one ceremony or celebration that defined his religious or political authority, rather, it was manifest throughout the city, and the various annual ceremonies.[3]

Both Emperor Wu and Augustus, building on the work of earlier rulers, attempted to centre the empire, and its religious institutions, around their own person, and in order to do so, they employed those who could, and would, assist them. But following the convergence, there is a divergence. Readers familiar with the histories will know that these reforms to religious institutions had very different paths.

The expansion of cult that began in the Qin and culminated in the extensive sacrifices of Emperor Wu was dismantled in the second half of the Western Han. The reasons for this are manifold, but primarily stem from the ongoing conflict between "modernists" and "reformists" at court, and the power vacuum which followed the death of Emperor Wu.[4] The reformist faction, who ultimately came to dominate the court, argued for a return to traditional practices, as elucidated in the ritual texts, and disliked the extravagant imperial cult practiced by the Qin and early Han emperors. At the end of Emperor Wu's reign, a witchcraft scandal broke out in Chang'an, and for two years, 92–91 BCE, major political disturbances led to the execution of many high officials, as well as the suicides of Empress Wei 衛子夫 and her son, the heir apparent, Liu Ju 劉據 in 91.[5] Following the death of Emperor Wu in 87 BCE, rather than being succeeded by his designated heir, Liu Ju, who was 38 at the time of his death and had extensive experience governing in Chang'an, the emperor was succeeded by his youngest son, the eight-year-old Emperor Zhao 漢昭帝. A triumvirate of regents was appointed, with Huo Guang 霍光 at their head, who effectively controlled the government until his death in 68 BCE under the reign of Emperor Xuan, the grandson of Liu Ju, whom Huo Guang had selected to be emperor in 74. Emperor Xuan, after the death of the regent, continued many of the sacrifices performed by his great-grandfather, and ensured that the Five Sacred Peaks and four rivers all had regular sacrifices.[6] He also toured the empire, sacrificing on several occasions to Great Unity at Ganquan, and to Sovereign Earth in Hedong, and periodically issuing amnesties on receiving favourable omens.[7] Emperor Xuan also held court at Ganquan, and with the final submission of the Xiongnu to the Han, caused the Shanyu to visit Ganquan.[8] Emperor Yuan initially continued the traditions established by Emperor Wu, but over the course of his reign, the sacrificial program saw a number of reversals: at times, influenced by the *ru* scholars who maintained that the current sacrifices were not in accordance with antiquity, sacrifices were stopped, but after becoming ill, he reinstituted the sacrifices which had been cancelled.[9] This back and forth between maintaining the sacrifices performed by Emperor Wu and limiting the number and types of sacrifices continued until the end of the Western Han.[10] Debates during the reign of Emperor Cheng would eventually set the precedent for the imperial sacrifices that existed in the Eastern Han, and resulted in the establishment of altars to Heaven and Earth to the north and south of the capital, and the end of the imperial sacrificial processions.

In 32 CE, the reformist Kuang Heng 匡衡 proposed a major reform of the imperial ritual system that would eradicate numerous cults and move the major sacrifices of state to the suburbs of the imperial capital at Chang'an. He argued that the sacrifices of the Qin and early Han had no precedent in the Zhou tradition, and that they were rather an invention of the Qin state, and thus should not be followed. He objected to the lavish expenditure on sacrifice and the elaborate altars, which had contributed to the ruin of the Han's finances. He protested that the roads to travel to these remote locations to offer sacrifice were perilous, and the processions brought hardship to the people of the empire.[11] The emperor permitted Kuang Heng to discuss the possibility of ritual reform with others. These men noted that the sacrifices themselves were taking place in the wrong locations, according to Yin-Yang theory: Heaven, dominant Yang, should be sacrificed to in the south, while Earth should be offered sacrifice in the north, associated with Yin. In so arguing, they not only argued that the cult practiced by the early Han emperors was not in alignment with contemporary cosmological thinking, but shifted the emphasis away from the High Gods and Great Unity (representing Heaven) and the cult of Sovereign Earth (representing Earth), to the worship of Heaven and Earth directly.[12] The reforms thus established shrines to Heaven and Earth to the south and north of the capital, respectively, where the emperor would personally offer sacrifice. According to Michael Loewe:

> The reforms were represented as restoring old and proper practices from which departures had been made; they were to uphold the position of the

emperor and save him from unnecessary indignity and hardship; and they were to bring economies to the state and reduce the exacting contributions of the populace to the maintenance of the ceremonies.[13]

Additionally, the reforms were intended to bring the imperial sacrifices under the domain of the *ru* scholars at court, and prevent any further usurpation of the roles of ritual advisors by the *fangshi*.[14] Significantly, the reforms established once and for all that the emperor should be the one to offer the most important sacrifices of state, perhaps inadvertently reinforcing the precedent that had been established by Emperor Wu. However, Kuang Heng's reforms, while enacted by the emperor, were not met with unanimous approval. Many objected to the proposed reforms, and the spirits seem to have agreed: on the day the reforms were enacted, a major storm destroyed the Bamboo Palace at Ganquan, and uprooted over one hundred trees in the sacrificial area.[15] The emperor consulted Liu Xiang劉向 (77–6 BCE), who informed him that many objected to his discontinuation of these sacrifices, and that it was dangerous to abandon cults that had been established by one's ancestors, particularly cults that had long pre-dated the Han.[16] In 14 BCE, the former sacrifices were reinstated, and the emperor went to personally perform them.[17] Throughout the rest of the Western Han, the emperors' worship alternated between these two systems, but the reforms of 32 proved to be the death knell of the imperial cult worshiped under the Qin and Western Han: in the Eastern Han, imperial cult was established according to Kuang Heng's reforms, with sacrifices to Heaven and Earth offered at altars to the south and north of the new capital at Luoyang.[18] As Tian Tian has argued, as the central government became better at governing the extremities of the empire, it was no longer necessary for the emperor to travel such great distances in order to demonstrate his authority,[19] but, the inspection tours of Emperor Wu did help to reinforce this authority, and, perhaps ironically, contributed to not only the centralization of government, but to the ultimate centralization of cult around the capital.

The *feng* and *shan* sacrifices, the most important sacrifices offered by Emperor Wu, were not seen again until the Eastern Han, when they were performed by Emperor Guangwu in 56 CE. While the specifics of Guangwu's sacrifice are not preserved, we know that he basically followed the model established by Emperor Wu, though he included more people in the *feng* sacrifice at the summit of Mt. Tai. The *feng* and *shan* sacrifices remained rare and it was not until the Tang that they were performed again.[20] They remained an important part of the mythology surrounding Emperor Wu and the Mandate of Heaven, and his ability to perform them with Heaven's approval testified to the glory of his reign.

In Rome, the system of priestly colleges was maintained without further change into the next centuries; indeed, the colleges themselves were of such antiquity that such a continuation was almost inevitable. However, the Augustan precedent of establishing the *princeps* as a member of each of the colleges continued, and the Augustan system provided a "framework for the rest of the imperial period."[21] Both Gaius and Lucius, Augustus' adopted sons, were made members of the Augural and Arval colleges towards the end of the first century BCE, and likely would have been co-opted into the other colleges if not for their untimely deaths, Gaius in 4 CE and Lucius in 2 CE. Augustus' eventual successor, Tiberius came to power at fifty-six years of age with extensive experience in governing, and within the priestly colleges. The smooth succession of power, unlike in the Han, may have contributed to the longevity of Augustus' reforms. Tiberius had been added to the Pontifical college in 22 BCE, he became member of the Arval Brothers in 23/22 BCE, during its revival, and would go on to become an Augur in 4 CE, and a member of the *quindecimvir* and *epulo* colleges in 14 CE. Following the death of Augustus, he became *pontifex maximus* in 15 CE, and while his election to this post followed Republican procedures, paying heed to tradition, it was surely a foregone conclusion.[22] Tiberius was incorporated into each of these colleges over a long period of time, but it did eventually become precedent for the *princeps*, and his heir, to automatically become members of *omnia collegia*. The first literary reference to a *princeps* being incorporated as such does not come until the reign of Titus (r. 79–81 CE),[23] yet on the occasion of Nero's adoption by Claudius, in 50 CE, coins were issued with symbols indicating that he had been co-opted as a supernumerary member of each college, thus making visible the imperial family's claim over all religious activity in the city of Rome.[24]

Despite his membership in each of the colleges, Tiberius attempted to minimize his religious authority, and avoided both religious and political accolades, to the extent that Suetonius described him as being "somewhat neglectful of the gods and of religious matters."[25] According to Suetonius, he forbade the voting of temples and other honours to his person, and would not allow his birthday to be recognized during the Plebian games.[26] Additionally, he ended the precedent of having a month of the year named after the *princeps*: he refused the month of September for himself, and October for Livia,

Augustus' widow.[27] However, he remained concerned with maintaining the "traditional" religious institutions; he attempted to abolish foreign cults, particularly those of the Egyptians and Jews, and he banished astrologers from the city of Rome, though he himself was said to have been "addicted to astrology."[28] He also sought to maintain the religious institutions, by ensuring that important priesthoods remained filled, and was willing to update outdated laws in order to do so. As he, like others before him, found it difficult to find anyone willing to serve as *flamen Dialis*, the high priest of Jupiter, he modified the marriage requirements for the post, so that more men would be willing to occupy it.[29] Membership in the colleges was maintained, but, as in the late-Augustan period, the Pontifical College was still considered the most prestigious. The *princeps*, and later emperor, as a member of each of these colleges, and as the *pontifex maximus*, was present and visible at all important sacrifices and celebrations.

The main development under the reign of Tiberius, the worship of the dead emperor's *numen*, had its roots in the Augustan period. While the worship of the divine emperor began with the deification of Julius Caesar, it was under Tiberius, with the worship of the divine Augustus, that emperor worship became a larger part of the state's religious affairs.[30] Before Augustus' death, in ca. 6 CE, Tiberius dedicated an altar on the Palatine to the *numen* of Augustus, next to his home there, to which all four colleges were required to offer sacrifices.[31] While Augustus had been worshiped as divine in the provinces prior to his death,[32] and Julius Caesar was sacrificed to in Rome, this was the first time that Augustus had been offered sacrifice in the city. During the reign of Tiberius, the deceased Augustus received a number of honours usually reserved for the gods: a temple was dedicated to him between the Capitoline and Palatine, a *flamen* was appointed from Augustus' own family, and a new college, the *sodales Augustales*, was formed, staffed with the leading members of the senatorial elite.[33] Here, too, precedent was set, beginning with Augustus' promotion of the cult to Julius Caesar, and followed by Tiberius. According to Beard, North, and Price,

> the practices of the Augustan age established the basic framework which prevailed for the rest of the imperial period. Emperors and members of their families were given divine honours by vote of the senate only after their death and then only in recognition of the fact (so the official version went) that they had, by their merits, actually become gods.[34]

Between Augustus and Constantine (r. 306–337 CE), approximately half of the new temples built in Rome were dedicated to deified rulers, establishing their prominence in marble in the city of Rome itself.[35] Ultimately, the worship of emperors became, for Cassius Dio, one of the most important unifying factors in the empire.[36]

Although subsequent iterations of the *ludi saeculares* were based on some elements of Augustan precedent, the games were far too important a political tool to escape manipulation. While the discussions preparing for the Augustan celebration had determined the length of a *saeculum* to be one-hundred or one-hundred and ten years, the longest possible lifespan of a man, later emperors attempted to interpret this differently, so as to be able to inaugurate their own *saeculum*. Claudius, initiating the games in 47 CE, argued that the *saeculum* designated a century, and thus held the games to commemorate the eight-hundredth anniversary of the founding of the city of Rome.[37] His celebration was mocked, however, when heralds invited spectators to "a spectacle such as they had never seen before," as the Augustan games were within living memory for many in Rome, and some actors performed in both the Augustan and Claudian games.[38] Domitian (r. 81–96 CE), celebrated the games in 88 CE, following the Augustan designation of the *saeculum* and effectively ignoring the Claudian celebration.[39] Subsequent *ludi* were performed under Septimus Severus (204 CE) and Philip (248 CE).[40] While the interval of a *saeculum*, established by Augustus, was not followed by the emperors, the basic ritual script for the performance followed the Augustan version.[41] It seems that there was more competition over the right to hold the games and thus initiate a new *saeculum* than there was over the religious message they delivered. Like the *feng* and *shan* sacrifices, the *ludi saeculares* were not available to any emperor: a convergence of favourable omens and a sufficient interval of years was required before an emperor had the opportunity to renew this festival.

Ultimately, the different longevities of the religious reforms matter less to us than the effects they had. The centralization of authority that took place under Emperor Wu, in part due to his expansion of imperial cult, lasted beyond his reign, though power ultimately devolved to the court elite rather than remaining with the emperors. What might have happened if, like Augustus, Emperor Wu had been replaced by a strong heir who shared his father's vision for imperial power? As we have seen, Augustus was able to achieve so much due in part to his long life, and many of the institutions he established were carried on as a result of a strong line of succession. What fate would have befallen the new imperial structures in Rome had Augustus, instead of recovering, died from the illness that afflicted him in 23 BCE? There is, of course, no real point to speculating about what might have happened if circumstances had been different for either ruler. However, it is worth considering whether or not we should see the reversals of Emperor Wu's cult practice in the first century BCE as a complete failure. While it is clear that no Han emperor enjoyed such immense personal authority after Emperor Wu, his cult reforms, in many respects achieved their goals. The cult system established by Kuang Heng in 31 BCE meant that the emperor no longer travelled to the spirits, but this was, perhaps, because it was no longer necessary for the emperor to travel. Having incorporated the important spiritual sites under the supervision of the Superintendent of Ceremonial, and with the lack of any rebellions threatening the Han court, the lavish inspection tours and attempts to contact a variety of spirits were no longer necessary. Henceforth, the spirits would travel to Chang'an rather than the emperor to them. While the Han imperial cult changed shape, in both cases, the *princeps* and later emperors of Rome and the emperors of Han remained the central figure in their cult institutions, as well as their empires.

Notes

Chapter 1

1. *Shiji* 28.1403. All references to the *Shiji* and *Hanshu* refer to the Zhonghua shuju editions. Translations from the Chinese, unless otherwise indicated, are my own. The Director of Sacrifices, *taizhu* 太祝, was an official under the Superintendent of Ceremonial *fengchang* 奉常 (after the reign of Emperor Wu, the title of this post was changed to *taichang* 太常). *Hanshu* 19A.
2. Suet. *Aug.* 30–31; of these only the *ludi saeculares* is mentioned by Augustus in his *Res Gestae*.
3. While Octavian Augustus only came to be known by the epithet Augustus in 27 BCE, for the sake of consistency, this monograph will use the title Augustus throughout.
4. Throughout the monograph, I refer to some of the premodern states as "Chinese," however in so doing it is not my intention to argue for a monolithic Chinese state that spans the millennia from antiquity to the present. While this claim is made by the CCP and the standard histories of each dynasty promote this idea, the histories of the states that existed within the modern borders of the PRC are far from linear, nor are they teleological.
5. Science and knowledge: Geoffrey E. R. Lloyd, *Adversaries and Authorities: Investigations into Ancient Greek and Chinese Science* (Cambridge: Cambridge University Press, 1996); *The Ambitions of Curiosity: Understanding the World in Ancient Greece and China* (Cambridge: Cambridge University Press, 2002); *Ancient Worlds, Modern Reflections: Philosophical Perspectives on Greek and Chinese Science and Culture* (Cambridge: Cambridge University Press, 2004); *Principles and Practices in Ancient Greek and Chinese Science* (Aldershot: Ashgate/Variorum, 2006); Geoffrey E. R. Lloyd and Nathan Sivin, *The Way and the World: Science and Medicine in Early China and Greece* (New Haven, CT: Yale University Press, 2002); art, aesthetics, and philosophy: Francois Jullien, *Detour and Access: Strategies of Meaning in China and Greece* (New York: Zone Books, 2000); *A Treatise on Efficacy: Between Western and Chinese Thinking* (Honolulu: University of Hawai'i Press, 2004); *The Impossible Nude: Chinese Art and Western Aesthetics* (Chicago: University of Chicago Press, 2007); philosophy: David L. Hall and Roger Ames, *Thinking through Confucius* (Albany: SUNY Press, 1987); *Thinking from the Han: Self, Truth, and Transcendence in Chinese and Western Culture* (Albany: SUNY Press, 1998); historiography: Thomas R. Martin, *Herodotus and Sima Qian: The First Great Historians of Greece and China, a Brief History with Documents* (Boston: Bedford/St. Martin's, 2010); Robert Bonnaud, *Victoires sur le temps. Essais Comparatistes. Polybe le Grec et Sima Qian le Chinois* (Paris: La ligne d'ombre, 2007); Fritz-Heiner Mutschler, "Tacite (et Tite-Live) et

Sima Qian: La vision politique d'historiens latins et chinois." *Bulletin de l'Association Guillaume Budé* 2 (2008): 123–55: Fritz-Heiner Mutschler and Achim Mittag, eds., *Conceiving the Empire: China and Rome Compared* (Oxford: Oxford University Press, 2008); rhetoric: Xing Lu, *Rhetoric in Ancient China, Fifth to Third Century BCE: A Comparison with Classical Greek Rhetoric* (Columbia: University of South Carolina Press, 1998); Michael Puett, *To Become A God: Cosmology, Sacrifice, and Self-divinization in Early China* (Cambridge, MA: Harvard University Press, 2002); military, Hsing, I-tien, "Rome and China: The Role of the Armies in the Imperial Succession. A Comparative Study." PhD Diss., University of Hawai'i at Manoa, 1980. For a detailed overview of the different approaches in Sino-Hellenic studies, see Jeremy Tanner, "Ancient Greece, Early China; Sino-Hellenic Studies and Comparative Approaches to the Classical World, A Review Article," *Journal of Hellenic Studies* 129 (2009): 89–109. See also the bibliography compiled by Lisa Raphals (2018, https://faculty.ucr.edu/~raphals/pubs/2018%20Oxford%20Bibliographies.pdf accessed 21 June 2022) and Alexander Beecroft (2016, https://www.oxfordhandbooks.com/view/10.1093/oxfordhb/9780199935390.001.0001/oxfordhb-9780199935390-e-14?rskey=gF2J1R&result=3 accessed 21 June 2022).
6. Lloyd and Sivin, *The Way and the World*, xi.
7. Lloyd and Sivin, *The Way and the World*, 1–2.
8. Lloyd and Sivin, *The Way and the World*, 2.
9. On divination, Lisa Ann Raphals, *Divination and Prediction in Early China and Ancient Greece* (Cambridge: Cambridge University Press, 2013); literature and gender, Yiqun Zhou, *Festivals, Feasts, and Gender Relations in Ancient China and Greece* (Cambridge: Cambridge University Press, 2010); ethnicity, Hyun Jin Kim, *Ethnicity and Foreigners in Ancient Greece and China* (London: Duckworth, 2009), Ryan Russel Abrecht, "My Neighbor the Barbarian: Immigrant Neighborhoods in Classical Athens, Imperial Rome, and Tang Chang'an." PhD. Diss. University of California, Santa Barbara, 2014.
10. Walter Scheidel, "Introduction," in *Rome and China: Comparative Perspectives on Ancient World Empires*, ed. Walter Scheidel (Oxford: Oxford University Press, 2009), 3–10; *State Power in Ancient China and Rome* (Oxford: Oxford University Press, 2015).
11. See, for example, Bruce Trigger, *Understanding Early Civilizations: A Comparative Study* (Cambridge: Cambridge University Press, 2003).
12. Scheidel, *State Power in Ancient China and Rome*, 3.
13. Jack Goldstone, *Revolution and Rebellion in the Early Modern World* (Berkeley: University of California Press, 1991), 57.
14. Goldstone, *Revolution and Rebellion in the Early Modern World*, 55.
15. Goldstone, *Revolution and Rebellion in the Early Modern World*, 57.
16. So few, in fact, that a volume on *Military Culture in China* contains very little to do with military culture itself. Nicola Di Cosmo, ed., *Military Culture in Imperial China* (Cambridge: Harvard University Press, 2009). Some narratives of battles do exist, but primarily from pre-Qin sources. See Mark Edward Lewis, *Sanctioned Violence in Early China* (Albany: SUNY Press, 1990) and Rebecca Zerby Byrne, "Harmony

and Violence in Classical China: A Study of the Battles of the *Tso-chuan*." PhD Diss. University of Chicago, 1974.
17. Studies of cosmology have tended to focus on comparisons between China and Greece, where there is a great deal more literature on the subject. While Cicero (*De Natura Deorum*; *De Haruspicum Responsis*) and others do comment on the nature of the universe and the gods, metaphysical questions of correlationism are not central to the discussion.
18. Herbert Franke, "Some Remarks on the Interpretation of Chinese Dynastic Histories," *Oriens* 3, no. 1 (1950): 8. While the *Shiji* and *Hanshu* were not official histories in the later sense of the term, they were written from within the court environment.
19. Tanner, "Ancient Greece, Early China," 2009, 91.
20. Matthew Lange, *Comparative-historical Methods* (Los Angeles, Sage, 2013), 2; 182.
21. Trigger, *Understanding early Civilizations*, 15.
22. Filippo Marsili, *Heaven Is Empty: A Cross-Cultural Approach to "Religion" and Empire in Ancient China* (Albany: SUNY, 2018), 3. State religion in Rome will be discussed in further detail in Chapter 4.
23. In particular, Roy Rappaport has argued for the cultural universality of ritual and religion, but while he provides a universal definition for ritual, he does not attempt to do so for the more problematic category of religion. Roy A. Rappaport, *Ritual and Religion in the Making of Humanity* (Cambridge: Cambridge University Press, 1999).
24. Marsili, *Heaven is Empty*, 23–58.
25. Marsili, *Heaven is Empty*, 27.
26. Kenneth E. Brashier, *Ancestral Memory in Early China* (Cambridge, MA: Harvard University Asia Center, 2011), 35.
27. See Chapter 4.
28. For such a discussion, the reader is referred again to Marsili, who, while arguing for the importance of an evaluation of the Chinese source materials in their own right, also shows how this can free other ancient religious traditions from the tentacles of the Abrahamic traditions.
29. For good overviews of the religions of early China and Rome in this period, see Poo Mu-chou, *In Search of Personal Welfare: A View of Ancient Chinese Religion* (Albany: SUNY, 1998) and Clifford Ando, *The Matter of the Gods: Religion and the Roman Empire* (Berkeley: University of California Press, 2008).
30. Sima Qian was deeply influenced by the tradition of the *Spring and Autumn Annals*, attributed to Confucius. On the structure of the *Shiji* see Grant Hardy, *Worlds of Bronze and Bamboo: Sima Qian's Conquest of History* (New York: Columbia University Press, 1999), particularly Chapter 5 on the Confucian influence. See also Griet Vankeerberghen, "Texts and Authors in the *Shiji*," in *China's Early Empires: A Reappraisal*, ed. Michael Nylan and Michael Loewe (Cambridge, Cambridge University Press, 2010), 461–79.
31. *Shiji* 130.3319. Endymion Wilkinson notes that many of the dates in the *Shiji* have been challenged by historians from the Han period onwards, and most of the dates which are challenged are in the "tables" section. *Chinese History: A New Manual* (Cambridge, MA: Harvard University Press, 2013), 706.

32. This is the common translation of the title which is used in translations of the *Shiji*, and while it does reflect Sima Qian's role as archivist, belies the fact that his official role was primarily concerned with observing and recording astronomical phenomena.
33. See particularly Bo Shuren 薄樹人, "Taolun Sima Qian de tianwenxue sixiang" 討論司馬遷的天文學思想, *Shixueshi yanjiu* 3 (1982): 7–15, on Sima Qian's astronomical theory.
34. See Jin Dejian 金德建, *Sima Qian suojian shukao* 司馬遷所見書考 (Shanghai: Shanghai renmin chubanshe, 1963), on the types of works he may have been able to consult. The question of Sima Qian's motivations has been long debated, with some arguing that his work is an "accurate history," while others see the text as a means of promoting his own name. See Stephen W. Durrant, *The Cloudy Mirror: Tension and Conflict in the Writings of Sima Qian* (Albany: SUNY Press, 1995). Michael Nylan provides a religious explanation for his writing of the text, arguing that this was the epitome of filial piety. Nylan, "Sima Qian: A True Historian?" *Early China* 23–24 (1998–1999): 203–46.
35. Due to the Li Ling affair, recounted in "Sima Qian's letter to Ren An," included in the *Hanshu* biography of Sima Qian, *Hanshu* 62.2725–36. On the textual history of this letter, see Stephen Durrant et al., eds., *The Letter to Ren An and Sima Qian's Legacy* (Seattle: University of Washington Press, 2016).
36. See particularly Durrant, *The Cloudy Mirror*, 29–60.
37. On the textual overlap and differences between the *Shiji* and *Hanshu*, Pak Chae-u, "Shiji" "Hanshu" *bijiao yanjiu* "史記" "漢書" 比較研究 (Beijing: Zhongguo wenxue chubanshe, 1994). A. F. P. Hulsewé has argued that we need to be "circumspect when dealing with textual contradictions or irregularities," as both texts have their own independent traditions, and thus irregularities must be compared between the two histories. These irregularities may sometimes result from a copyist's error, rather than intentional manipulation by an author or editor. A. F. P. Hulsewé, "A Striking Discrepancy between the Shih chi and the Han shu," *T'oung Pao* 76, no. 4–5 (1990): 323.
38. The *Liji* is a text made up of forty-nine chapters that discuss various aspects of ritual theory and performance. Kenneth Brashier has described the text as a loose-leaf binder, a text "into which chapters and their commentarial notes were inserted, shuffled, and removed," over time, including chapters from texts from written from the Late Spring and Autumn and Warring States periods (Brashier, *Ancestral Memory*, 48–49). The various chapters of the text were extant during the Han period, though it is possible that they were not combined into one text named the *Liji* before 102 CE. Within the text, it is nearly impossible to determine the origins of individual chapters. Jeffrey K. Riegel, "*Li Chi* 禮記," in *Early Chinese Texts: A Bibliographical Guide*, ed. Michael Loewe (Berkeley, CA: Society for the Study of Early China and Institute of East Asian Studies, 1993), 294–95. See also Michael Nylan, *The Five "Confucian" Classics* (New Haven, CT: Yale University Press, 2001), 187–88; and Michael Puett, "Combining the Ghosts and Spirits, Centering the Realm: Mortuary Ritual and Political Organization in the Ritual Compendia of Early China," in *Early Chinese Religion, Part One: Shang through Han (1250 BC–220 AD)*, ed. John Lagerwey

and Marc Kalinowski, vol. 2. (Leiden: Brill, 2009), 696. For one example on the complexities of the evolution of *Liji* chapters, see Edward Shaughnessy, "Rewriting the *Zi Yi*: How One Chinese Classic Came to Read as It Does," in *Rewriting Early Chinese Texts* (Albany: SUNY Press, 2006).

39. Over the past several decades, in addition to caches of documents unearthed by archaeologists in mainland China, there have been a number of collections of texts, probably looted from tombs, that have found their way onto the antiquities market in Hong Kong, where they have been purchased and then donated to mainland universities, usually by anonymous alumni. Western scholars are largely divided in opinion as to whether or not one should use these documents; scholars in China generally agree that they are valuable sources for our understanding of early China and should not be disregarded. It is far beyond the scope of the present monograph to enter into this debate.

40. The most comprehensive work on this is now Anthony Barbieri-Low and Robin D. S. Yates, *Law, State, and Society in Early Imperial China: A Study with Critical Edition and Translation of the Legal Texts from Zhangjiashan Tomb no. 247*, 2 Vols. (Leiden: Brill, 2015).

41. For an overview of texts in this genre, see Donald Harper and Marc Kalinowski, eds., *Books of Fate and Popular Culture in early China: the Daybook Manuscripts of Warring States, Qin, and, Han* (Leiden: Brill, 2017).

42. On the authorship and composition of early texts: Michael Loewe, ed. *Early Chinese Texts: A Bibliographical Guide* (Berkeley: University of California Press, 1993).

43. John Thornton, "Pragmatic History," in *The Encyclopedia of Ancient History*, ed. Roger S. Bagnall et al. (Malden: Wiley-Blackwell, 2013), 5499.

44. Thornton, "Pragmatic History," 5499.

45. Ronald Mellor, *The Roman Historians* (London: Routledge, 1999), 9.

46. On Roman historiography, see the overviews by Mellor; Andreas Mehl, *Roman Historiography: An Introduction to Its Basic Aspects and Development* (Malden, MA: Wiley-Blackwell, 2011); Andrew Feldherr, ed., *The Cambridge Companion to the Roman Historians* (Cambridge: Cambridge University Press, 2009); John Marincola, ed., *A Companion to Greek and Roman Historiography* (Malden, MA: Blackwell, 2007). The scholarship on individual authors and texts is too vast to cite here; pertinent studies will be referred to throughout the book.

47. Mellor, *The Roman Historians*, 64. This, of course, was subject to his own criteria for believability.

48. Mellor, *The Roman Historians*, 69; Mehl, *Roman Historiography*, 109.

49. Mellor, *The Roman Historians*, 70; Mehl, *Roman Historiography*, 100.

50. Mellor, *The Roman Historians*, 71.

51. Mellor, *The Roman Historians*, 71.

52. Ronald Syme, 'Livy and Augustus', *Harvard Studies in Classical Philology* 64 (1959): 27–87.

53. Mehl, *Roman Historiography*, 152.

54. Mehl, *Roman Historiography*, 152. The most conspicuous case is the discussion between Agrippa and Maecenas over the Roman constitution.

55. Peter Michael Swan, *The Augustan Succession: An Historical Commentary on Cassius Dio's Roman History, Books 55–56 (9 B.C.–A.D. 14)*, American Classical Studies, no. 47 (Oxford: Oxford University Press, 2004), 15.
56. Mellor, *The Roman Historians*, 149–51.
57. On Plutarch's use of sources, see Philip A. Stadter, *Plutarch and the Historical Tradition* (London: Routledge, 2002).
58. Peter Brunt and J. M. Moore, ed. and trans., Res gestae divi Augusti: *The Achievements of the Divine Augustus* (London: Oxford University Press, 1967).
59. Cic. *Brut*. 262. *Sed dum voluit alios habere parata, unde sumerent qui vellent scribere historiam.*
60. It is worth noting that our translation of the title *Huangdi* 皇帝 as "August Emperor" is indebted to Augustus' choice of name for himself.
61. An exception, which exceeds the scope of the present monograph, is Augustus' sanctioning of cults which worshipped him outside of Rome, particularly in the East, where ruler worship was well established. For an introduction, see S. R. F. Price, *Rituals and Power: The Roman Imperial Cult in Asia Minor* (Cambridge: Cambridge University Press, 1984). The self-divinization of emperors has been discussed from a comparative perspective in Michael Puett's chapter, "Ghosts, Gods, and the Coming Apocalypse: Empire and Religion in Early China and Ancient Rome," in *State Power in Ancient China and Rome*, ed. Walter Scheidel (Oxford: Oxford University Press, 2015), 230–59.

Chapter 2

1. David Engels, "Historical Necessity or Biographical Singularity? Some Aspects in the Biographies of C. Iulius Caesar and Qin Shi Huang Di," in *Rulers and Ruled in Greece, Rome, and China*, ed. Hans Beck and Griet Vankeerberghen (Cambridge: Cambridge University Press, 2021), 328–68, compares the biographies of Caesar and the First Emperor, while Yakobson, "The First Emperors: Image and Memory," in *Birth of an Empire: The State of Qin Revisited*, ed. Yuri Pines et al. (Berkeley: University of California Press, 2014), 280–300, examines Augustus in comparison with the First Emperor of Qin.
2. While the break between Republic and Empire is most commonly seen in the actions of Julius Caesar in his usurpation of dictatorial power in the mid-first century BCE, the transformation of the Republic had, in fact, been long underway. Harriet Flower argues that we should not view Roman history in terms of a "Republic" becoming an Empire, but rather look at a series of "Roman Republics" and transitional periods, rather than view the rule of Caesar as a single point of rupture. Harriet I. Flower, *Roman Republics* (Princeton, NJ: Princeton University Press, 2010).
3. The Han never fully eradicated the kingdoms within the empire, though the territory they possessed was substantially limited after the reigns of Emperor Jing and Emperor Wu.

4. Arthur M. Eckstein, *Mediterranean Anarchy, Interstate War, and the Rise of Rome* (Berkeley: University of California Press, 2006), 245.
5. This is a simplification and an idealization, based on the example of the Italian peninsula. Not all conquered territories were as easily assimilated, and the process of Romanization was often long, difficult, and never entirely one-sided. See Jean-Michel David, *The Roman Conquest of Italy* (Oxford: Blackwell, 1996) on the process of the integration of the Italian peninsula. The connection of local elites to the capital in Rome eventually became an important source of prestige. On this phenomenon in the Imperial period, see Carlos Noreña, *Imperial Ideals in the Roman West* (Cambridge: Cambridge University Press, 2011). The literature on Romanization is vast and subject to much debate. See, for example, Peter Brunt, "The Romanization of the Local Ruling Classes in the Roman Empire," in *Assimilation et résistance à la culture gréco-romaine dans le monde ancien*, ed. D. M. Pippidi (Bucuresti: Editura Academiei, 1976), 161–73; Ramsey Macmullen, *Romanization in the Time of Augustus* (New Haven, CT: Yale University Press, 2000); Greg Woolf, "Becoming Roman, Staying Greek. Culture, Identity and the Civilizing Process in the Roman East," *Proceedings of the Cambridge Philological Society* 40 (1994): 116–43; Andrew Wallace-Hadrill, *Rome's Cultural Revolution* (Cambridge: Cambridge University Press, 2008).
6. William V. Harris, *War and Imperialism in Republican Rome, 327–70 B.C.* (Oxford: Clarendon Press, 1979), 18.
7. On the many functions of the consul, Francisco Pina Polo, *The Consul at Rome: The Civil Functions of the Consuls in the Roman Republic* (Cambridge: Cambridge University Press, 2011).
8. On the role of the Plebs and the constitution of "the people" as a political concept rather than as a physical reality, see H. H. Mouritsen, *Plebs and Politics in the Late Roman Republic* (Cambridge: Cambridge University Press, 2001); and Karl-Joachim Hölkeskamp, *Senatus populusque romanus: Die politische Kultur der Republik: Dimensionen und Deutungen* (Wiesbaden: Franz Steiner Verlag, 2004).
9. Flower, *Roman Republics*.
10. Polybius. *Hist.* 6.11. On the monolithic view of the Republic in modern scholarship, see Flower, *Roman Republics*, 9–10.
11. Timothy Cornell argues that the Roman kingship was abolished in the fifth century by the aristocrats who wanted to keep power distributed amongst the aristocracy, to guard against the rise of a popular figure, i.e., to limit the power of the plebians and ensure a more balanced distribution of power amongst the elites. *The Beginnings of Rome: Italy and Rome from the Bronze Age to the Punic Wars (c. 1000–264 BCE)* (London: Routledge, 1995), 203. The intricacies of the republican system and its constituent parts are beyond the scope on this brief discussion. For an overview of the republican system, see Andrew Lintott, *The Constitution of the Roman Republic* (Oxford: Clarendon Press, 1999).
12. Karl-Joachim Hölkeskamp, *Reconstructing the Roman Republic: An Ancient Political Culture and Modern Research* (Princeton, NJ: Princeton University Press, 2010), 19.
13. This is not to say that the people did not matter in Roman politics, but that the system which claimed to represent them was in actuality one which protected the interests of

the aristocrats. Due to the organization of the voting assemblies (*comitia*), the wealthy held great influence, despite the fact that suffrage extended to all citizens. On voting assemblies, see Lily Ross Taylor, *Roman Voting Assemblies from the Hannibalic War to the Dictatorship of Caesar* (Ann Arbor: University of Michigan Press, 1966).

14. During the early to mid-Republic, although elite competition was a fundamental part of Roman politics, external pressures led to the development of an aristocracy which was competitive, but also cohesive, Kurt A. Raaflaub, "Born to Be Wolves? Origins of Roman Imperialism," in *Transitions to Empire: Essays in Greco Roman History*, ed. Robert W. Wallace and Edward Monroe Harris (Norman: University of Oklahoma Press, 1996), 291. The cohesion of the aristocracy began to break down in the second century BCE, and would continue to devolve until the end of the first century BCE.
15. Flower, *Roman Republics*, 114–26.
16. Flower, *Roman Republics*, 137.
17. Pina Polo, *The Consul at Rome*, 248–90.
18. Flower, *Roman Republics*, 32.
19. Flower, *Roman Republics*, 149.
20. Pina Polo, *The Consul at Rome*, 317.
21. Flower, *Roman Republics*, 151.
22. There is debate as to whether or not this was a law enacted by Sulla. See Pina Polo, *The Consul at Rome,* 225–29.
23. Pina Polo, *The Consul at Rome*, 307.
24. Pina Polo, *The Consul at Rome*, 249.
25. He was first appointed dictator in 49 BCE, but held the position for only 11 days, while in 48 he was again appointed dictator for an undefined amount of time. In 46, he was given a ten-year term as dictator, and he held this position for the rest of his life.
26. Suet. *Iul.* 76; Dio 44.8.
27. See Dio 44.4–6 for the complete list of honours offered to him.
28. Suet. *Iul.* 76–79.
29. For a broad overview of the assassination and its aftermath, see John S. Richardson, *Augustan Rome 44 BC to AD 14: The Restoration of the Republic and the Establishment of the Empire* (Edinburgh: Edinburgh University Press, 2012), 10–46.
30. Aug. *Res Gest.* 13. On the struggle for power and wars, see Dio, 47–51. See also Richardson, *Augustan Rome*, 47–79; Andrew Lintott, *The Romans in the Age of Augustus* (Malden, MA: Wiley-Blackwell, 2010), 67–76.
31. There was no single way in which Augustus was able to legitimize his rule, and throughout his reign, he was continuously trying to balance his position as effective monarch with the appearance of popular rule. Here we are concerned only with the actions he took in the field of imperial cult and religious ideology. Numerous excellent studies have discussed the formation of the Principate, and the reader is referred to Richardson, *Augustan Rome*; Karl Galinsky, ed., *The Cambridge Companion to the Age of Augustus* (Cambridge: Cambridge University Press, 2005); Werner Eck, *The Age of Augustus* (Malden, MA: Wiley-Blackwell, 2007); Lintott, *The Romans in the Age of Augustus*. On the cultural transformations, see Andrew Wallace-Hadrill, *Rome's Cultural Revolution*.

32. Michael Nylan, "The Rhetoric of 'Empire' in the Classical Era in China," in *Conceiving the Empire: China and Rome Compared*, ed. Fritz-Heiner Mutschler and Achim Mittag (Oxford: Oxford University Press, 2008), 47–48.
33. On the Western Zhou bureaucracy, see Li Feng, *Bureaucracy and the State in Early China: Governing the Western Zhou* (Cambridge: Cambridge University Press, 2008).
34. Lothar von Falkenhausen, *Chinese Society in the Age of Confucius (1000–250 BC): The Archaeological Evidence* (Los Angeles: University of California Press, 2006), 2. See also Jessica Rawson, "Western Zhou Archaeology," in *The Cambridge History of Ancient China*, ed. Michael Loewe and Edward L. Shaughnessy (Cambridge: Cambridge University Press, 1999), 433–40.
35. Von Falkenhausen, *Chinese Society in the Age of Confucius*, 49–50.
36. Von Falkenhausen, *Chinese Society in the Age of Confucius*, 251.
37. On the cultural construction of "Chinese" identity in opposition to "barbarians," see Yuri Pines, "Beasts or Humans: Pre-Imperial Origins of the Sino-Barbarian Dichotomy," in *Mongols, Turks, and Others: Eurasian Nomads and the Sedentary World*, ed. Reuven Amitai and Michal Biran (Leiden: Brill, 2004), 59–102.
38. Li *Bureaucracy and the State*, 238; 246–49.
39. During the Spring and Autumn period, there were numerous small states, but over time, fifteen became dominant. This number was reduced to seven in the Warring States period. On the politics of the Spring and Autumn period, see Cho-yun Hsu, "The Spring and Autumn Period," in *The Cambridge History of Ancient China: From the Origins of Civilization to 221 B.C.*, ed. Michael Loewe and Edward L. Shaughnessy (Cambridge: Cambridge University Press, 1999); Yuri Pines, *Foundations of Confucian Thought: Intellectual Life in the Chunqiu Period 722–453 B.C.E.* (Honolulu: University of Hawai'i Press, 2002). On the blood covenants sworn between states and between rulers and subjects, see Susan R. Weld, "The Covenant Texts from Houma and Wenxian," in *New Sources of Early Chinese History: An Introduction to the Reading of Inscriptions and Manuscripts*, ed. Edward L. Shaughnessy (Berkeley: University of California Press, 1997).
40. At the beginning of the Spring and Autumn period, ministers were often appointed for life, but over time, changes of ministers were frequent. According to Hsu, this indicates the "growing power of rulers and the decreasing authority of chancellors." Cho-yun Hsu, *Ancient China in Transition: An Analysis of Social Mobility, 722–222 B.C.* (Stanford: Stanford University Press, 1965), 51.
41. On social mobility, see Hsu, *Ancient China in Transition*; Yuri Pines, *Envisioning Eternal Empire: Chinese Political Thought of the Warring States Era* (Honolulu: University of Hawai'i Press, 2009), 115–84.
42. Advisors could fairly easily leave a ruler with whom they disagreed and seek employment at another court. Pines, *Envisioning Eternal Empire*, 172. Barry Blakeley has written extensively on court politics and competition in the state of Chu, see, for example "King, Clan, and Courtier in Ancient Ch'u," *Asia Major* Third Series, 5.2 (1992).
43. See Pines, 2009, and, more recently *The Everlasting Empire: The Political Culture of Ancient China and Its Imperial Legacy* (Princeton, NY: Princeton University Press,

2012), which argues for a continuity in the idea of imperial ideology for the *longue durée* of Chinese history.
44. Steven F. Sage, *Ancient Sichuan and the Unification of China* (Albany: SUNY Press, 1992), 145.
45. On the various reasons for Qin's success, see Derk Bodde, "The State and Empire of Ch'in," in *The Cambridge History of China: The Ch'in and Han Empires, 221 BC–AD 220*, ed. Denis Twitchett and John K. Fairbank (Cambridge: Cambridge University Press, 1987), 46–50.
46. *Shiji* 6.239. Mark Edward Lewis, *The Construction of Space in Early China* (Albany: SUNY Press, 2006), 170–73.
47. *Shiji* 6.239.
48. *Shiji* 6.236.
49. Bodde, "The State and Empire of 'Ch'in,'" 85–87. Many of these claims were made in the Han by officials seeking to promote their own systems of governance and promote the image of the Han emperors as benevolent rulers. New evidence of the Qin administrative system has been found in many excavated texts which presents a very different portrait of the Qin. See Robin D. S. Yates "The Qin Slips and Boards from Well No. 1, Liye, Hunan: A Brief Introduction to the Qin Qianling County Archives," *Early China* 35–36 (2012–13): 291–329 for a broad overview of some of these materials and the new perspectives they offer, as well as Anthony J. Barbieri-Low and Robin D. S. Yates, *Law, State, and Society in Early Imperial China: A Study with Critical Edition and Translation of the Legal Texts from Zhangjiashan Tomb No. 247*, Sinica Leidensia, 2 Vols. (Leiden: Brill, 2015).
50. Steven Sage argues that the Qin conquest of Sichuan had been effective precisely because care was taken to integrate the new land and adopt their policies of conquest to suit the area. Had the First Emperor taken more time to try to unite the states, and followed a more flexible model, he argues, the unification of the Warring States may have created a much longer-lasting empire. Sage, *Ancient Sichuan*, 139–55.
51. There were ten kingdoms recognized by Liu Bang at the beginning of the Han, most of which were in the east. By 196 BCE, all but one of the kings were replaced by relatives of the Liu family, in the hopes that this would strengthen the kingdoms' connection to the court. The kingdoms were expected to govern themselves, modelled on the central government, and to remit taxes to the centre. On the Han dynasty kingdoms and the consolidation of state power, see Tang Xiejun 唐燮軍 and Weng Gongyu 翁公羽, *Cong fenzhi dao jiquan: xi Han de wangguo wenti jiqi jiejue* 從分治到集權：西漢的王國問題及其解決 (Hangzhou: Zhejiang daxue chubanshe, 2012).
52. Emperor Jing's imperial counsellor, Chao Cuo, had advised the emperor to take steps to reduce the power of the regional lords, however, his political rivals at court convinced the emperor to have him executed to stave off rebellion. While Chao Cuo was executed, it did not prevent rebellion, and the rebellion was only supressed by military engagement.
53. Telly H. Koo, "The Constitutional Development of the Western Han Dynasty," *Journal of the American Oriental Society* 40 (1920): 185. See also Michael Loewe, "The Former Han Dynasty," in *The Cambridge History of China Volume 1: The*

Ch'in and Han Empires, 221 B.C.–A.D. 220, ed. Denis Twitchett and Michael Loewe (Cambridge: Cambridge University Press, 1986), 103–222..

54. Nylan, "The Rhetoric of 'Empire,'" 49.
55. Kathleen D. Morrison, "Sources, Approaches, Definitions," in *Empires: Perspectives from Archaeology and History*, ed. Susan E. Alcock et al. (Cambridge: Cambridge University Press, 2011), 3.
56. Jane Burbank and Frederick Cooper, *Empires in World History: Power and the Politics of Difference* (Princeton, NJ: Princeton University Press, 2010), 4.
57. Burbank and Cooper, *Empires in World History*, 2.
58. Greg Woolf emphasizes this lack of homogeneity and the tolerance of regional diversity as one of the characteristics of the early Roman empire, and, perhaps, one of the keys to its longevity. Greg Woolf, "Inventing Empire in Ancient Rome," in *Empires: Perspectives from Archaeology and History*, ed. Susan E. Alcock et al. (Cambridge: Cambridge University Press, 2011), 311.
59. Burbank and Cooper, *Empires in World History*, 10. The authors note that this idea of a nation state is, of course, itself a product of a particular type of history, "of a state that through institutional and cultural initiatives convinced its members to think of themselves as a single people."
60. Burbank and Cooper, *Empires in World History*, 8.
61. Burbank and Cooper, *Empires in World History*, 15.
62. Burbank and Cooper, *Empires in World History*, 3.
63. Robin D. S. Yates, "Cosmos, Central Authority, and Communities in the Early Chinese Empire," in *Empires: Perspectives from Archaeology and History*, ed. Susan E. Alcock et al. (Cambridge: Cambridge University Press, 2011), 353 and 368.
64. The use of Caesar as a surname took place during the middle of Augustus' reign, Werner Eck, *The Age of Augustus* (Malden, MA: Wiley-Blackwell, 2007), 57. Woolf notes that subsequent emperors adopted the name, and the title was subsequently adopted and modified by many European rulers. Woolf, "Inventing Empire in Ancient Rome," 313.
65. Numerous studies on Romanisation and Hellenization discuss the spread of cultures in the ancient Mediterranean. See, for example, Brunt, "The Romanization of the Local Ruling Classes in the Roman Empire"; Macmullen, *Romanization in the Time of Augustus*; and Wallace-Hadrill, *Rome's Cultural Revolution*, who explores the ways in which Greek and Roman culture shaped each other in the late Republic and early Empire.
66. Woolf, "Inventing Empire in Ancient Rome," 314–15.
67. See Noreña, *Imperial Ideals in the Roman West*, on the spread of imperial iconography on coins.
68. Yates, "Cosmos, Central Authority, and Communities."
69. There was, of course, much debate on how a ruler should rule, and many emperors who chose to leave the affairs of state to their ministers, or who were too young to rule themselves. While for the most part the people of early China did not participate in political decisions through popular votes, the importance of the people cannot be entirely ruled out. The one exception to this is the occasional ad-hoc voting

assemblies during the Spring and Autumn period, open to the *guoren* 國人, the "Capital Dwellers." These were not open and democratic votes, in the Greek sense, and while the *Zuo zhuan* contains numerous examples of the people expressing their will, on many of these occasions popular expression is ignored by the ruler, or popular will was manipulated to further an elite individual's personal cause. Ultimately, final decision making was considered to be the responsibility of the ruler. See Pines, *Envisioning Eternal Empire*, 192–97 on the *guoren*, and 187–218 on the relationship between the ruler and the people in the Spring and Autumn and Warring States periods. On the *guoren*, see also Cai Feng 蔡鋒, "Guoren de shuxing ji qi huodong dui Chunqiu shiqi guizu zhengzhi de yingxiang" 國人的屬性及其活動對春秋時期貴族政治的影響, *Beijing daxue xuebao (zhexue shehui kexue ban)*, 3 (1997): 113–21; Chao Fulin 晁福林, "Lun Zhou dai guoren yu shumin shehui shenfen de bianhua" 論周代國人與庶民社會身分的變化, *Renwen zazhi*, 3 (2000): 98–105; and Lewis, *Construction of Space*, 136–50.

Chapter 3

1. See *Divine Institutions* which convincingly argues that temples, as a form of infrastructure, were a fundamental part of shaping Roman identity. Dan-el Padilla Peralta, *Divine Institutions: Religions and Community in the Middle Roman Republic* (Princeton: Princeton University Press, 2020).
2. Poo, *In Search of Personal Welfare*.
3. The reforms in late Western Han are discussed by Michael Loewe, *Crisis and Conflict in Han China, 104 BC to AD 9* (London: Allen & Unwin, 1974), 154–92; Kaneko Shūichi 金子修一, *Chūgoku kodai kōtei saishi no kenkyu* 中國古代皇帝祭祀の研究 (Tokyo: Iwanami Shoten, 2006), 123–219; Gan Huaizhen 甘懷真, *Huangquan, liyi yu jingdian quanshi: Zhongguo gudai zhengzhishi yanjiu* 皇權，禮儀與經典詮釋：中國古代政治史研究 (Shanghai: Huadong shifan daxue chubanshe, 2008); Tian Tian, "The Suburban Sacrifice Reforms and the Evolution of the Imperial Sacrifice," in *Chang'an in 26 BCE: An Augustan Age in China*, ed. Michael Nylan and Griet Vankeerberghen (Seattle: University of Washington Press, 2015), 270–84, has argued that there only became a settled system with Wang Mang's 5 CE reform. While there were numerous reversals and restorations, the blueprint for imperial cult was drawn up at this time. Marianne Bujard, "State and Local Cults in Han Religion," in *Early Chinese Religion*, vol. 2, ed. John Lagerway and Marc Kalinowski (Leiden: Brill, 2008), 777–811.
4. Sarah A. Queen and John S. Major, trans., *Luxuriant Gems of the Spring and Autumn: Attributed to Dong Zhongshu* (New York: Columbia University Press, 2016), 506.
5. For reasons of space and to make a more fruitful comparison with Rome, I do not discuss ancestral worship performed by the emperors. For a recent discussion of ancestral worship under the Han, see Kenneth E. Brashier, *Ancestral Memory in Early China* (Cambridge: Harvard University Press, 2011). For the role of ancestors in

Republican Rome, see Harriet I. Flower, *Ancestor Masks and Aristocratic Power in Roman Culture* (Oxford: Clarendon Press, 1999).

6. Mu-chou Poo, "Religion and Religious Life of the Qin," in *Birth of an Empire: The State of Qin Revisited*, ed. Yuri Pines et al. (Berkeley: University of California Press, 2014), 192.
7. Marianne Bujard, "State and Local Cults in Han Religion."
8. Chen Shuguo 陳戌國, *Zhongguo lizhi shi: Qin-Han juan* 中國禮制史：秦漢卷 (Changsha: Hunan jiao yu chu ban she, 2002 [1993]), 17.
9. Watson notes that this lengthy quotation was likely included to demonstrate that "even in the most ancient of the Confucian Classics there is no detailed account of the Feng and Shan sacrifices." While this is certainly a part of it, it is also possible that this description of the earliest sacrificial programs of the sages was also included to provide a certain amount of continuity with the subsequent inspection tours under the First Emperor and Emperor Wu, and it is also important with regard to Emperor Wu's desire to take control over the rites at the Five Sacred Peaks (see Chapter 5). Burton Watson, *Records of the Grand Historian of China: Han Dynasty*, vol. 2 (Columbia: Columbia University Press, 1993 [1961]), 4.
10. *Shiji* 28.1355; *Hanshu* 25A.1191.
11. *Shiji* 28.1356; *Hanshu* 25A.1191.
12. *Hanshu* 25A.1193. While Sima Qian includes the system of King Cheng in his history, the comment on the harmony of the way of the kings is only in the *Hanshu* chapter.
13. 而諸侯祭其疆內名山、大川，大夫祭門、戶、井、灶、中霤五祀，士、庶人祖考而已 *Hanshu* 25A.1193–94. A similar comment is included in the *Shiji* prior to the discussion of the reign of King Cheng, but is phrased slightly differently: 天子祭天下名山大川，五嶽社三公，四瀆社諸侯，諸侯祭其疆內名山大川。*Shiji* 28.1357. The *Shiji* chapter does not connect the worship of the named mountains and rivers to the stipulation that people of certain rank (below the regional lords) could only worship up to a certain generation of ancestors. This idea is ubiquitous in various ritual texts and discussions of ritual, see Brashier, *Ancestral Memory*, 64ff.
14. The *Shiji* claims to cite the *Rites of Zhou* 周禮, which states that the Son of Heaven continued inspection tours and sacrifices to the great mountains and rivers. However, there is no such passage in the *Rites of Zhou*, and Sima Qian provides no specific information about Zhou rulers going on inspection tours.
15. *Shiji* 28.1367–68. The Eight Lords were the Lord of Heaven, Lord of Land, Lord of Arms (who was worshipped by sacrificing to Chi You), Lords of Yin and Yang, Lords of the Moon and Sun, and the Lord of the Four Seasons.
16. Sanft, "Progress and Publicity." This aspect of the sacrificial tours will be considered in greater detail in Chapter 6.
17. Tian, "The Suburban Sacrifice Reforms."
18. *Shiji* 6, "The Basic Annals of Qin Shi Huang" 秦始皇本紀. Only six of the inscriptions are recorded in the *Shiji*, a seventh text was known in the Tang and has been preserved in fourteenth-century inscription collections. See Kern, *The Stele Inscriptions of Ch'in Shih-huang*, 2, for details.
19. Kern, *The Stele Inscriptions of Ch'in Shih-huang*, 109–11.

20. The seven texts have been translated by Martin Kern, *The Stele Inscriptions of Ch'in Shih-huang: Text and Ritual in Early Chinese Imperial Representation*.
21. On the Qin biblioclasm, see Jens Østergard Peterson, "Which Books Did the First Emperor of Ch'in Burn? On the Meaning of Pai Chia in Early Chinese Sources," *Monumenta Serica* 43 (1995): 1–52.
22. Lord Xiang was given the territory and made a regional lord for the assistance he provided to the Zhou after their defeat by the Quanrong 犬戎 in 771, when they were forced to move their court east to Luoyang.
23. *Shiji* 28.1358; *Hanshu* 25A.1194.
24. *Shiji* 28.1358; *Hanshu* 25A.1194. The *Shiji* mentions that there had previously been important altars in the region of Yong, and that this area in the highlands had a reputation for being a good land for gods (神明之隩). *Shiji* 28.1359; *Hanshu* 25A.1195.
25. *Shiji* 28.1358; *Hanshu* 25A.1194.
26. *Jiao* has frequently been translated as the "suburban" or "border" sacrifice, as the word "*jiao*" had this meaning before the Han, and the *jiao*-sacrifice took place in the suburbs of the Qin capital before the formation of the First Empire. In later times, the *jiao* sacrifice also took place in the suburbs of the Han capital. However, in the period under discussion, and throughout the *Shiji* and *Hanshu* treatises, the term *jiao* is used to refer to major sacrifices to heavenly spirits, usually using the three sacrificial animals, described above. Marianne Bujard has argued that the *jiao* in *Shiji* and *Hanshu* simply means "sacrifice," however the term is not used to refer to sacrifices to earthly spirits, which were buried rather than burned. Marianne Bujard, "Le 'Traité des sacrifices' du Hanshu et la mise en place de la religion d'État des Han," *Bulletin de l'Ecole française d'Extrême-Orient* 84 (1997): 111–27.
27. This complement of three sacrificial animals was also called a *tailao* 太牢 (or *dalao* 大牢) *Liji* "Jiao te sheng," *Liji jijie* juan 25, *Xuxiu siku quanshu*, vol. 104, 34. The use of an ox, colt, and goat suggests that there may have been regional variation in what three animals were sacrificed.
28. *Shiji* 28.1360; *Hanshu* 25A.1196. While Sima Qian begins his history of the cult practice at Yong with the creation of the shrine to the White Emperor under Lord Wen, Tian Tian ("Chunqiu, Zhanguo, Qinguo ci si kao," 40) notes that with the cult of Chen Bao located in the region, the area had a much lengthier history of cult. The cult to Chen Bao was established under Lord Wen (r. 765–716). See also Tian Yaqi 田亞岐 "Qin-Han zhi zhi yanjiu" 秦漢置時研究, *Kaogu yu wenwu*, 3 (1993): 53–59, for a discussion of the development of cults practiced at and around Yong under the Qin. On the cult of Chen Bao, see also Marianne Bujard, "Le culte du Joyau de Chen: Culte historique—culte vivant," *Cahiers d'Extrême-Asie: Culte des sites et culte des saints en Chine* 10 (2008),
29. A distinction must be made here between the Yellow Thearch, the legendary culture hero who was said to have lived during the second millennium BCE, and the Yellow Emperor, who was one of the five gods worshipped at Yong (*shangdi* 上帝).
30. *Shiji* 28.1364; *Hanshu* 25A.1199.
31. To the sun, moon, Orion, Antares, the southern dipper, the northern dipper, Mars, Venus, Jupiter, Mercury, the twenty-eight lodges *ershi ba xiu* 二十八宿, the wind,

rain, four seas, nine vassals, fourteen vassals, and the various others. *Hanshu* 25A.1206–07. The *Shiji* does not record the Second Emperor's sacrifices at Yong.
32. *Shiji* 28.1378; *Hanshu* 25A.1210.
33. *Shiji* 8.343ff. Gaozu did establish a few new shrines at Chang'an, including one to the spirit Chi You 蚩尤, who was associated with warfare and weapons. This spirit had previously received sacrifice under the Qin, and the altar established at Chang'an remained in use until the reforms of 31 BCE. *Shiji* 28.1378–79; *Hanshu* 25A.1210–11. On Chi You, see Loewe, *Divination, Mythology, and Monarchy*, 242–46; Lewis, *Sanctioned Violence in Early China*, 165ff.
34. *Shiji* 28.1378; *Hanshu* 25A.1210. The text here is not clear if Gaozu was declaring himself to actually be the Black Emperor 於是高祖曰：「吾知之矣，乃待我而具五也。」乃立黑帝祠，名曰北畤 or if he saw his role simply as completing the set of altars. As he himself did not offer personal sacrifice to the five emperors, Chen Shuguo (*Zhongguo lizhi shi*, 109) has argued that he believed himself to be the Black Emperor, as it would be inappropriate to offer sacrifice to oneself. However, as there was no fixed rule that the emperor must offer sacrifice at Yong, it is also possible that he simply thought it to be the task of the sacrificial officials. Moreover, there is no mention of Gaozu receiving sacrifice at Yong, and after his death, he, like other Han emperors, received sacrifices at his Chanling mausoleum. On the worship of deceased ancestors, see Michael Loewe, *Divination, Mythology and Monarchy in Han China* (Cambridge: Cambridge University Press, 1994) 267–99; Brashier, *Ancestral Memory*, 102–83; and Wu Hung, "From Temple to Tomb: Ancient Chinese Art and Religion in Transition," *Early China* 13 (1988), on the shift of focus for ancestral worship from temples to tombs in the late Eastern Zhou.
35. The *Shiji* and *Hanshu* refer to this collection of spirits at Yong as the High Gods *Shangdi* 上帝 before the fifth temple was established and after the establishment of the shrine to the Black Emperor 黑帝, the text alternates between *Shangdi* and *Wudi* 五帝. For the sake of simplicity, I refer to these spirits who were offered sacrifice together at Yong and other locations as High Gods throughout. Although the *Shangdi* of the Zhou referred to a singular spirit, in the Qin and Han it is clear that *Shangdi* is used in the plural and, as Robert Eno has argued, this may reflect earlier, Shang practice. Robert Eno, "Was there a High God *Ti* in Shang Religion?" *Early China* 15 (1990): 1–26.
36. At least until the end of Emperor Wu's reign. See Chapter 7 and the conclusion for the evolution of the altars of the High Gods.
37. *Shiji* 28.1381; *Hanshu* 25A.1212.
38. This is seen in direct contrast to Emperor Wu, who, we are led to believe by Sima Qian, frequently believed advisors who fabricated omens. See Chapter 5 for details. *Shiji* 28.1381–83; *Hanshu* 25A.1212–14.
39. *Shiji* 28.1381–82; *Hanshu* 25A.1214. The *Shiji* does not specify the month, only that this visit took place in the summer.
40. HS 19A.726; Bielenstein, 18.
41. HS 19A.726.

42. Bielenstein, 17. There were many other responsibilities assigned to this office, including the evaluation of examination candidates, but these are beyond the scope of the present discussion.
43. Officials were dismissed in 117 and 107 for "failure to keep sufficient sacrificial animals" for the sacrifices at Yong. These sacrificial animals had to be kept in excellent condition and it can be assumed that a large part of the daily activities of the sacrificial officials involved caring for the animals. Loewe, *Men Who Governed*, 756.
44. The origins of Roman religion with Numa was a question that was debated during the Republic, particularly with the discovery in 181 BCE of a chest containing writings, supposedly composed by Numa. These texts were destroyed, as it was feared they would challenge the authority of the senatorial elite. See Hans Beck, "The Discovery of Numa's Writings: Roman Sacral Law and the Early Historians," in *Omnium Annalium Monumenta: Historical Writing and Historical Evidence in Republican Rome*, ed. Kaj Sandberg and Christopher Smith (Leiden: Brill, 2018).
45. The designation of colleges as "major" (*collegia maiora*) is an expression dating to the imperial period, but reflects the perceived importance of the colleges in the late Republic.
46. The *Flamines*, priests who were attached to a cult of an individual god, were under the supervision of the pontifical college, but due to the individual nature of their duties, did not form a college unto themselves. These *flamines* were often subject to various legal restrictions, and were primarily concerned with officiating rites to the object of their cult. See Mary Beard and John North, ed., *Pagan Priests: Religion and Power in the Ancient World* (London: Duckworth), 17ff; John Scheid, "Les prêtres officiels sous les empereurs julio-claudiens," in *Aufstieg und Niedergang de römischen Welt* II.16.1: 610–54 (Berlin: Walter de Gruyter, 1978). Women, while very important in a number of rituals, "could not take on any representative religious function on behalf of the state"; Scheid, *An Introduction to Roman Religion*, 131. The exception to this being the Vestal Virgins, who were charged with maintaining the sacred fire of Vesta and with many other purification rites for important state sacrifices. However, given the Vestal's unique position, separated from society, their role is not representative of women in Rome in general. On the Vestal Virgins, see Mary Beard, "The Sexual Status of Vestal Virgins," *The Journal of Roman Studies* 70 (1980): 12–27, and Robin Lorsch Wildfang, *Rome's Vestal Virgins: A Study of Rome's Vestal Priestesses in the Late Republic and Early Empire* (London: Routledge, 2006).
47. Liv. 10.6.6–12; Jörg Rüpke notes that this law "did not diminish the number of patrician priests but simply added plebian pontifices and augurs," in *Religion in Republican Rome*, 13; see also Karl J. Hölkeskamp, "Das Plebiscitum Ogulnium de sacerdotibus: Überlegungen zu Authentizität und Interpretation der livianischen Überlieferung," *Rheinisches Museum für Philologie*, Neue Folge, 131 (1988); Beard, North, and Price, *Religions of Rome*, 130–31; Martha W. Hoffman Lewis, *The Official Priests of Rome under the Julio-Claudians: A Study of the Nobility from 44 B.C. to 68 A.D.* (Rome: American Academy in Rome, 1955).
48. Cic. *Har. Resp.* 9. The Etruscan Haruspices were not an official priestly college, though they were to a certain extent organized, and they were ultimately organized as a

profession under Tiberius. See Beard, North, and Price, *Religions of Rome*, 101, and R. M. Ogilvie, *The Romans and Their Gods in the Age of Augustus* (New York: Norton, 1970), 67. The "ancient prophecies" refers to the Sibylline books, which could be consulted by the *quindecimviri*, discussed in Chapter 5.

49. This practice of election began in the third century, and was extended to the other priestly colleges with the *lex Domitia* in 104 BCE. A special electoral assembly was convened which consisted of seventeen of the thirty-five tribes. The *lex Domitia* may have been revoked by Sulla, but we know that by the time of Caesar's somewhat scandalous victory in the election of 63 BCE, that the right to elect the *pontifex maximus* had been restored. Lily Ross Taylor, "The Election of the Pontifex Maximus in the Late Republic," *Classical Philology* 37, no. 4 (1942): 421–24. On Caesar's election, see Ronald Syme, "Caesar as *Pontifex Maximus*," in *Approaching the Roman Revolution: Papers on Republican History* (Oxford: Oxford University Press, 2016): 189–95.

50. Beard, North, and Price, *Religions of Rome*, vol. 2, 205.

51. Beard, North, and Price, *Religions of Rome*, vol. 1, 100; Ogilvie, *The Romans and Their Gods in the Age of Augustus*, 106–09; Rüpke, *Fasti sacerdotum*, 7; and for a general overview of the college, Françoise Van Haeperen, *Le collège pontifical: 3e s. av. J.-C.- 4e s. ap. J.-C.: contribution à l'étude de la religion publique romaine* (Bruxelles-Rome, Institut historique belge de Rome, 2002).

52. Ogilvie, *The Romans and Their Gods in the Age of Augustus*, 106–09.

53. After the *lex Ogulnia* in 300 BCE, their numbers were fixed at nine, this was increased to fifteen under Sulla, and up to sixteen under Julius Caesar, though the numbers of this college, like the others, were highly inconsistent throughout the years. Hoffman Lewis suggests that in the early empire, there could be as many as 25 members in each of the major colleges, *The Official Priests of Rome under the Julio-Claudians*, 12.

54. Scheid, *An Introduction to Roman Religion*, 133.

55. It was often difficult to find patricians who both met the requirements and were willing to fill some of these offices. Particularly in the case of the Rex Sacrorum and the major Flamines, there were very strict restrictions placed on the priest, making it very difficult for him to become a magistrate and advance through the *cursus honorum*. See Jesse Benedict Carter, "The Reorganization of the Roman Priesthoods at the Beginning of the Republic," *Memoirs of the American Academy at Rome* 1 (1915); Cornell, however, suggests that the position may have been created prior to the start of the Republic, with power divided between a religious *rex* and a ruling tyrant (*magister populi*), *The Beginnings of Rome*, 235–36.

56. Olga Tellegen-Couperus, "Introduction," in *Law and Religion in the Roman Republic* (Leiden: Brill, 2011), 1; Beard, "Priesthood in the Roman Republic," in *Pagan Priests*, 36–37.

57. Beard, "Priesthood in the Roman Republic," 36. See also Cic. *Dom*. 1–4, and on the ritual authority of the *pontifices*, Beard, "Priesthood in the Roman Republic," 136.

58. Cic. *Dom*. 33. As Jerzy Linderski notes, the question of secret knowledge within the colleges is complicated: Cicero did not claim to know whether or not the augurs had secret books, only that "should the augurs have any books of recondite character, he

is not prying into them"; "The *Libri Reconditi*," *Harvard Studies in Classical Philology* 89 (1985): 208. This suggests that Cicero suspected that the augurs did have such texts, but that, as he had not yet been co-opted into the college, he had no concrete knowledge of the existence of the texts, or what they contained. In addition to the *libri reconditi*, the colleges maintained their own archives, and these were likely "relatively accessible to interested scholars," Jerzy Linderski, "The Augural Law," in *Aufstieg und Niedergang der römischen Welt*. II.16.3 (Berlin: Walter de Gruyter 1986): 2245.

59. Linderski, "The *Libri Reconditi*," 221.
60. Cic. *Att*. 74. "All the Pontifices who were Senators were called in. Marcellinus, who was very strongly on my side, as the first called upon, asked them to give reasons for their decree. M. Lucullus, speaking for all his colleagues, then replied that the Pontifices had been judges of the religious issue, but the Senate was judge of the law. His colleagues and himself had given their verdict on the former; on the latter they would decide in the Senate, as Senators." *Adhibentur omnes pontifices qui erant senatores. a quibus Marcellinus, qui erat cupidissimus mei, sententiam primus rogatus quaesivit quid essent in decernendo secuti. Tum M. Lucullus de omnium collegarum sententia respondit religionis iudices pontifices fuisse, legis esse senatum; se et collegas suos de religione statuisse, in senatu de lege statuturos cum senatu. Itaque suo quisque horum loco sententiam rogatus multa secundum causam nostram disputavit*. For an earlier example, see also the case of the *pontifex maximus* Cornelius Barbatus, who, in 304 BCE, was compelled, by the force of the people to instruct a magistrate (Cn. Flavius) on the correct way to dedicate a temple, although he had attempted to obstruct this (Liv. 9.46.6-7). See Eric M. Orlin, *Temples, Religion, and Politics in the Roman Republic* (Leiden: E. J. Brill, 1997), 163–65.
61. Beck, "The Discovery of Numa's Writings."
62. Ibid. See also the discussion on these *Annales Maximi* and their relationship with the *tabula dealbata* in Timothy J. Cornell, ed., *The Fragments of the Roman Historians* (Oxford: Oxford University Press, 2013), vol. 1, 144–48.
63. Hoffman Lewis, *The Official Priests of Rome under the Julio-Claudians*, 102.
64. Cic. *Leg*. 3.19.
65. Beard, "Priesthood in the Roman Republic," 40.
66. Beard, "Priesthood in the Roman Republic," 39–40. On *templum* as link between heaven and earth, Varro, *Ling*. 8.8–10.
67. Beard, "Priesthood in the Roman Republic," 40.
68. Cic. *Dom*. 39. "I proceed now to the augurs, into whose books, such of them at least as are secret, I forbear to pry. I am not curious to inquire into augural regulations. There are some, however, of which I share the knowledge with the populace, which have often been revealed, in answer to inquiry, in mass meetings, and with these I am familiar." *Venio ad augures, quorum ego libros, si qui sunt reconditi, non scrutor: non sum in exquirendo iure augurum curiosus: haec, quae una cum populo didici, quae saepe in contionibus responsa sunt, novi*. See Linderski, "The *Libri Reconditi*," on Cicero's knowledge of these books.

69. While the historicity of the acquisition of the texts is impossible to verify, it testifies to the antiquity of the office (Dion. Hal. 4.62). The Sibylline Books themselves will be discussed further in Chapter 5. The expansion to ten men is recorded in Livy 6.42.12. Caesar added a priest *supernumerarii* in 44 BCE (Dio. 43.51.9). As the college was known as the *quindecimviri* during the times of Julius Caesar and Augustus, I use this name throughout. See also Lintott, *The Constitution of the Roman Republic*, 183–85.
70. Lintott, *The Constitution of the Roman Republic*, 184.
71. See, for example, Hoffman Lewis, *The Official Priests of Rome under the Julio-Claudians*, 103, who ranks the *quindecimviri* as the third most prestigious college; Rüpke, *Fasti Sacerdotum*, 8, "these two [*pontifices* and *augures*] were always more prestigious" than the *quindecimviri*; Likewise, Beard's discussion of the priestly colleges focuses only on the *pontifices* and *augures*, "Priesthood in the Roman Republic," 19–48.
72. Lintott, *The Constitution of the Roman Republic*, 184.
73. Livy, 33.42.1, Dio, 43.51.9; Rüpke presents the possibility that the number was increased to seven under Sulla. Rüpke, *Fasti Sacerdotum*, 8.
74. Cic. *Orat*. 3.9. "But just as the old pontifices owing to the vast number of sacrifices decided to have a Banquet Committee of three members, though they had themselves been appointed by Numa for the purpose among others of holding the great Sacrificial Banquet of the Games." *Sed ut pontifices veteres propter sacrificiorum multitudinem tres viros epulones esse voluerunt, cum essent ipsi a Numa ut etiam illud ludorum epulare sacrificium facerent institute.*
75. Gel. Att. XII.8.
76. "Septemviri—Brill Reference." Online.
77. Ogilvie, *The Romans and Their Gods in the Age of Augustus*, 110.
78. Varro *Ling*. 5.85.
79. Ronald Syme, *Some Arval Brethren* (Oxford: Clarendon Press, 1980), 2.
80. On the difficulty of dating this revival, see John Scheid, *Les Frères Arvales: Recrutement et origine sociale sous les empereurs Julio-Claudiens* (Paris: Presses Universitaires de France, 1975), 335–36. Scheid argues that the revival of the Arvals took place alongside other religious reforms of 31/29, and must have been accomplished by 27, when the Octavian took the title Augustus.
81. Rüpke, *Fasti Sacerdotum*, 8.
82. For example, with the revival of the college in 29 BCE, nine out of the twelve members already held other priesthoods, fairly evenly distributed between the *ponifices*, *augures*, *quindecimviri*, and *epulones*, and one member would attain membership in the pontifical college shortly thereafter. Following the membership lists in Rüpke, *Fasti Sacerdotum*, 136. Of the seventeen members during the reign of Augustus, eleven held membership in another college. See Scheid, *Les Frères Arvales*, 304.
83. In this way, Scheid argues that the Arvals were a precursor to the later imperial priests. Scheid, *Les Frères Arvales*, 340. See also Beard, North, and Price, *Religions of Rome*, vol. 1, 195; J. H. W. G. Liebeschuetz, *Continuity and Change in Roman Religion* (Oxford, Clarendon Press, 1979), 63.

84. There are several comprehensive monographs on the Arval Brothers for the imperial period, particularly, Scheid, *Les Frères Arvales*; John Scheid, *Romulus et ses frères: Le collège des Frères Arvales, modèle du culte public dans la Rome des empereurs* (Rome: Ecole française de Rome, 1990); Syme, *Some Arval Brethren*.
85. Beard, North, and Price, *Religions of Rome*, 136. Potential members were nominated by the college, but then had to be voted in. In 81 BCE, Sulla, in his capacity as dictator, revived the practice of cooptation to the priestly colleges, but elections were later restored by Caesar.
86. Pierre Bourdieu, *Outline of a Theory of Practice* (Cambridge: Cambridge University Press, 1977), 195.
87. Richard Gordon, "From Republic to Principate: Priesthood, Religion and Ideology," in *Roman Religion*, ed. Clifford Ando (Edinburgh: Edinburgh University Press, 2003), 77–78. This expenditure on religious ceremonies was in addition to the vast sums that magistrates would spend on public affairs as they climbed the *cursus honorum*.
88. Hoffman Lewis, *The Official Priests of Rome under the Julio-Claudians*, 10.
89. Rüpke, *Fasti Sacerdotum*, 57, emphasis added.
90. W. Jeffrey Tatum, *Always I Am Caesar* (Malden: Blackwell, 2008), 68.
91. Significantly, the *quindecimviri* could only consult the Sibylline books by order of the Senate.
92. Rüpke's *Fasti Sacerdotum* compiles and reconstructs enrolment records for the colleges. Much of this information is now available in digital format, up to the year 31 BCE, via the Digital Prosopography of the Roman Republic project at King's College London: https://romanrepublic.ac.uk/.
93. Rüpke, *Fasti Sacerdotum*, 8.
94. Little is known of the *flamines minors* other than there were twelve. Rüpke, *Fasti Sacerdotum*, 8.
95. A list of the taboos related to the *flamen Dialis* is preserved in Aulus Gellius, NA. 10.15. As the restrictions on the *flamen Dialis* were the most extreme, we know more about them than for other priesthoods. For an overview of this priesthood, see Jens H. Vanggaard, *The Flamen: A Study in the History and Sociology of Roman Religion* (Copenhagen: Museum Tusculanum Press, 1988).
96. Tac. *Ann.* 3.58.
97. Tac. *Ann.* 3.58; Rüpke, *Religion in Republican Rome*, 36–37.
98. John Scheid, "Sacrifices for Gods and Ancestors," in *The Blackwell Companion to Roman Religion*, ed. Jörg Rüpke (Malden: Blackwell, 2007), 264.
99. Scheid, "Sacrifices," 268. Likewise, in the Qin and Han commoners could purchase sacrificial meat.
100. This is a broad generalization of the main features of Roman sacrifice, and there was of course many variations in the specific rites offered to individual gods or on particular occasions.
101. Richard C. Beacham, *Spectacle Entertainments of Early Imperial Rome* (New Haven, CT: Yale University Press, 1999), 3.

Chapter 4

1. Michael Puett, *To Become a God: Cosmology, Sacrifice, and Self-divinization in Early China* (Cambridge: Harvard University Press, 2002), 307.
2. Puett, *To Become a God*, 245.
3. *Liji*, "Li Yun."
4. See, for example, *Zuozhuan*, Lord Ai, year 6. According to the *Lunyu* 論語, it was inappropriate to sacrifice to spirits that were not your own ("Wei Zheng" 為政).
5. Michael Puett has argued that Emperor Wu was attempting to himself "become a god," through his territorial and sacrificial expansion. What constituted immortality is itself a complicated question, discussed by Puett (2002 and 2015), and Yü Ying-shi, "Life and Immortality in The Mind of Han China," *Harvard Journal of Asiatic Studies* 25 (1964–1965): 80–122. Emperor Wu's own conception of his possible divinization is not of immediate concern in this chapter; what is of greater interest to me is the way this pursuit of immortality shaped imperial authority.
6. Wang Jing 王靜 and Liang Yong 梁勇, "Qin-Han shiqi fangshu, fangshi yu zhengzhi wenhua zhi guanxi" 秦漢時期方術, 方士與政治文化之關係, *Journal of Hebei University (Philosophy and Social Science)* 35, no. 3 (2010): 39. There is no evidence that the *fangshi* considered themselves to be a distinct group in this period. For overviews of the *fangshi* see Chen Pan 陳槃, "Zhanguo Qin Han jian fangshi kaolun" 戰國秦漢間方士考論, *Zhongyang yanjiuyuan, lishi yuyan yanjiusuo jikan* 17 (1948): 7–57; Ngo, *Divination, magie et politique*; and Mark Csikszentmihalyi, "Fangshi 方士 'Masters of Methods,'" in *The Encyclopedia of Taoism*, ed. Fabrizio Pregadio (London: Routledge, 2008), 406–09; Kenneth DeWoskin, *Doctors, Diviners, and Magicians of Ancient China: Biographies of* Fang-shih (New York: Columbia University Press, 1983).
7. The *fangshi* Shaoweng was executed after he was caught having fed a prophetic text to a sacrificial cow, with the intention that it would be discovered in the cow's stomach after its sacrifice. Shaoweng would have gotten away with it, too, had a pesky colleague not noticed that the text was written in Shaoweng's own hand. The *fangshi* Luan Da was also executed after many years of failing to deliver immortal spirits to the emperor.
8. *Shiji* 28.1403–04. "The Son of Heaven was increasingly unsatisfied with the strange and circuitous speech of the *fangshi*, but he became increasingly bound to them, without breaking [his ties], all the while hoping to find one who knew the truth. After this time, the *fangshi* who spoke of the spirits and sacrifices became increasingly numerous, but the effects are as we have seen." 天子益怠厭方士之怪迂語矣，然羈縻不絕，冀遇其真。自此之後，方士言神祠者彌眾，然其效可睹矣。
9. *Shiji* 28.1390; 29.1409, 1412–04. See Rebecca Robinson, "Repairing the Yellow River Breach at Huzi: Flood Control and Immortality during the reign of Han Wudi," *Etudes Chinoises* (forthcoming).
10. On the new cults and the *feng* and *shan* sacrifices, see Chapter 7.
11. Suet. *Aug.* 31.3–4.

12. Suet. *Aug.* 31.5. *Proximum a dis immortalibus honorem memoriae ducum praestitit, qui imperium p. R. ex minimo maximum reddidissent.*
13. "For ten years in succession I was one of the triumvirs for the re-establishment of the constitution] To the day of writing this I have been *princeps senatus* for forty years. I have been pontifex maximus, augur, a member of the fifteen commissioners for performing sacred rites, one of the seven for sacred feasts, an arval brother, a sodalis Titius, a fetial priest." *(Princeps senatus fui usque ad eum diem, quo scrip)seram 45(haec,)* ‖ *(per annos quadraginta. Pontifex maximus, augur, quindecimviru)m sacris (faciundis,)* | *(septemvirum epulonum, frater arvalis, sodalis Titius, fetiali)s fui.*
14. Dio, 53.17.9.
15. Sulla was likely, according to Rüpke, both a *decemvir* and an *augur*, though his membership in the colleges is still under debate. Caesar was both a Pontiff and Augur. See Rüpke, *Fasti Sacerdotum*, 645 and 734–35 for details.
16. Rüpke, *Fasti Sacerdotum*, 58.
17. The approximate dates for Augustus' co-optation are as follows (all dates BCE): Pontifical College, 47; Augural College, 43; *quindecimviri*, 39 or 37; *epulones*, 29, Arval Brothers, 29, and Sodalis Titii, 30. While Lepidus had been exiled and effectively stripped of all priestly power, he could not be stripped of the title of *pontifix maximus* itself.
18. Martha W. Hoffman Lewis, "The College of Quindecimviri (Sacris Faciundis) in 17 B. C.," *The American Journal of Philology* 73, no. 3 (1952): 289. While evidence for this exists in the *quindecimviri* lists, the Arval lists frequently deviate from it. Rüpke, *Fasti Sacerdotum*, 19 n.6.
19. With the exception of the colleges of *quindecimviri* and *Arvales*, which were revived in 29 BCE, with Augustus as a founding member. While there was no formal position of prominence in the Augural College comparable to the *pontifex maximus*, the most senior member of the *augures* did have some influence. Tacitus notes a case in 22 CE when the senior Augur, Cn. Cornelius Lentulus entered into a dispute with the *pontifex maximus* (Tiberius) over the question of a Flamen Dialis receiving a province. Tac. *Ann.* 3.58–59.
20. While it had been voted that Caesar's heir should succeed him as *pontifex maximus*, through the negotiations of the triumvirs, Lepidus was given this honour, and it would not be until the death of Augustus that the office became hereditary. Dio 44.5.3.
21. Many of these awards of priesthoods were the result of military negotiations, notably Sextus Pompeius (Augur) at the Treaty of Misenum (39 BCE), who was also promised a future consulship, and Valerius Messalla (Augur, enrolled *supernumerari* in 36 BCE, later to be co-opted into the Arval Brothers [20 BCE]). Dio 48.36; 49.16.
22. In 36 BCE. Dio. 49.15.
23. Cic. *Fam.* 3.10 states that the friendship between priests must extend beyond the colleges, and that no priest could be co-opted into a college if he had some enmity with one of the existing members.
24. Frederico Santangelo, "Enduring Arguments: Priestly Expertise in the Early Principate," *Transactions of the American Philological Association* 146 (2016): 355.
25. See Scheid, "Les restaurations religieuses d'Octavien/Auguste," 125; and on the role of the Arval Brothers, Scheid, *Les Frères Arvales*, 344; 348–51.

26. The list of members has been reconstructed by Hoffman Lewis, whose observation that the *fasti* lists for the colleges were organized according to date of co-optation has significantly aided our understanding of co-optation and membership in the colleges. See also the prosopographical information in Rüpke, *Fasti Sacerdotum*, and at the Kings College London digital humanities project *Digital Prosopography of the Roman Republic*, with data available for years up to 31 BCE. Accessible at www.romanrepublic.ac.uk.
27. Following the reconstructions in Rüpke. The new appointees for whom we have biographical information can be linked to Augustus, though there are also many priests for whom we lack further information. The majority of new appointments were made to the college of the *quindecimviri*, which Augustus raised in prestige, so it is reasonable to assume that the unknown priests were also close allies of Augustus. See below on the college of *quindecimviri* and its changing status during the *principate*. One of the new priests, Asinius Gallus, who was co-opted to the *quindecimviri* in the early 20s at a very young age was married to Vipsania Agrippina, Agrippa's daughter. Rüpke, *Fasti Sacerdotum*, 547.
28. The First Emperor actively pursued immortal spirits and offered many sacrifices himself, while Caesar was a member of both the pontifical and augural colleges, and, for a time, the *flamen Dialis*.
29. This can be most clearly seen during the calendrical reforms of 105/4 BCE, when Sima Qian's calendrical expertise was brushed aside in favour of a man from the provinces who created a calendrical system more in line with the emperor's wishes. On the calendar reforms see Christopher Cullen, "Motivations for Scientific Change in Ancient China: Emperor WU and the Grand Inception Astronomical Reforms of 104 B.C.," *Journal for the History of* 24, no. 3 (1993): 185–203; and Rebecca Robinson, "Employing Knowledge: A Case Study in Calendar Reforms in the Early Han and Roman Empires," in *Rulers and Ruled in Ancient Greece, Rome, and China*, ed. Griet Vankeerberghen and Hans Beck (Cambridge: Cambridge University Press, 2021), 369–96, for a comparison between the calendrical reforms that took place in early China and Rome.

Chapter 5

1. Wu Hung, "From Temple to Tomb," 101–02.
2. See also the discussion and translation of *Hanshu* 25B in Marianne Bujard, *Le sacrifice au ciel*.
3. For an overview of the promulgation of Roman religion in the provinces and the problems inherent in exporting Roman religion, see Ando, "Exporting Roman Religion," in *A Companion to Roman Religion*, 429–45. The worship of the divinized emperors did spread through the provinces, and was an important factor in connecting the provinces to Rome. Augustus, however, did not encourage the worship of himself during his own lifetime, and the topic remains outside of the scope of the monograph. See Ittai Gradel, *Emperor Worship and Roman Religion* (Oxford: Clarendon Press, 2002); Simon R. F. Price, *Rituals and Power*.

4. Yang, "Qin Han diguo de shenquan tongyi," 6–7.
5. Yang, "Qin Han diguo de shenquan tongyi," 6–7.
6. There are two mountains worshipped under Emperor Wu whose names transliterate to the pinyin *heng*. To avoid confusion, I follow other translators in rendering *heng* 恆 as Hengg, and *heng* 衡 as Heng.
7. *Shiji* 28.1371.
8. See Yang "Qin Han diguo de shenquan tongyi," 7.
9. *Shiji* 28.1377: 郡縣遠方祠者，民各自奉祠，不領於天子之祝官。
10. *Shiji* 28.1381. The text implies that after the kingdoms were reestablished, the kings were again responsible for sacrifices.
11. "Wang zhi" *Liji jijie* juan 12, *Xuxiu siku quanshu*, Vol. 103, 943. Legge, trans., Vol. 27, 217.
12. Mark Edward Lewis, "The *feng* and *shan* Sacrifices of Emperor Wu of the Han," in *State and Court Ritual in China*, ed. Joseph P. McDermott (Cambridge: Cambridge University Press, 1999), 79. Lewis argues that the emperor traced this "mandala" on his inspection tours, while this may have been the idealized vision of the tours, there was little to no consistency in the route or timing of Emperor Wu's inspection tours.
13. *Shiji* 28.1355–56. The inspection tours are treated in greater detail in Chapter 6.
14. *Shiji* 28.1387, *Hanshu* 25A.1219.
15. *Hanshu* 44.2155–56. Ord notes that "The king's real offense was failure to take a hint." Edmund Burke Holladay Ord, "State Sacrifices in the Former Han Dynasties According to the Official Histories," PhD Dissertation, University of California, Berkeley (1967), 232.
16. *Shiji* 28.1387, *Hanshu* 25A.1219; 53.2434–36. *Hanshu* 53, "Biographies of the Thirteen Sons of Emperor Jing" 景十三王傳 describes the affair. After abolishing the kingdom, the King of Changshan's son was made ruler of the region of Zhending真定, within the former territory of the king, so that he could maintain ancestral sacrifices. The chapter indicates that the emperor was lenient in assigning territory to each of the sons of King Xian, choosing to blame the offence on the licentious queen, rather than on the misguided sons. The section on the king of Changshan is very concise and makes no mention of the emperor's acquisition of Mt. Hengg.
17. *Shiji* 28.1387, *Hanshu* 25A.1219.
18. The King of Jibei, the nephew of Liu An and Liu Ci, Kings of Huainan and Hengshan, respectively, was also likely eager to avoid being charged with rebellion after the execution of his uncles. For more on the events of 123–122 BCE, see Griet Vankeerberghen, *The Huainanzi and Liu An's Claim to Moral Authority* (Albany: State University of New York Press, 2001), 55–60.
19. *Hanshu*, 44.2157.
20. *Shiji* 28.1388, *Hanshu* 25A.1219.
21. Charles Sanft, "Debating the Route of the Qin Direct Road (Zhidao): Text and Excavation," *Frontiers of History in China* 6.3 (2011): 326–27; *Shiji* 6.241.
22. *Shiji* 88.2566–67.
23. The area remained contested until the campaigns during Emperor Wu's reign, in 166 BCE, the fourteenth year of Emperor Wen's reign, the Xiongnu Shanyu led forces into

Han territory and scouts went as far as Ganquan palace. *Shiji* 110.2901. On the development of the site, see also Yao Shengmin 姚生民, "Xi Han Ganquan gong zai Ganquanshan xia" 西漢甘泉宮在甘泉山下, *Qin-Han Yanjiu* 6 (2012): 66–70.

24. In 119 BCE, on the advice of the *fangshi* Shaoweng, he built at Ganquan, and again in 118 BCE, on the advice of a shaman, in order to cure his illness. cf. Li Ling, "An Archaeological Study of Taiyi (Grand One) Worship," trans. Donald Harper, *Early Medieval China* 2 (1995–1996): 4; *Sanfu Huangtu*, 70–71.

25. *Shiji* 28.139; *Hanshu* 25A.1230. 其後黃帝接萬靈明庭。明庭者，甘泉也。This is also noted in the *Sanfu Huangtu*, which, citing the "Guanfu Ji" states that the "Yellow Thearch would sacrifice to Heaven at the round mound at Ganquan." 黃帝以來圜丘祭天處; *Sanfu Huangtu*, 47.

26. The new cult of Great Unity will be discussed in Chapter 7.

27. *Hanshu* 6.199. The *Hanshu* records the receiving of these accounts in two other years, 106 BCE and 98 BCE, both at the *mingtang* at Mt. Tai.

28. *Hanshu* 6.206.

29. *Hanshu* 25B.1253. The use of Ganquan palace corresponds to the end of Nicola di Cosmo's "second phase" of Han expansion in the north west, and the pursuit of further expansion after consolidating the northern border. Nicola Di Cosmo, *Ancient China and Its Enemies: The Rise of Nomadic Power in East Asian History* (Cambridge: Cambridge University Press, 2004), 241–44. The Xiongnu did not formally accept Han superiority until 51 BCE, during the reign of Emperor Xuan; see Di Cosmo, *Ancient China and Its Enemies*, 206.

30. Guan Donggui 管東貴, "Qin-Han Ganquan gong xiaoshi" 秦漢甘泉宮小識", in *Kaogu yu lishi wenhua: Qingzhu Gua Quxun xiansheng bashi dashou lunwen ji (xia)* 考古與歷史文化：慶祝刮去尋先生八十大壽論文集（下）(Taipei: Chengchung shuju, 1991), 54, and *Sanfu Huangtu*, 46–50; 67–82 on the importance of the site and its various palaces.

31. See for example *Shiji* 110, *Hanshu* 96, and *Huainanzi* 11. Sima Qian, however, identified an alternate site for the Xiongnu's worship of heaven, at Longcheng 籠城, which Di Cosmo places in modern Inner Mongolia. *Shiji* 11.2892; Nicola DiCosmo, *Ancient China and Its Enemies*, 189.

32. *Shiji* 28.1369–70.

33. Wang and Liang, 41.

34. To give but the example of Yong, neither of the Qin emperors sacrificed personally to the *Shangdi*; Gaozu established a fifth shrine, but did not sacrifice; Emperor Wen increased the sacrifices at Yong, and sacrificed on one occasion, before establishing a second temple to the *Shangdi* north of the Wei river; Emperor Wu sacrificed frequently, but not according to a fixed schedule.

35. This position, occupied by a holder of noble rank, was often dangerous, and there are many instances wherein the holder of this post was accused of ritual impropriety, and stripped of his rank and title, suggesting that perhaps this position was highly politicized. See Griet Vankeerberghen, "Of Gold and Purple: Nobles in Western Han China and Republican Rome," in Hans Beck and Griet Vankeerberghen, eds., *Rulers and Ruled in Greece, Rome, and China* (Cambridge: Cambridge University Press 2021), 25–69, and *Hanshu* 19B.771ff.

36. *Hanshu* 19A.726, Hans Bielenstein, *The Bureaucracy of Han Times*, 17–23.
37. As Luke Habberstad has demonstrated, the responsibilities of the Superintendent of Ceremonial declined dramatically with the ritual reforms in the late Western Han. Habberstad, "Legalizing Ritual: Critiques of Imperial Cults and the Ascendance of Ritual over Law During the Western Han," paper delivered at the "Empire and the Media of Religion" Workshop, UCLA, May 2015.
38. *Shiji* 28.1380; *Hanshu* 25A.1212.
39. A document excavated from the Xuanquan 懸泉 site discusses the loss of a travel pass given to an official who had been sent to oversee an official sacrifice in 39 BCE. Charles Sanft, *Literate Community in Early Imperial China* (Albany: SUNY, 2019), 58–59. See also Zhang Defang 張德芳, "Xuanquan Han jian zhong de 'chuanxin jian' kaoshu" 懸泉漢簡中的'傳信簡'考述, in *Chutu wenxian yanjiu* 出土文獻研究 7. ed. Zhongguo wenwu yanjiusuo (Shanghai: Shanghai guji chubanshe, 2005), 65–81 for more on the relevant slips.
40. *Shiji* 12.474; 28.1397; *Hanshu* 6.190. According to Roel Sterckx, this would have amounted to a population of approximately 1,500 people to provide sacrifice at this one mountain. Roel Sterckx, *Food, Sacrifice, and Sagehood in Early China* (Cambridge: Cambridge University Press, 2011), 136. The establishment of towns to maintain sacrifices was particularly common near mausoleums; see Michael Loewe, "The Tombs Built for Han Chengdi and Migrations of the Population," in *Chang'an 26 BCE: An Augustan Age in China*, Michael Nylan and Griet Vankeerberghen, eds. (Seattle: University of Washington Press, 2015), 201–17.
41. Michael Loewe, "The Former Han Dynasty," in *The Cambridge History of China Volume 1: The Ch'in and Han Empires, 221 B.C.–A.D. 220* (Cambridge: Cambridge University Press, 1986), 159; Brashier, *Ancestral Memory*, 114–23; *Hanshu* 6.187.
42. Tian Tian, *Qin-Han guojia jisi shigao* 秦漢國家祭祀史稿 (Beijing: Xin zhi san lian shudian, 2015), 270.
43. The court's ties to the capital began to change in the late Western Han, particularly under the reign of Emperor Cheng. See the recent volume *Chang'an in 26 BCE* (Nylan and Vankeerberghen, eds.) for the development of the capital in the late Western Han.
44. Mark Edward Lewis, "Public Spaces in Cities in the Roman and Han Empires," in *State Power in Ancient China and Rome*, ed. Walter Scheidel (Oxford: Oxford University Press, 2015), 205.
45. Suet. *Lives*. II.28.
46. Lewis, "Public Spaces," 222.
47. G. W. Bowersock, "The Pontificate of Augustus," in *Between Republic and Empire: Interpretations of Augustus and His Principate*, ed. Kurt A. Raaflaub (Berkeley: University of California Press, 1990), 382.
48. Ronald Syme, "Augustus did not strip him [Lepidus] of that honour [the pontifex maximus], ostentatious in scruple when scruple cost him nothing. He could wait for Lepidus' death. Better that he should—in recent history the dignity of pontifex maximus, in no way the reward of merit, was merely a prize in the game of politics." *The Roman Revolution* (Oxford: Oxford University Press, 2002), 447; Bowersock, "The Pontificate of Augustus," 380.

49. Bowersock, "The Pontificate of Augustus," 72.
50. The importance of the inauguration of the new *saeculum*, as well as the timing, will be discussed in detail in Chapter 7.
51. Scheid, *Les Frères Arvales*; Val. Max. 8.11.2 records him as being a pontiff on the Ides of March, 44, though the exact date of his co-optation is unknown. He was consul in 53 and 40 BCE, and celebrated a triumph in 36.
52. See Scheid, *Les Frères Arvales*, 40–43; and Scheid, *Romulus et ses frères*, 690–732.
53. They were consulted in 38 BCE (Dio, 48.44; Tac. *Ann.* 1.10; in 37 BCE, (Dio, 48.53.4–6); in 47 CE, (Tac. *Ann.* 11.15); and in 49 CE, (Tac. *Ann.* 12.8), though they continued to advise on affairs concerning family religion and burials. See Liebeschuetz, *Continuity and Change in Roman Religion*, 63.
54. See Scheid, "Les Restaurations religieuses d'Octavien/Auguste," *in Le principat d'Auguste: Réalités et représentations du pouvoir autour de la Res publica restituta* eds. Fréderic Hurlet and Bernard Mineo (Rennes: Presses universitaires de Rennes), 126–27.
55. Tac. *Ann.* 3.58; Gordon, "From Republic to Principate: Priesthood, Religion, and Ideology," in *Pagan Priests*, 183. Gordon notes that this evocation of the religious activity of Numa is also connected to Augustus' closing of the temple of Janus in 29 BCE.
56. These parallel lineages were emphasised by Augustus and can be particularly seen in the narrative created during the Augustan reforms to the calendar. See Rebecca Robinson, "To Reverently Bestow the Seasons: Calendrical Narratives in Early China and Rome," in *Intersections of Religion and Astronomy*, eds. Aaron Ricker et al. (Oxon: Routledge, 2021), 27–35.
57. Prior to this period, the *pontifices* and *augures* held more consulships than members of other colleges. See David E. Hahm, "Roman Nobility and the Three Major Priesthoods, 218–167 BC," *Transactions and Proceedings of the American Philological Association* 94 (1963): 73–85.
58. Alexander Yakobson demonstrates that the élites were often divided at the polls, and that it was therefore necessary to gain the support of the lower classes. While the elections in the Augustan period were far less open than in the earlier Republic, competition and rivalry amongst the elites remained fierce, and it was necessary for Augustus to try to control the conversation. Yakobson, "Petitio et Largitio: Popular Participation in the Centuriate Assembly of the Late Republic," *The Journal of Roman Studies* 82 (1992): 32–52.
59. Displays of this sort were useful in demonstrating one's importance in a highly competitive, public setting. Wilfried Nippel, *Public Order in Ancient Rome* (Cambridge: Cambridge University Press, 1995), 32.
60. According to Rüpke, banquets had long been an important part of the priests' functions. Rüpke, *Religion in Republican Rome*, 83–84. The banquets of the rich, according to John H. D'Arms, were theatrical performances, where elites would display their wealth and status. Participation in these banquets was thus a mark of status, and exclusion from them representative of a loss of power. John H. D'Arms, "Performing Culture: Roman Spectacle and the Banquets of the Powerful," in *The Art of Ancient Spectacle*, ed. Bettina Ann Bergmann et al. (Washington, DC: National Gallery of Art, 1999), 301–19.

61. "Ce rapprochement fut d'après nous dans l'intention de souder en un bloc homogène la nobles sénatoriale en réunissant ses 'chefs de file'." Scheid, *Les Frères Arvales*, 351.
62. Frédéric Hurlet, "Consulship and Consuls under Augustus," in *Consuls and Res Publica: Holding High Office in the Roman Republic*, ed. Hans Beck et al. (Cambridge: Cambridge University Press, 2011), 329.
63. Hurlet, "Consulship and Consuls under Augustus."
64. Hurlet, "Consulship and Consuls under Augustus," 331; cf. Yakobson, "Petitio et Largitio," for the importance of the lower orders in consular elections.
65. Hurlet, "Consulship and Consuls under Augustus," 331–32.
66. On the distribution of authority amongst the priestly colleges, see Frederico Santangelo, "Enduring Arguments: Priestly Expertise in the Early Principate," *Transactions of the American Philological Association* (2016), 349–76.
67. Orlin, *Temples, Religion, and Politics in the Roman Republic*, 79; H. W. Parke, *Sibyls and Sibylline Prophecy in Classical Antiquity*, B. C. McGing, ed. (London, Routledge, 1988), 137.
68. Cicero (*Div*. 2.112) records that the texts were determined authentic based on whether or not they used an acrostic.
69. Orlin, *Temples, Religion, and Politics in the Roman Republic*, 82–83.
70. Liv. 42.2.
71. Dio 54.17: "The Sibylline verses, which had become indistinct through lapse of time, should be copied off by the priests with their own hands, in order that no one else might read them."
72. See details in Chapter 7.
73. Suet. *Aug*. 31. "After he finally had assumed the office of pontifex maximus . . . he collected whatever prophetic writings of Greek or Latin origin were in circulation anonymously or under the names of authors of little repute, and burned more than two thousand of them, retaining only the Sibylline books and making a choice even among those; and he deposited them in two gilded cases under the pedestal of the Palatine Apollo." *Postquam vero pontificatum maximum, . . ., quidquid fatidicorum librorum Graeci Latinique generis nullis vel parum idoneis auctoribus vulgo ferebatur, supra duo milia contracta undique cremavit ac solos retinuit Sibyllinos, hos quoque dilectu habito; condiditque duobus forulis auratis sub Palatini Apollinis basi.*
74. We have no direct evidence of what staff were stationed to maintain sacrifices, but as most of the sacrifices were annual and required substantial preparation as well as general upkeep of the shrines, it is safe to assume that they were officially, if not permanently, incorporated into the oversight of the Superintendent of Ceremonial.

Chapter 6

1. What constituted "the people" of course differed in each society, as did the respective governments' reliance on their support. See Hans Beck and Griet Vankeerberghen, "Introduction," in *Rulers and Ruled in Greece, Rome, and China* (Cambridge: Cambridge University Press, 2021), 1–21.

2. This argument was made by Kuan Heng, who reformed imperial ritual so that the emperor did not need to leave the capital region. *Hanshu* 25B.1253–57. This topic will be discussed further in the Conclusion; see also Loewe, *Crisis and Conflict,* 154–92 for details of the reform.
3. Although Augustus is usually credited with a new, marble urban landscape, the city of Rome was itself quite spectacular before his interventions, and his new vision of the city was rooted in centuries of architectural tradition. See John North Hopkins, *The Genesis of Roman Architecture* (New Haven, CT: Yale University Press, 2016).
4. Clifford Geertz, *Negara: The Theatre State in Nineteenth Century Bali* (Princeton, NJ: Princeton University Press, 1980), 102. James Laidlaw provides discussion of the dangers of applying Geertzian theory to Imperial Chinese ritual: "On Theatre and Theory: Reflections on Ritual in Imperial Chinese Politics," in *State and Court Ritual in China*, ed. Joseph P. McDermott (Cambridge: Cambridge University Press, 1999). Laidlaw's primary argument is that the imperial Chinese rituals, unlike the Balinese rites, were not public affairs. However, as we shall see in Chapter 7, while the Han sacrifices were not performed in front of "the people," there was nonetheless an important audience. Angela Zito explores the role of the audience in her monograph on Qing imperial rituals, and shows that the performance of the rituals in front of an audience of the elite was an important component in the ritual enactment of Qing authority. Angela Zito, *Of Body & Brush: Grand Sacrifice as Text/Performance in Eighteenth-Century China* (Chicago: University of Chicago Press, 1997).
5. Geertz, *Negara*, 125.
6. Geertz, *Negara*, 102.
7. Umberto Eco, "Function and Sign: The Semiotics of Architecture," in *Rethinking Architecture: A Reader in Cultural Theory*, ed. Neil Leach (London: Routledge, 1997), 182.
8. Eco, "Function and Sign," 187.
9. Eco, "Function and Sign," 187.
10. Of course, as Walter Benjamin has argued, the message conveyed by any form of media cannot be completely controlled by its designer, nor does it remain static in time. The architecture of imperial Rome and the imperial processions of Emperor Wu took on very different meanings in later times. Walter Benjamin, "The Work of Art in the Age of Mechanical Reproduction," in *Illuminations,* ed. Hanna Arendt, trans. Harry Zhon (New York: Harcourt, Brace & World, 1968): 217–51.
11. Michael Suk-young Chwe, *Rational Ritual: Culture, Coordination, and Common Knowledge* (Princeton, NJ: Princeton University Press, 2001), 3.
12. Chwe, *Rational Ritual*, 4.
13. Chwe, *Rational Ritual*, 4.
14. In the 2013 edition of the book, Chwe explores how the generation of common knowledge has changed in the Internet age.
15. Chwe, *Rational Ritual*, 19.
16. Chwe, *Rational Ritual*, 20–21.
17. Suet. *Aug.* 28.
18. Dio. 56.

19. Aug. *Res Gest.* 19–21. For the use of architecture in the Augustan period, the definitive account is Paul Zanker, *The Power of Images in the Age of Augustus* (Ann Arbor: University of Michigan Press, 1988); see also, Diane G. Favro, *The Urban Image of Augustan Rome* (Cambridge: Cambridge University Press, 1998); T. J. Luce, "Livy, Augustus, and the Forum Augustum," in *Between Republic and Empire: Interpretations of Augustus and His Principate*, ed. Kurt A. Raaflaub and Mark Toher (Berkeley: University of California Press, 1990); Wallace-Hadrill, *Rome's Cultural Revolution*, ch. 4: "Vitruvius: Building Roman Identity," 144–210.
20. Aug. *Res Gest.* 20. Augustus states that this was undertaken in his sixth consulship.
21. Beard, North, and Price, *Religions of Rome*, 196–97. See Peralta's important study which demonstrates how important the elite participation in temple dedication and construction contributed to the formation of Roman identity in the middle republic. Peralta, *Divine Institutions*.
22. Zanker, *The Power of Images*, 106–07.
23. Zanker, *The Power of Images*, 105.
24. Beard, North, and Price, *Religions of Rome*, 197.
25. Beard, North, and Price, *Religions of Rome*, 197. The temple to *divus Julius* was dedicated by Augustus in 29 BCE, and the temple to *divus Augustus* after his death, was dedicated in 37 CE.
26. Suet. *Aug.* 29.
27. Hekster and Rich have argued that the announcement of his intention to build the temple in 36 BCE was the beginning of Augustus' propaganda associating himself with the god. The announcement of the Temple of Apollo Palatinus connected to his house was the result of a series of fortuitous circumstances, primarily a lightning strike on the hill, which the harsupices interpreted as Apollo's wish to have a temple dedicated there. Oliver Hekster and John Rich, "Octavian and the Thunderbolt: The Temple of Apollo Palatinus and the Roman Tradition of Temple Building," *The Classical Quarterly New Series* 56, no. 1 (2006): 149–68. The association between Augustus and Apollo, as well as the Sibylline Books stored in the new temple will be discussed further below. It is worth noting too, as Dan-el Padilla Peralta has shown, that Augustus' rebuilding of Rome's temples also gave him unprecedented access to the city's written documents, allowing him to edit, discard, or forge them according to his needs. Padilla Peralta, "Monument Men: Buildings, Inscriptions, and Lexicographers in the Creation of Augustan Rome," 90–91, in *The Cultural History of Augustan Rome*, ed. Loar et al. (Cambridge: Cambridge University Press, 2019).
28. The temple of Jupiter Tonans was dedicated by Augustus to the god out of thanks for his safety after a close encounter with a thunderbolt, which struck and killed the enslaved man carrying his torch. Suet. *Aug.* 29.
29. Augustus' ability to reshape the urban landscape of Rome and promote his authority through it is well established, however, recent scholarship has demonstrated that the process of creating this narrative was neither simple nor uncontested. Much of what we know of Augustus' monumental architecture comes from contemporary poets, who often had a complicated relationship with the *princeps*, and attempted to balance this relationship in their works. See Nandini B. Pandey, *The Poetics of Power in Augustan*

Rome: Latin Poetic Reponses to Early Imperial Iconography (Cambridge: Cambridge University Press, 2018).
30. Flower, *The Dancing Lares*, 258–59. There has been much debate even at the time about the *lares* and their origin, and this is reflected in contemporary scholarship. Harriet Flower's 2017 monograph provides the most detailed and thorough discussion of the *lares* and my discussion relies heavily on her work.
31. Flower, *The Dancing Lares*, 258–59.
32. Flower, *The Dancing Lares*, 1.
33. Flower, *The Dancing Lares*, 17–24.
34. Flower, *The Dancing Lares*, 76–86.
35. Flower, *The Dancing Lares*, 116.
36. Flower, *The Dancing Lares*, 136.
37. While many scholars have previously taken the name *lares augusti* to mean that this cult was associated with the *genius* of Augustus, Flower and others have recently argued that the worship of the *lares augusti* was in no way connected to the worship of Augustus' own household *lares* or *genius*. Instead, *augusti* should be read as an adjective: the August, or Holy, *lares*, but that the name shared by these new *lares* and the princeps created a clear and strong association between the two. Flower, 288ff and 299–310; J. Bert Lott, *The Neighborhoods of Augustan Rome* (Cambridge: Cambridge University Press, 2004), 107–13.
38. One of the primary reasons for redistricting the city was to improve the city's fire response, but, as with other opportunities, Augustus used it to his own advantage. The *vici* had existed during the Republic as informal neighbourhood organizations and divisions. Suet. *Aug.* 30. On the redistricting of the city, see Lott, *The Neighborhoods of Augustan Rome*, ch. 4, "The Reforms of Augustus," 81–127; Karl Galinksy, *Augustan Culture: An Interpretive Introduction* (Princeton, NJ: Princeton University Press, 1996), 300–12. Wallace-Hadrill, *Rome's Cultural Revolution*, 264–69.
39. Flower, *The Dancing Lares*, 271. Flower notes that Augustus did not himself sponsor any of the new gods (including *lares*) to take the adjective *augustus*, but neither did he discourage the practice. Flower, *The Dancing Lares*, 335.
40. Lott, *The Neighborhoods of Augustan Rome*, 117.
41. On the exportation of Roman Religion, see Clifford Ando, "Exporting Roman Religion," in Jörg Rüpke, ed. *Blackwell Companion to Roman Religion* (Malden, MA: Blackwell, 2007), 429–45.
42. Price, *Rituals and Power*, 70–100.
43. Price, *Rituals and Power*, 1.
44. Carlos Noreña, "Coins and Communication," in *The Oxford Handbook of Social Relations in the Roman World*, ed. M. Peachin (Oxford: Oxford University Press, 2011): 253.
45. Christopher T. H. R. Ehrhardt, "Roman Coin Types and the Roman Public." *Jahrbuch für Numismatik und Geldgeschichte* 34 (1984): 46.
46. Erhardt, "Roman Coin Types," 46.
47. The inspection tour was again revived in modern China, when Deng Xiaoping 邓小平 made his famous Southern Tour南巡 in 1992 to revive the "Reforms and Opening

Up" policy after the 1989 Tiananmen Square Protests. See Suisheng Zhao, "Deng Xiaoping's Southern Tour: Elite Politics in Post-Tiananmen China," *Asian Survey* 33, no. 8 (1993): 739–56.
48. He Pingli何平立, *Xunshou yu fengshan: fengjian zhenzhi de wenhua guiji* 巡狩與封禪：封建的文化軌跡 (Jinan: Qi Lu shushe, 2003): 118.
49. See for example, Charles Sanft, "Progress and Publicity," 21–37 on the First Emperor's tours, He Pingli, *Xunshou yu fengshan*, 150, and Tian Tian, *Qin-Han guojia jisi shigao*, 270. Sanft discusses the importance of communication and coordination in the Qin empire in more detail in *Communication and Cooperation in Early Imperial China: Publicizing the Qin Dynasty* (Albany: State University of New York Press, 2014).
50. He, *Xunshou yu fengshan*, 100.
51. *Shiji* 6.249, 55.2034; *Hanshu* 6.204.
52. *Hanshu* 25B.1253. Edouard Chavannes, *Le T'ai Chan: Essai de monographie d'un culte chinois* (Paris: Farnborough, Gregg, 1969 [1910]) provides a description of the difficult terrain surrounding Mt. Tai in the early twentieth century, with a discussion of the role of the mountain in China's religious history.
53. *Hanshu* 6.196.
54. Yuanfeng 3rd Year (108), Taichu 4th Year (101), and Taishi 1st Year (96).
55. To Yong in Yuanguang 2nd and 6th year (134 and 130), Yuanshuo 1st and 2nd Year (122, 121), and to Ganquan in Yuanshuo 4th year (125).
56. He Pingli, *Xunshou yu fengshan*, 169. These will be discussed in greater detail in Chapter 7.
57. Sanft, "Progress and Publicity," using Michael Suk-young Chwe's theory, argues that communicating the knowledge of a new regime was essential to the longevity of that regime.
58. The *zhuhou wang* had an obligation to travel to the court at certain times of the year, but Emperor Wu's sacrificial schedule frequently changed the location of these meetings.
59. In Yuanshou 6 (117 BCE). *Hanshu* 6.180.
60. *Shiji* 28.1396; *Hanshu* 25A.1232. A similar comment is made in both histories' "Treatise on Food and Money"; *Shiji* 30.1438; *Hanshu* 24B.1173, that in preparation for the *feng* and *shan* sacrifice, all the commanderies and kingdoms repaired their roads and readied their palaces for an imperial visit, awaiting the imperial visit.
61. E.g., the *Liji* chapters, "Royal Regulations" (Wang zhi 王制) and "the Single Victim at the *Jiao* Sacrifice," provide instructions on imperial visits.
62. McKnight has demonstrated that the use of amnesties in the Han followed precedent set by the Qin state, particularly in issuing amnesties on the ascension of a new ruler, though in the Han this later changed to a commemoration of a ruler's death. It has previously been assumed that there were no such amnesties under the First Emperor, as Sima Qian makes this claim in *Shiji* 6.238, see also, Brian E. McKnight, *The Quality of Mercy: Amnesties and Traditional Chinese Justice* (Honolulu: University of Hawai'i Press, 1981), 14–15. However, recent archaeological evidence indicates that there were some amnesties under the Qin; see, for example, the evidence in the Yuelu slips in Thies Staack and Ulrich Lau, *Legal Practice in the Formative Stages of the*

Chinese Empire: An Annotated Translation of the Exemplary Qin Criminal Cases from the Yuelu Academy Collection (Leiden: Brill, 2016), 130.
63. McKnight demonstrates the cosmological and political reasons for the increasing use of general amnesties under the early Han emperors. While this study focuses primarily on amnesties granted to the entire empire, he does note that on some occasions, more localized amnesties were granted for political purposes. McKnight, *The Quality of Mercy*, 12–36.
64. Chen *Zhongguo lizhi shi*, 4. While the origins of the periods of "universal drinking" may have derived from military celebrations, it later became an opportunity for officials and commoners to drink together, which was forbidden under Qin law. See William Nienhauser et al., trans., *The Grand Scribe's Records*, Vol. 1 (Bloomington: Indiana University Press, 1994), 134 n. 118.
65. In 140, 134, 131, 128, 126, 122, 120, 116, 112, 109, 106, 100, 98, 96, 93, 90, and 88. The amnesties were usually granted in the spring.
66. In 133, 126, 116, 103, and 94.
67. One step of rank was given to commoner men in 140 and 134. In 110, one step of rank was given to people within the five commanderies that Emperor Wu had travelled through. Gifts were given in 122 to the filially pious, in 118, to All under Heaven, according to rank, in 109 to the regions through which the emperor had travelled, and again in 109 to the whole empire, in honour of the discovery of fungus at Ganquan. As Moonsil Lee Kim has shown in her study of the legislation surrounding food distribution, in many cases, what was recorded by the historical texts was what the legislators *hoped* to be able to distribute, but the actual distribution of food (or other gifts) did not always meet what was specified in the written records. Additionally, she notes that oftentimes gifts were paid out in cash, rather than kind. See Moonsil Lee Kim, "Food Redistribution during China's Qin and Han Periods: Accordance and Discordance among Ideologies, Policies, and their Implementation," PhD Diss., University of California, Santa Barbara (2014), ch. 3.
68. Benjamin, "The Work of Art in the Age of Mechanical Reproduction," 241.
69. Chwe, *Rational Ritual*, 10; 4.
70. The emperor in China was himself not visible to the general public, unlike Augustus in Rome, who appeared frequently before the crowds. However, what these tours made visible in China was imperial authority itself, rather than the person of the emperor. See Sanft, "Progress and Publicity."

Chapter 7

1. *Shiji* 28.1403.
2. The sacrifices were prohibited during the reign of Emperor Cheng, along with several others, as part of Kuang Heng's ritual reforms. *Hanshu* 25B.1257–58.
3. He made an additional trip to Yong in 129, but the *Hanshu* does not record a sacrifice in that year.
4. *taiyi* 太壹, *taiyi* 泰一, and *dayi* 大一 are common variants of *taiyi* 太一.

5. *Shiji* 28.1355–1404; *Hanshu* 25.1189–1272.
6. It is mentioned, for example, in the *Xunzi*, *Lüshi Chunqiu*, and *Zhuangzi*. See also Li "An Archaeological Study of Taiyi," 1–2.
7. Li, "An Archaeological Study of Taiyi," 1. See also the discussion in Tian Tian, "'Xi Han Tai Yi jisi yanjiu" 西漢太一祭祀研究, *Shi Xue Yue Kan*, no. 4 (2014): 39–51.
8. Li, "An Archaeological Study of Taiyi," 25.
9. Li Du-du argues that Great Unity was only defined during the discussions about sacrifice during the early years of Emperor Wu's reign. Li Du-du, "Ganquan yu xi Han zhongqi de guojia jisi," *Shihezi daxue xuebao (zhexue shehui kexue ban)* 25, no. 5 (2011): 117. The sacrifice to Great Unity established under Emperor Wu was dismantled later in the Western Han, and the concept continued to evolve in different traditions.
10. *Shiji* 27.1289. See Li "An Archaeological Study of Taiyi"; David Pankenier, "A Brief History of Beiji 北極 (Northern Culmen), With an Excursus on the Origin of the Character Di 帝," *Journal of the American Oriental Society* 124, no. 2 (2004): 211–36, and Tian Tian, "Xi Han Tai Yi jisi yanjiu" on the various identifications of Great Unity in cosmological thought and Tian Tian, "Western Han Sacrifices to Taiyi 泰一," in *Technical Arts in the Han Histories: Tables and Treatises in the* Shiji *and* Hanshu, ed. Mark Csikszentmihalyi and Michael Nylan, trans. Michael Nylan (Albany: SUNY, 2021), 281–305.
11. Particularly the Guodian Chu Manuscript "Taiyi sheng shui" 太一生水, in which Great Unity is credited with creating Heaven and Earth. For a broad overview of this manuscript, see Sarah Allan, "The Great One, Water, and the Laozi, New Light from Guodian," *T'oung Pao*, 89, no. 4 (2003): 237–85.
12. *Shiji* 28.1386; *Hanshu* 25A.1218. Here the text refers to the spirits as the "Five Emperors," but the later movement of the sacrifice to the five *Shangdi* at Yong to the site at Ganquan suggests that they were one and the same.
13. *Shiji* 28.1386; *Hanshu* 25A.1218. Liang Yun believes that this site may have been discovered in 1971, 4.5 km southeast of Chang'an. Liang Yun 梁雲, "Dui luanting shan jisi yizhi suo aidi de chubu renshi," 對鸞亭山祭祀遺址所在地的初步認識, *Zhongguo lishi wenwu* 5 (2005): 15–31.
14. *Shiji* 28.1386; *Hanshu* 25A.1218.
15. Tian Tian, "Xi Han Tai Yi jisi yanjiu," 42.
16. *Shiji* 28.1393; *Hanshu* 25A. 1227.
17. *Shiji* 28.1394; *Hanshu* 25A. 1228.
18. *Hanshu* 22.1045.
19. The relationship between musical harmonics and cosmology was very complex in early China. For an overview of the political implications of music, see Erika Fox Brindley, *Music, Cosmology, and the Politics of Harmony in Early China* (New York: SUNY, 2012). The collection of nineteen hymns written for the *jiao* and *si* sacrifices is recorded in the *Hanshu* "Treatise on Ritual and Music" 禮樂志, though we know that there were additional hymns written for other sacrifices which have not been preserved. The "Nineteen Songs for the Jiao and Si Sacrifices" 郊祀歌十九章 have been

translated into French by Edouard Chavannes, *Les Memoires historique*, vol. 3, and German by Martin Kern, *Die Hymnen der chinesischen Staatsopfer: Literatur und Ritual in der politischen Repräsentation von der Han-Zeit bis zu den Sechs Dynastien* (Stuttgart: Franz Steiner, 1997). See also partial translations in English in Martin Kern, "In Praise of Political Legitimacy: The miao and jiao Hymns of the Western Han," *Oriens Extremus* 39, no. 1 (1996): 29–67, and the discussion in Zhang Shuguo 張樹國, "An Investigation of the Evolution of the National Sacrifice System during the Reign of Emperor Wu of Han Dynasty and the Creation of the Nineteen Suburban Sacrifice Songs" 漢武帝時代國家祭祀的逐步確立與"郊祀歌"十九章創制時地考論, *Hangzhou shifan daxue xuebao: Shehui kexue ban* 2 (2009): 49–57.

20. *Shiji* 28.1395; *Hanshu* 25A.1231.
21. It is odd that none of the *fangshi* attribute the sacrifice to the Great Unity to the Yellow Thearch. Miu Ji, who first introduced the sacrifice, claimed only that the Sons of Heaven of antiquity performed the sacrifice.
22. *Sanfu Huangtu*, 46–50, 67–82. See details in Chapter 5.
23. *Shiji* 28.1395; *Hanshu* 25A.1231.
24. The *feng* and *shan* sacrifices, as we will see below, were considered to be the most important sacrifices to be offered by Emperor Wu, but these could only be performed by the emperor himself. Other sacrifices, such as those to the Great Unity and Sovereign Earth were performed by government officials in the years that the emperor did not personally offer sacrifice.
25. For a discussion on the identity of Sovereign Earth in pre-Qin literature, see Xiang Jinwei 向晉衛 and Mu Wei 穆葳, "Qin Han Shiqi de Houtu Chongbai—Jianlun Fenyin Houtu Ci de Jianzhi Beijing 秦漢時期的后土崇拜—兼論汾陰后土祠的建置背景," *Nandu Xuetan (Renwen Shehui Kexu Xueban)* 35, no. 1 (2015): 16; Tang Xiaofeng 唐曉峰, "Fenyin Houtu ci de diaocha yanjiu" 汾陰后土祠的調查研究, in *Jiuzhou* Vol. 4. *Zhongguo dilixue shi zhuanhao* (Beijing, Shang wu yin shu guan, 2007). Niu Jingfei 牛敬飛 argues that previous cults to Sovereign Earth had existed in the Qin and early Han, though they had taken different names. "The Exaggerated Pre-Suburban Sacrifice Era—An Exploration of the Misuse of Historical Records in the *Qin and Han State Sacrifices: A Draft History*" 被誇大的前郊祀時代— 從 《秦漢國家祭祀史稿》對史料的誤用說起, *Qinghua Daxue xuebao (zhexue shehui kexue ban)* 1, no. 32 (2017): 82–83.
26. In the 1930s, archaeologists determined that the site was located at Wanquanjie Mountain, in modern Shanxi. See Yao Yuanyuan 姚媛媛"On Fenyin Hou Tu Sacrifice in Han Dynasty" 論漢代的汾陰后土祭祀, 13, for details.
27. *Shiji* 28.1382. See also Chapter 3.
28. Tian, *Qin-Han guojia ji si shigao*, 154.
29. Seven months after the establishment of the shrine in the tenth month, which was then the beginning of the year.
30. See Table 5.1.
31. *Shiji* 28.1392; *Hanshu* 25A.2335–36.

32. *Shiji* 28.1392; *Hanshu* 25A.2335–36. While the harvest had improved in the past year, the emperor had not performed a thanksgiving sacrifice, and therefore did not believe he should receive such a good omen.
33. *Shiji* 28.1393; 1395. Tian Tian notes that the discovery of the tripod was likely the impetus to build a new Great Unity altar. Tian Tian, "Xi Han Taiyi jisi yanjiu," 44.
34. Sovereign Earth was considered to be a female deity, while the Great Unity represented the male. This is made clear in the second of nineteen hymns composed during Emperor Wu's reign, preserved in the *Hanshu* Treatise on Rites and Music: "The Sovereign Earth is an abundant mother" 后土富媼.
35. Suet. *Aug*. 30–31; of these only the *ludi saeculares* is mentioned by Augustus in his *Res Gestae*.
36. Tac. *Ann*. 12.23.
37. Dio. 37.24.
38. Steven J. Green, "Malevolent Gods and Promethean Birds: Contesting Augury in Augustus's Rome," *Transactions of the American Philological Association* 139 (2009): 149.
39. Dio. 37.24. Dio also comments that it was "absurd" that the augury was taken when there was so much in-fighting among the Roman senatorial elite.
40. Cic. *Div*. 1.105. Cicero here refers to the Cataline conspiracy.
41. Rosalinde Kearsley, "Octavian and Augury: The Years 30–27 B.C." *The Classical Quarterly* 59, no. 1 (2009): 150.
42. Dio links these two events to 29 BCE, though the peace following the Battle of Actium in 31 BCE was what allowed the gates to be closed.
43. Presumably Augustus would not have been pleased with the taking of the augury had it proved to be unfavourable. While there remains a strong commitment to the idea that auguries were frequently manipulated by the *augures* to produce favourable results, Lindsay Driediger-Murphy, using the failed *augurium Salutis* of 63 BCE, convincingly argues that these auguries were serious affairs, and while there was a certain amount of manipulation, once taken and accepted, the results of an augury were difficult to change. Driediger-Murphy, *Roman Republican Augury: Freedom and Control* (Oxford: Oxford University Press, 2018), see particularly Chapter 3 on the Augury of Safety.
44. Dio. 51.20.
45. Kearsley, "Octavian and Augury," 150.
46. Aug. *Res Gest*. 13. Augustus notes that the gates were closed on three occasions during his time as princeps, despite only having been closed on two previous occasions in Roman history.
47. Kearsley, "Octavian and Augury," 152.
48. Tac. *Ann*. 12.23.
49. For a short overview of the festival, see Hopkins, 314–15. Ovid describes the festival in detail in *Fasti* 2.267–452.

50. Keith Hopkins, "From Violence to Blessing: Symbols and Rituals in Ancient Rome," in *Sociological Studies in Roman History*, ed. Christopher Kelly (Cambridge: Cambridge University Press, 2017): 314. On the fifth century debate over the Lupercalia, see Neil McLynn, "Crying wolf: the Pope and the *Lupercalia*." *Journal of Roman Studies* 98 (2008): 161–75.
51. Hopkins, "From Violence to Blessing," 315.
52. Cic. *Phil.* 3.12.
53. Cicero himself was so disgusted by the image that he continued to taunt Antony with his nude speech upon the Rostra. Cic. *Phil.* 2.87. Timothy Peter Wiseman, "The God of the Lupercal," *The Journal of Roman Studies* 85 (1995): 15.
54. Suet. *Aug.* 31.
55. Dion. Hal. *Rom. Ant.* 1.80 describes the earliest Luperci as running "around the village naked, their loins girt with the skins of the victims just sacrificed." As all references to the Lupercalia from the Augustan period and before refer to the Luperci as *nudi*, Holleman argues that the introduction of loincloths was an Augustan innovation. He further argues that Ovid's frequent references to the nudity of the Luperci can be seen as mocking this new requirement, which surely took the fun out of the ritual for the male participants, though perhaps not for the female spectators. Aloysius Wilhelmus Jozef Holleman "Ovid and the Lupercalia," *Historia: Zeitschrift für Alte Geschichte* 22, no. 2 (1973), 261–63.
56. Ovid *Fasti* 2.282.
57. Plut. *Rom.* 111, Aul. Gel. *Att.* X.15. Aulus Gellius only mentions a prohibition on she-goats.
58. Holleman, "Ovid and the Lupercalia," 228.
59. The *flamen Dialis* was subject to numerous restrictions that made it impossible for the priest to have a political career.
60. See Chapter 6.
61. Flower, *The Dancing Lares*, 262.
62. Dion. Hal. IV.15.
63. Flower, *The Dancing Lares*, 160.
64. In the later imperial period, the festival's dates were fixed to 3–5 January, but Macrobius, in the fifth century CE, still records it as a moveable feast. Mac. *Sat.* 1.6; see Flower, *The Dancing Lares*, 165, for details
65. Gel. *Att.* X.24. "*populo Romano Quiritibus*"
66. Flower, *The Dancing Lares*, 160.
67. Flower, *The Dancing Lares*, 169.
68. Flower, *The Dancing Lares*, 166–70.
69. Mac. *Sat.* 1.34. According to Macrobius, the human sacrifice was replaced with heads of garlic and poppy after the reign of Tarquin; Flower, *The Dancing Lares*, 166–70.
70. Flower, *The Dancing Lares*, 169.
71. Flower, *The Dancing Lares*, 191.
72. Flower, *The Dancing Lares*, 263.

73. Flower, *The Dancing Lares*, 269. Flower notes that the establishment of the cult of the *lares augusti* was a radical act which broke from his pattern of reviving ancient religious practices by establishing an entirely new cult.
74. Suet. *Aug.* 31.
75. Aug. *Res. Gest.* 8.
76. An extended comparison of the *feng* and *shan* and *ludi saeculares* can be found in Rebecca Robinson, "Spectacular Power in the Early Han and Roman Empires," *The Journal of World History* 29, no. 3 (2018): 343–68.
77. Cens. 17.2, citation in John F. Hall, "The *Saeculum Novum* of Augustus and its Etruscan Antecedents," in *Aufstieg und Niedergang der römischen Welt*, II.16.3 (Berlin, Walter de Gruyter, 1986), 2567.
78. Richard C. Beacham, *Spectacle Entertainments of Early Imperial Rome* (New Haven, CT: Yale University Press, 1999), 114.
79. In the 7th century BCE, the hegemon (*ba* 霸), Duke Huan of Qi 齊桓公 (r. 685–643 BCE), was dissuaded from offering the *feng* and *shan* sacrifices on the advice of Guan Zhong, who reported to him that although he had hegemony over the rulers and territories, he had not received sufficient omens legitimizing his right to rule. *Shiji* 28.1361.
80. As the games could only be performed once per *saeculum*, there was an element of messianic timing in who could host them.
81. Howard J. Wechsler, *Offerings of Jade and Silk: Ritual and Symbol in the Legitimation of the T'ang Dynasty* (New Haven, CT: Yale University Press, 1985), 170.
82. Wechsler, *Offerings of Jade and Silk*, 170.
83. Lewis, "The *feng* and *shan* Sacrifices," 53.
84. Lewis, "The *feng* and *shan* Sacrifices," 53. While much has been made of the individual performance of the sacrifice, I have not found any documentation of a requirement that it be performed by the emperor in isolation. The sources do not indicate what was written on the text that was buried.
85. Mark Edward Lewis separates out the various streams of thought that were involved in the early Han iteration of the sacrifice, "The *feng* and *shan* Sacrifices."
86. In *Shiji* Guan Zhong states that there were seventy-two rulers, of whom twelve names were recorded. By the time of the writing of the *Shiji*, the First Emperor's name would have been added to this list.
87. *Shiji* 28.1361, 1364.
88. *Shiji* 28.1363–64. Sima Qian then includes a modified quotation from the *Lunyu* III.11, referring to the Great Ancestral Sacrifice, though the connection between the feng and the di sacrifice is not clear. "Someone asked about the meaning of the Great Sacrifice. The master said: "I do not know. One who knew its meaning would be able to govern All under Heaven as easily as this!" as he pointed to his hand." 或問禘之說。子曰：「不知也。知其說者之於天下也，其如示諸斯乎！」指其掌。
89. Lewis, "The *feng* and *shan* Sacrifices," 52.
90. *Shiji* 28.1366.
91. *Shiji* 28.1366–67.
92. *Shiji* 28.1367.

93. The discussion of the First Emperor's performance of the *feng* is, in my opinion, quite unsatisfactory. We have nothing but Sima Qian's account of it, and the way in which it was described in the *Shiji* bears such similarity to the account of Emperor Wu, that is becomes suspect. Mark Edward Lewis has suggested that Sima Qian's account of the First Emperor's sacrifice is perhaps just a part of the critique of Emperor Wu, and that he had no real knowledge of the First Emperor's ritual (Lewis, "The *feng* and *shan* Sacrifices," 64). While the First Emperor erected a stele at the summit of Mt. Tai (the text of which is included in *Shiji* 6), he left engraved stelae at the summits of all of the mountains at which he sacrificed on his inspection tours, and in the Mt. Tai inscription itself, there is nothing to indicate that this sacrifice was in any way different or more significant than the others. Martin Kern, while following Sima Qian in calling the sacrifice a *feng*, does indicate that there is still some question as to whether or not the Mt. Tai stele was in fact erected by the First Emperor, or his son, Er Shi. Kern, 4. If the First Emperor did not perform a *feng* sacrifice, this would be in keeping with Michael Loewe's recent, though controversial, argument that the Qin did not consciously adopt a colour and power, as the empire saw themselves as something completely new and different from previous Chinese dynasties. (Loewe, *The Men Who Governed Han China*, 496–502). However, there is not enough evidence to refute Sima Qian's claim, and the fact remains that by the time of Emperor Wu, it was believed that the First Emperor had performed (successfully or not) this important sacrifice.
94. Michael C. J. Putnam, *Horace's* Carmen Saeculare: *Ritual Magic and the Poet's Art* (New Haven, CT: Yale University Press, 2001), 52–53.
95. Plut. *Sull.* 7.7. Stefan Weinstock, *Divus Julius* (Oxford: Oxford University Press, 1971), 192. On the Etruscan roots of the *ludi saeculares*, see Hall, The *Saeculum Novum* of Augustus," 1986. Pierre Brind'Amour also notes the possible Egyptian origin of the one hundred and ten-year *saeculum*, "L'origine des jeux séculaires," in *Aufstieg un Niedergang der röischen Welt*. II.16.2 (1978): 1335–39.
96. Liebeschuetz, 84.
97. Weinstock, *Divus Julius*, 192–93.
98. Hall, "The *Saeculum Novum*," 2577.
99. Weinstock notes that there is no definitive evidence for this, but that a number of portents and discussions indicate that there was likely some speculation about the dawning of a new *saeculum* under Julius Caesar. See Weinstock, *Divus Julius*, 191–98 for details.
100. Weinstock, *Divus Julius*, 195.
101. Of course, the Sibylline books could be read in such a way as to provide the desired response, though there was less overt manipulation of prodigies than one might suspect in Rome. Lindsey Driediger-Murphy discusses the question of omen manipulation in *Roman Republican Augury: Freedom and Control*, and determines that while interpretations of auguries may be shaped by the motivations of actors, this was only possible to a certain extent, and that omens were rarely directly fabricated or misconstrued. While her discussion concerns the practice of augury, it is likely that this holds for the Sibylline Books. The Books could be interpreted in various ways, but the priests could not outright invent a prophesy.

102. Hall, "The *Saeculum Novum*," 2575. Other texts from the time site a different chronology, e.g., Valerius Antias: 509, 348, 249, and 149. Varro rejects the possibility of games being held in 509 BCE. Palmer (cited in Hall) suggests that the games were never fixed to a precise schedule of either 100 or 110 years, and that they were to occur roughly once per century. The *quindecimviri* date of 126 was likely a fabrication (with games actually occurring in 149 or 146) to provide a more exact sequence of repetitions every 110 years, leading up to the games of 17 BCE, though there is no explanation offered as to why they were celebrated in 17, rather than 16. Hall, "The *Saeculum Novum*," 2575–76. Dio 54.18.4 records the 17 BCE games as the fifth celebration of the games, though the sources only record two prior celebrations (249 and 149/6). See also Susan Satterfield, "The Prodigies of 17 B.C.E. and the *Ludi Saeculares*," *Transactions of the American Philological Society* (2016): 325–48, on the timing of the games in 17 BCE. Satterfield notes that 17 BCE also marked the ten years which had passed since Augustus had consolidated his power in 28–27 BCE.

103. Suet. *Aug.* 31.4.

104. Geoffrey S. Sumi, *Ceremony and Power: Performing Politics in Rome between Republic and Empire* (Ann Arbor: University of Michigan Press, 2005), 243.

105. *Shiji* 28.1384.

106. *Shiji* 28.1398; *Hanshu* 25A.1235.

107. The coachman also performed a sacrifice, but fell ill and died shortly thereafter, an event which only increased the air of mystery surrounding the sacrifices. *Shiji* 28.1398; *Hanshu* 25A.1235.

108. *Shiji* 28.1398; *Hanshu* 25A.1235. The animals were brought to Mt. Tai for the sacrifice, but taken away after.

109. At the time of the first performance of the *feng* sacrifice, Sima Tan held the position of Grand Astronomer, and would have been present at the ceremony, but was unable to attend, due to illness, and died shortly thereafter. This perhaps explains the paucity of the account, though Sima Qian would have attended the later renewals of the sacrifice. *Shiji* 130.3295.

110. *Shiji* 28.1398. *Hanshu* 25A.1235.

111. *Shiji* 28.1398; *Hanshu* 25A.1235.

112. *Shiji* 28.1398; *Hanshu* 25A.1235.

113. *Shiji* 28.1398. A slightly modified version appears in *Hanshu* 6.191.

114. *Shiji* 28.1398; *Hanshu* 25A.1236. The *Hanshu* attributes the edict to the "records of Wu" 武記.

115. He also travelled to Mt. Tai in 109 and 105 BCE but the *Shiji* does not mention a renewal of the *feng*. *Hanshu* 6. He Pingli has suggested that the emperor performed the *feng* every time he visited Mt. Tai, but it is not specifically stated in the *Hanshu* biography that he performed a *feng* sacrifice, only that he sacrificed to Mt. Tai. (He, *Xunshou yu fengshan*, 168).

116. *Hanshu* 6.196, 6.204. We are not given any explanation as to why the regional lords were not present for the first performance of the *feng*. It is possible that the emperor was concerned that it would fail, as it perhaps had for the First Emperor, and therefore wanted to avoid having too many witnesses if it did. On failure in rituals in early China more broadly, see Michael David Kaulana Ing, *The Dysfunction of Ritual in Early Confucianism* (Oxford: Oxford University Press, 2012).

117. Lewis, "The *feng* and *shan* Sacrifices," 78–79.
118. Scheid, "Les restauration religieuse d'Octavian/Auguste," 122.
119. Sumi, *Ceremony and Power*, 244. On the *quindecimviri*, see Chapters 4 and 5.
120. *CIL* 6.32323. The relevant inscriptions are reconstructed in Ionnes Baptista Pighi, *De ludis saecularibus populi Romani Quiritium libri sex* (Amsterdam: Verlag P. Schippers NC, 1965), 107–19. See Hoffman Lewis, "The College of Quindecimviri," on the reconstruction of the lists of *quindecimviri*.
121. The Oracle is preserved in Zos. 2.6.
122. *CIL* 6.32323:50–63, translated in Kitty Chisholm and John Ferguson, ed., *Rome: The Augustan Age* (Oxford: Oxford University Press, 1986), 151–52.
123. *CIL* 6.32323:50–63. *pe[rti]nere ad conseruandam memoriam tantae b[enuolentiae deorum commentarium ludorum] saecularium in colum[n]am aheneam et marmoream inscribe, st[atuique ad futuram rei memoriam utramque]*. Pighi, 112.
124. *CIL* 6.32323:50–63. The *Lex Julia de maritandis ordinibus* of 18 BCE attempted to restore traditional republican *mores* through the regulation of marriage and encouragement of procreation. According to Beth Severy, this legislation was intended to not only increase the population, but to strengthen class lines by discouraging the elite from marrying below them. Dio 54.30.1; Suet. *Aug.* 27; *Res Gest.* 6. Severy, *Augustus and the Family at the Birth of the Roman Empire* (New York: Routledge, 2003), 50–56.
125. The *Carmen* was inscribed on marble and can be found in CIL 6.32323: 64–168. Michael Putnam argues that the *Carmen* was a celebration of the city of Rome, and that while the hymn may have been commissioned by Augustus for the occasion, the poem itself should be read as a hoary celebration rather than as a piece of political propaganda. Putnam, *Horace's "Carmen Saeculare,"* 5.
126. Putnam, *Horace's "Carmen Saeculare,"* 5.
127. Hall, "The *Saeculum Novum*," 2565.
128. On the relationship between the *Ara Pacis* and Augustus' position of Pontifex Maximus, see Bowersock, "The Pontificate of Augustus."
129. Bowersock, "The Pontificate of Augustus," 382.
130. In particular, Augustus did not intervene in the calendar, where intercalary days were being inserted once every three years rather than every four. He waited until 8 BCE to reform the calendar, after he had become pontifex maximus. This calendrical reform was also a significant part of Augustus' consolidation of authority; Rebecca Robinson, "Employing Knowledge."
131. Bowersock, "The Pontificate of Augustus," 382. On the absence of Lepidus in this period, see Ronald T. Ridley, "The Absent Pontifex Maximus," *Historia* 54, no. 2 (2005).
132. Augustus here made a grand claim to religious authority, but he was also careful to emphasize his piousness in other ways. Particularly, after claiming the title of Augustus, he preferred to be portrayed in priestly garb, rather than military or senatorial. Zanker, *The Power of Images*, 127.
133. Putnam, *Horace's "Carmen Saeculare,"* 52–53.
134. Putnam, *Horace's "Carmen Saeculare,"* 52–53.
135. *CIL* 6.32323. See also the description of events in John Miller, *Apollo, Augustus, and the Poets* (Cambridge: Cambridge University Press, 2009), 270–74. Sacrifices at night were a distinctly Greek tradition, and both the Moerae and Ilithyiae were also

considered to be Greek rather than Roman, though not necessarily associated with the night themselves.
136. CIL 6.32323.
137. The Campus Martius was the traditional location for the *ludi;* Augustus's new daytime sacrifices expand the festival into the heart of Rome. Michael Lipka, *Roman Gods: A Conceptual Approach* (Leiden: Brill, 2009), 151–53.
138. Denis Feeney, "The *Ludi Saeculares* and the *Carmen Saeculare*," in *Roman Religion*, ed. Clifford Ando (Edinburgh: University of Edinburgh Press, 2000), 107.
139. "Your own Apollo now is king!" *tuus iam regnat Apollo.* Vir. *Ecl.* 4.10. As Miller notes, Augustus was not the only one to try to claim the support of Apollo, Antony, and others, also tried to associate themselves with the image of this god. Miller, *Apollo, Augustus, and the Poets,* 254.
140. Augustus began to associate himself with Apollo in 36 BCE, when a lightning bolt struck the hill and was interpreted as a sign that Apollo desired a temple there. Hekster and Rich, "Octavian and the Thunderbolt," 149–68; Robert Gurval, *Actium and Augustus: The Politics and Emotions of Civil War* (Ann Arbor: University of Michigan Press, 1995), 91–113.
141. Julia Dyson Hejduk's recent monograph *The God of Rome: Jupiter in Augustan Poetry* illustrates the connection between Augustus and Jupiter in poetry (Oxford: Oxford University Press, 2020). I am grateful to the author for providing me with a copy of the book when COVID-19 restrictions hindered library access.
142. Yakobson, "Petitio et Largito," 35.
143. Five types of coins were issued for the games in 17 BCE, in gold and silver. See John Scheid, "Déchiffrer des monnaies: Réflexions sur la représentation figurée des Jeux séculaires," in *Images romaines: Actes de la table ronde organise à l'École normale supérieure, Tome 9,* C. Auvray-Assayas, ed. (Paris, Presses de l'École normale supérieure, 1998). This type of iconography would be mimicked by later emperors.
144. *CIL* 6.32323:50–63: *pe[rti]nere ad conseruandam memoriam tantae b[enuolentiae deorum commentarium ludorum] saecularium in colum[n]am aheneam et marmoream inscribe, st[atuique ad futuram rei memoriam utramque].* Pighi, 112.
145. This point is made most clearly by James Laidlaw: "This feature of ritual traditions—that their basic building blocks and reference points are acts, which are felt to have their own history and character and to be beyond the particular intentions and purposes of actors—effectively prevents ritual performances from being merely the expression of a meaning or a message." Laidlaw, "On Theatre and Theory," 410.
146. We know, for example, that Sima Tan was devastated to not be able to witness the *feng* and *shan* sacrifices.
147. See Peralta, *Divine Institutions,* on the importance of religion in establishing Roman identity in the middle Republic.
148. This point is modified from Hobsbawm, who writes that invented traditions "seek to inculcate certain values and norms of behavior by repetition, which automatically implies continuity with the past." "Introduction: Inventing Traditions," in *The Invention of Tradition,* ed. Eric Hobsbawm and Terence Ranger (Cambridge: Cambridge University Press, 1992 [1983]), 1.
149. Zanker, *The Power of Images,* 127.

Chapter 8

1. Scheid, 2009, 128. Scheid offers his own view, that the religious reforms offered the Roman people to see immediate results from the princeps' reforms, and that rather than being religion or politics, the rebuilding of temples and restitution of sacrifices was a means of giving the people what they wanted.
2. This is of course not to say that Augustus' imperial image did not spread outside of the capital, only that the institutions or Roman religion were not the means through which it was spread.
3. Beard, North, and Price, *Religions of Rome*, Vol. 1, 206.
4. The terms "modernist" and "reformist" are Michael Loewe's, *Crisis and Conflict in Han China*.
5. Loewe, *Crisis and Conflict*, ch. 2, provides the most comprehensive discussion of the witchcraft scandal, the political intrigues, and the shifts in power during this period. See also Cai Liang on the effects of the witchcraft scandal on the shape of the Han court. Cai Liang, *Witchcraft and the Rise of the First Confucian Empire* (Albany: SUNY, 2014).
6. The *Hanshu* suggests that these sacrifices were opposed by Huo Guang, who exerted his influence over both the young Emperor Zhao and the early years of Emperor Xuan's reign. According to the *Hanshu*, Emperor Zhao did not travel the empire and perform sacrifices at all; this could simply be due to his young age. *Hanshu* 25B.1248.
7. *Hanshu* 25B.1248ff.
8. *Hanshu* 25B.1252–53.
9. *Hanshu* 25B.1253.
10. *Hanshu* 25B.1253.
11. *Hanshu* 25B.1253–54.
12. *Hanshu* 25B.1254. The *Hanshu* (25B.1253–57) contains lengthy transcripts of the responses submitted to the emperor, which have been largely translated in Loewe, *Crisis and Conflict*, 171–75. Loewe provides more detail about these debates and transformations to the cult, as does Tian Tian, *Qin-Han guojia jisi shigao*; "The Suburban Sacrifice Reforms and the Evolution of the Imperial Sacrifice."
13. Loewe, *Crisis and Conflict*, 166.
14. Fujikawa Masakazu 藤川正數, 漢代における礼学の研究, *Kandai ni okeru reigaku no kenkyū* (Tokyo: Kazama shobo, 1968), 204ff. According to the *Hanshu* (25B.1258), the *fangshi* who had been charged with seeking the immortals were dismissed and sent home at this time.
15. *Hanshu* 25B.1258; Loewe, *Crisis and Conflict*, 176
16. *Hanshu* 25B.1258.
17. *Hanshu* 25B.1259. The edict to reinstate the sacrifices was made by the Empress Dowager, and the *Hanshu* notes that this reversal of position was in part due to the fact that the emperor did not as yet have an heir.
18. Loewe, *Crisis and Conflict*, 179.
19. Tian Tian, "The Suburban Sacrifice Reforms," 270.
20. See details in Chapter 7.

21. Beard, North, and Price, *Religions of Rome*, Vol. 1, 168.
22. Danuta Musial, "The Princeps as the *Pontifex Maximus*. The Case of Tiberius," *Electrum* 21 (2014): 102; van Haeperen, "Des pontifes païens aux pontifes chrétiens," 150–53.
23. CIL 6.40453. This co-option as a supernumerary member continued until at least the 230s CE. Rüpke, *Fasti Sacerdotum*, 58.
24. Beard, North, and Price, *Religions of Rome*, Vol. 1 188.
25. Suet. *Tib*. 69. "*Circa deos ac religions neglegentior.*"
26. Suet. *Tib*. 26.
27. Suet. *Tib*. 26.
28. Suet. *Tib*. 36; 69.
29. The requirement that the *flamen Dialis* be married by the old *confarreatio* method of marriage was changed under Tiberius so that women would only be subordinate to their husbands for religious affairs, thus encouraging more patrician women to marry in this way. Hans-Friedrich Mueller, *Roman Religion in Valerius Maximus* (London: Routledge, 2002), 1–2. He did not, however, change the requirement that the *flamen Dialis* must remain in Rome, thereby prohibiting the priest from leaving the city to take up a governorship. Tac. *Ann*. 3.58–59. On Tiberius' decision-making process, see Musial, "The Princeps as the *Pontifex Maximus*," 103–05.
30. Julius Caesar had received divine honours prior to his death, which likely contributed to his assassination. Augustus, learning from Caesar's example, refused all such divine honours in Rome, but did ensure that *Divus Julius* received proper worship. The precedent to refer to the deceased emperor as *divi* was set by Caesar and reinforced by the Senate voting divine honours to Augustus after his death. See Gradel, *Emperor Worship* 54–72; 109–39.
31. Beard, North, and Price, *Religions of Rome*, Vol. 1, 207.
32. On the worship of Augustus in the provinces, see Gradel, *Emperor Worship*.
33. Beard, North, and Price, *Religions of Rome*, Vol. 1, 209.
34. Beard, North, and Price, *Religions of Rome*, Vol. 1, 209
35. Beard, North, and Price, *Religions of Rome*, Vol. 1, 253.
36. Beard, North, and Price, *Religions of Rome*, Vol. 1, 318. Dio 51.20.7–8.
37. Suet. *Claud*. 21.2.
38. Pliny, *HN*. 7.48.159.
39. Tac. *Ann*. 11.11.1; Suet. *Dom*. 4.3; Zos. 2.4.
40. For the source materials and commentary, see Pighi.
41. Melanie Grunow Sobocinski, "Visualizing Ceremony: The Design and Audience of the Ludi Saeculares Coinage of Domitian," *American Journal of Archaeology* 110, no. 4 (2006): 584. Sobocinski notes in particular that the coinage issued in commemoration of Domitian's games was intended to directly mimic the Augustan coins.

Bibliography

Premodern Chinese sources listed by title

Abrecht, Ryan Russell. 2014. "My Neighbor the Barbarian: Immigrant Neighborhoods in Classical Athens, Imperial Rome, and Tang Chang'an." PhD Diss. University of California, Santa Barbara.
Alcock, Susan E., Terence N. D'Altroy, Kathleen D. Morrison, and Carla M. Sinopoli, eds. 2001. *Empires: Perspectives from Archaeology and History*. Cambridge: Cambridge University Press.
Allan, Sarah. 2003. "The Great One, Water, and the Laozi, New Light from Guodian," *T'oung Pao*, 89.4: 237–85.
Amitai, Reuven, and Michal Biran, eds. 2004. *Mongols, Turks, and Others: Eurasian Nomads and the Sedentary World*. Leiden: Brill.
Ando, Clifford, ed. 2003. *Roman Religion*. Edinburgh: Edinburgh University Press.
Ando, Clifford. 2007. "Exporting Roman Religion," in *Blackwell Companion to Roman Religion*, Jörg Rüpke, ed., 429–45. Malden, MA: Blackwell.
Ando, Clifford. 2009. *The Matter of the Gods: Religion and the Roman Empire*. Berkeley: University of California Press.
Augustus. *Res Gestae Divi Augusti*. See Brunt and Moore.
Auvray-Assayas, C., ed. 1998. *Images romaines: Actes de la table ronde organise à l'École normale supérieure, Tome 9*. Paris: Presses de l'École normale supérieure.
Bagnall, Roger S., Kai Brodersen, Craige B. Champion, Andrew Erskine, and Sabine R. Huebner, eds. 2013. *The Encyclopedia of Ancient History*. First Edition. Malden, MA: Wiley-Blackwell.
Beacham, Richard C. 1999. *Spectacle Entertainments of Early Imperial Rome*. New Haven, CT: Yale University Press.
Beard, Mary. 1980. "The Sexual Status of Vestal Virgins," *The Journal of Roman Studies*, 70: 12–27.
Beard, Mary. 1990. "Priesthood in the Roman Republic," in *Pagan Priests: Religion and Power in the Ancient World*, Mary Beard and John North, eds., 17–48. London: Duckworth.
Beard, Mary and John North, eds. 1990. *Pagan Priests: Religion and Power in the Ancient World*. London: Duckworth.
Beard, Mary, John North, and Simon Price. 1998. *Religions of Rome*. 2 Vols. Cambridge: Cambridge University Press.
Beck, Hans, Antonio Duplá, Martin Jehne, and Francisco Pina Polo, eds. 2011. *Consuls and Res Publica: Holding High Office in the Roman Republic*. Cambridge: Cambridge University Press.
Beck, Hans. 2018. "The Discovery of Numa's Writings: Roman Sacral Law and the Early Historians," in *Omnium Annalium Monumenta: Historical Writing and Historical Evidence in Republican Rome*, Kaj Sandberg and Christopher Smith, eds., 90–112. Leiden: Brill.

Beck, Hans and Griet Vankeerberghen, eds. 2021. *Rulers and Ruled in Ancient Greece, Rome, and China.* Cambridge: Cambridge University Press.

Benjamin, Walter. 1968. "The Work of Art in the Age of Mechanical Reproduction," in *Illuminations,* Hanna Arendt, ed., Harry Zhon trans., 217–51. New York: Harcourt, Brace & World.

Bergmann, Bettina Ann and Christine Kondoleon, eds. 1999. *The Art of Ancient Spectacle.* Washington, DC: National Gallery of Art.

Bielenstein, Hans. 1980. *The Bureaucracy of Han Times.* Cambridge: Cambridge University Press.

Blakeley, Barry B. 1992. "King, Clan, and Courtier in Ancient Ch'u," *Asia Major, Third Series* 5, no. 2: 1–39.

Bo Shuren 薄樹人. 1982. "Taolun Sima Qian de tianwenxue sixiang" 討論司馬遷的天文學思想, *Shixueshi yanjiu* 史學史研究, 1982.3: 7–15.

Bodde, Derk. 1987. "The State and Empire of "Ch'in," in *The Cambridge History of China: The Ch'in and Han Empires, 221 BC–AD 220,* Denis Twitchett and John K. Fairbank, eds., 20–102. Cambridge: Cambridge University Press.

Bonnaud, Robert. 2007. *Victoires Sur le Temps. Essais Comparatistes. Polybe le Grec et Sima Qian le Chinois.* Paris: La ligne d'ombre.

Bourdieu, Pierre. 1977. *Outline of a Theory of Practice.* Cambridge: Cambridge University Press.

Bowersock, G. W. 1990. "The Pontificate of Augustus," in *Between Republic and Empire: Interpretations of Augustus and His Principate,* Kurt A. Raaflaub, ed., 380–94. Berkeley, CA: University of California Press.

Brashier, Kenneth E. 2011. *Ancestral Memory in Early China.* Cambridge, MA: Harvard University Asia Center.

Brind'Amour, Pierre. 1978. "L'origine des jeux séculaires," in *Aufstieg und Niedergang der römischen Welt* II.16.2: 1334–417, Wolfgang Haase, ed. Berlin: Walter de Gruyter.

Brindley, Erica Fox. 2011. *Music, Cosmology, and the Politics of Harmony in Early China.* Albany, NY: State University of New York Press.

Brisch, Nicole, ed. 2008. *Religion and Power: Divine Kingship in the Ancient World and Beyond.* Chicago, IL: Oriental Institute of the University of Chicago.

Brunt, Peter. 1976. "The Romanization of the Local Ruling Classes in the Roman Empire," in *Assimilation et résistance à la culture gréco-romaine dans le monde ancien,* D. M. Pippidi, ed., 161–73. Bucuresti: Editura Academiei.

Brunt, Peter and J. M. Moore, ed. and trans. 1967. *Res gestae divi Augusti: The Achievements of the Divine Augustus.* London: Oxford University Press.

Bujard, Marianne. 1997. "Le "Traité des sacrifices" du *Hanshu* et la mise en place de la religion d'État des Han," *Bulletin de l'École française d'Extrême-Orient,* 84: 111–27.

Bujard, Marianne. 2000. *Le sacrifice au Ciel dans la Chine ancienne: Théorie et pratique sous les Han occidentaux.* Paris: École française d'Extrême-Orient.

Bujard, Marianne. 2008. "Le culte du Joyau de Chen: culte historique—culte vivant," *Cahiers d'Extrême-Asie: Culte des sites et culte des saints en Chine,* 10: 131–81.

Bujard, Marianne. 2008. "State and Local Cults in Han Religion," in *Early Chinese Religion: Part One; Shang through Han (1250 BC–220 AD),* vol. 2, John Lagerway and Marc Kalinowski, eds., 777–811. Leiden: Brill.

Burbank, Jane and Frederick Cooper. 2010. *Empires in World History: Power and the Politics of Difference.* Princeton, NJ: Princeton University Press.

Byrne, Rebecca Zerby. 1974. "Harmony and Violence in Classical China: A Study of the Battles of the *Tso-chuan*." PhD Diss. University of Chicago.

Cai Feng 蔡鋒. 1997. "Guoren de shuxing ji qi huodong dui Chunqiu shiqi guizu zhengzhi de yingxiang" 國人的屬性及其活動對春秋時期貴族政治的影響, *Beijing daxue xuebao (zhexue shehui kexue ban)* 北京大學學報（哲學社會科學版）, 3: 113–21.

Cai, Liang. 2014. *Witchcraft and the Rise of the First Confucian Empire*. Albany, NY: State University of New York Press.

Carter, Jesse Benedict. 1915. "The Reorganization of the Roman Priesthoods at the Beginning of the Republic," *Memoirs of the American Academy at Rome*, 1: 9–17.

Censorinus. 1900. *De Die Natali*, trans. William Maude. New York: The Cambridge Encyclopedia Co.

Chao Fulin 晁福林. 2000. "Lun Zhou dai guoren yu shumin shehui shenfen de bianhua," 論周代國人與庶民社會身分的變化, *Renwen zazhi* 人文雜誌, 3: 98–105.

Chavannes, Edouard, trans. 1967. *Les Mémoires historiques de Se-ma Ts'ien*. 6 Vols. Paris: Librairie d'Amérique et d'Orient Adrien Maisonneuve.

Chavannes, Edouard, trans. 1969 (1910). *Le T'ai Chan: Essai de monographie d'un culte chinois*. Paris: Farnborough, Gregg.

Chen Pan 陳槃. 1948. "Zhanguo Qin Han jian fangshi kao lun" 戰國秦漢間方士考論, *Zhongyang yanjiuyuan, lishi yuyan yanjiusuo jikan* 中央研究院，歷史語言研究所集刊, 17: 7–57.

Chen Shuguo 陳戍國. 2002 (1993). *Zhongguo lizhi shi: Qin-Han juan*. 中國禮制史：秦漢卷. Changsha: Hunan jiao yu chu ban she.

Chen Zhi 陳直. 1982 (1980). *Sanfu huangtu jiaozheng* 三輔黃圖校證. Xi'an: Renmin chubanshe.

Chisholm, Kitty, and John Ferguson, eds. 1986. *Rome: The Augustan Age*. Oxford: Oxford University Press.

Chunqiu Zuozhuan zhengyi 春秋左傳正義. In *Shisanjing zhushu*. See Durrant et al., 2016.

Chwe, Michael Suk-young. 2001. *Rational Ritual: Culture, Coordination, and Common Knowledge*. Princeton, NJ: Princeton University Press.

Cicero. 1939 *Brutus: Orator*. Translated by G. L. Hendrickson, H. M. Hubbell. Loeb Classical Library 342. Cambridge, MA: Harvard University Press.

Cicero. *Letters to Atticus, Volume I*. Edited and translated by D. R. Shackleton Bailey. Loeb Classical Library 7. Cambridge, MA: Harvard University Press, 1999.

Cicero. *Letters to Friends, Volume I: Letters 1–113*. Edited and translated by D. R. Shackleton Bailey. Loeb Classical Library 205. Cambridge, MA: Harvard University Press, 2001.

Cicero. *Pro Archia. Post Reditum in Senatu. Post Reditum ad Quirites. De Domo Sua. De Haruspicum Responsis. Pro Plancio*. Translated by N. H. Watts. Loeb Classical Library 158. Cambridge, MA: Harvard University Press, 1923.

Cicero. 1923. *On Old Age. On Friendship. On Divination*. Translated by W. A. Falconer. Loeb Classical Library 154. Cambridge, MA: Harvard University Press.

Cicero. 1923. *Pro Archia. Post Reditum in Senatu. Post Reditum ad Quirites. De Domo Sua. De Haruspicum Responsis. Pro Plancio*. Translated by N. H. Watts. Loeb Classical Library 158. Cambridge, MA: Harvard University Press.

Cicero. 1928 *On the Republic. On the Laws*. Translated by Clinton W. Keyes. Loeb Classical Library 213. Cambridge, MA: Harvard University Press.

Cicero. 1933. *On the Nature of the Gods. Academics*. Translated by H. Rackham. Loeb Classical Library 268. Cambridge, MA: Harvard University Press.

Cicero. 1942. *On the Orator: Book 3. On Fate. Stoic Paradoxes. Divisions of Oratory*. Translated by H. Rackham. Loeb Classical Library 349. Cambridge, MA: Harvard University Press.

Cicero. 2010. *Philippics 1–6*. Edited and translated by D. R. Shackleton Bailey. Revised by John T. Ramsey and Gesine Manuwald. Loeb Classical Library 189. Cambridge, MA: Harvard University Press.

Cornell, Timothy J. 1995. *The Beginnings of Rome: Italy and Rome from the Bronze Age to the Punic Wars (c. 1000–264 BC)*. London: Routledge.

Cornell, Timothy J., ed. 2013. *The Fragments of the Roman Historians*. 3 Vols. Oxford: Oxford University Press.

Csikszentmihalyi, Mark. 2008. "*Fangshi* 方士 'Masters of Methods'," in *The Encyclopedia of Taoism*, Fabrizio Pregadio, ed., 406–09. London: Routledge.

Cullen, Christopher. 1993. "Motivations for Scientific Change in Ancient China: Emperor WU and the Grand Inception Astronomical Reforms of 104 B.C.," *Journal for the History of Astronomy Journal for the History of Astronomy*, 24.3: 185–203.

D'Arms, John H. 1999. "Performing Culture: Roman Spectacle and the Banquets of the Powerful," in *The Art of Ancient Spectacle*, Bettina Ann Bergmann, Christine Kondoleon, National Gallery of Art (U.S.), and Center for Advanced Study in the Visual Arts (U.S.), eds., 301–19. Washington, DC: National Gallery of Art.

David, Jean-Michel. 1996. *The Roman Conquest of Italy*. Antonia Nevill, trans. Oxford: Blackwell.

DeWoskin, Kenneth J. 1983. *Doctors, Diviners, and Magicians of Ancient China: Biographies of Fang-shih*. New York: Columbia University Press.

Di Cosmo, Nicola. 2004. *Ancient China and Its Enemies: The Rise of Nomadic Power in East Asian History*. Cambridge: Cambridge University Press.

Di Cosmo, Nicola, ed. 2009. *Military Culture in Imperial China*. Cambridge, MA: Harvard University Press.

Dio Cassius. 1914. *Roman History Volumes III–VII*. Translated by Earnest Cary, Herbert B. Foster. Loeb Classical Library 53. Cambridge, MA: Harvard University Press.

Dionysius of Halicarnassus. 1937. *Roman Antiquities, Volume I: Books 1–2*. Translated by Earnest Cary. Loeb Classical Library 319. Cambridge, MA: Harvard University Press.

Driediger-Murphy, Lindsay. 2018. *Roman Republican Augury: Freedom and Control*. Oxford: Oxford University Press.

Durrant, Stephen W. 1995. *The Cloudy Mirror: Tension and Conflict in the Writings of Sima Qian*. Albany, NY: State University of New York Press.

Durrant, Stephen W., Wai-yee Li, Michael Nylan, and Hans van Ess, eds. 2016. *The Letter to Ren An & Sima Qian's Legacy*. Seattle: University of Washington Press.

Durrant, Stephen W., Wai-yee Li, and David Schaberg, trans. 2016. *The Zuo Tradition/Zuozhuan* 左傳: *Commentary on the "Spring and Autumn Annals*. Seattle: University of Washington Press.

Eck, Werner, 2007. *The Age of Augustus*. Malden, MA: Wiley-Blackwell.

Eckstein, Arthur M. 2006. *Mediterranean Anarchy, Interstate War, and the Rise of Rome*. Berkeley: University of California Press.

Eco, Umberto. 1997. "Function and Sign: The Semiotics of Architecture," in *Rethinking Architecture: A Reader in Cultural Theory*, Neil Leach, ed., 182–202. London: Routledge.

Engels, David. 2021. "Historical Necessity or Biographical Singularity? Some Aspects in the Biographies of C. Iulius Caesar and Qin Shi Huang Di," in *Rulers and Ruled in Ancient Greece, Rome, and China*, Hans Beck and Griet Vankeerberghen, eds., 328–68. Cambridge: Cambridge University Press.

Eno, Robert. 1990. "Was There a High God *Ti* in Shang Religion?" *Early China*, 15: 1–26.

Ehrhardt, Christopher T. H. R. 1984. "Roman Coin Types and the Roman Public," *Jahrbuch für Numismatik und Geldgeschichte*, 34: 41–54.

von Falkenhausen, Lothar. 2006. *Chinese Society in the Age of Confucius (1000–250 BC): The Archaeological Evidence*. Los Angeles: University of California Press.

Favro, Diane G. 1996. *The Urban Image of Augustan Rome*. Cambridge: Cambridge University Press.

Feeney, Denis. 2000. "The *Ludi Saeculares* and the *Carmen Saeculare*," in *Roman Religion*, Clifford Ando, ed., 106–15. Edinburgh: University of Edinburgh Press.

Feldherr, Andrew, ed. 2009. *The Cambridge Companion to the Roman Historians*. Cambridge: Cambridge University Press.

Flower, Harriet I. 1999. *Ancestor Masks and Aristocratic Power in Roman Culture*. Oxford: Clarendon Press.

Flower, Harriet I. 2010. *Roman Republics*. Princeton, NJ: Princeton University Press.

Flower, Harriet I., ed. 2014. *The Cambridge Companion to the Roman Republic*. Second Edition. Cambridge: Cambridge University Press.

Flower, Harriet I. 2017. *The Dancing Lares and the Serpent in the Garden: Religion at the Roman Street Corner*. Princeton, NJ: Princeton University Press.

Franke, Herbert. 1950. "Some Remarks on the Interpretation of Chinese Dynastic Histories," *Oriens*, 3.1: 8; 114–22.

Fujikawa Masakazu 藤川正數. 1968. *Kandai ni okeru reigaku no kenkyū* 漢代における礼学の研究. Tokyo: Kazama shobo.

Galinsky, Karl. 1996. *Augustan Culture: An Interpretive Introduction*. Princeton, NJ: Princeton University Press.

Galinsky, Karl, ed. 2005. *The Cambridge Companion to the Age of Augustus*. Cambridge: Cambridge University Press.

Gan Huaizhen 甘懷真. 2008. *Huangquan, liyi yu jingdian quanshi: Zhongguo gudai zhengzhishi yanjiu* 皇權，禮儀與經典詮釋：中國古代政治史研究. Shanghai: Huadong shifan daxue chubanshe.

Geertz, Clifford. 1980. *Negara: The Theatre State in Nineteenth Century Bali*. Princeton, NJ: Princeton University Press.

Gellius. 1927. *Attic Nights, Volume II: Books 6–13*. Translated by J. C. Rolfe. Loeb Classical Library 200. Cambridge, MA: Harvard University Press.

Goldstone, Jack. 1991. *Revolution and Rebellion in the Early Modern World*. Berkeley: University of California Press.

Gordon, Richard. 2003. "From Republic to Principate: Priesthood, Religion and Ideology," in *Roman Religion*, Clifford Ando, ed., 62–83. Edinburgh: Edinburgh University Press.

Gradel, Ittai. 2002. *Emperor Worship and Roman Religion*. Oxford: Clarendon Press.

Green, Steven J. 2009. "Malevolent Gods and Promethean Birds: Contesting Augury in Augustus's Rome," *Transactions of the American Philological Association*, 139: 147–67.

Guan Donggui. 管東貴. 1991. "Qin-Han Ganquan gong xiaoshi" 秦漢甘泉宮小識, in *Kaogu yu lishi wenhua: Qingzhu Gua Quxun xiansheng bashi dashou lunwen ji (xia)* 考古與歷史文化：慶祝刮去尋先生八十大壽論文集（下）, 53–63. Taipei, Cheng chung shuju.

Gurval, Robert. 1995. *Actium and Augustus: The Politics and Emotions of Civil War*. Ann Arbor: University of Michigan Press.

Habberstad, Luke. 2015. "Legalizing Ritual: Critiques of Imperial Cults and the Ascendance of Ritual over Law during the Western Han." Paper delivered at the "Empire and the Media of Religion" Workshop, University of California, Los Angeles, May 2015.

van Haeperen, Françoise. 2002. *Le collège pontifical: 3e s. av. J.-C.- 4e s. ap. J.-C.: contribution à l'étude de la religion public romaine*. S.1.: Institut historique belge de Rome.

van Haeperen, Françoise. 2003. "Des pontifes païens aux pontifes chrétiens. Transformations d'un titre: entre pouvoirs et représentations," *Revue Belge de Philologie et d'Histoire*, 81: 137–59.

Hahm, David E. 1963. "Roman Nobility and the Three Major Priesthoods, 218–167 BC," *Transactions and Proceedings of the American Philological Association*, 94: 73–85.

Hall, John F. III. 1986. "The *Saeculum Novum* of Augustus and its Etruscan Antecedents," in *Aufstieg und Niedergang der römischen Welt*. II.16.3: 2564–89. Berlin: Walter de Gruyter.

Hall, David L., and Roger Ames. 1987. *Thinking through Confucius*. Albany: State University of New York Press.

Hall, David L., and Roger Ames. 1998. *Thinking from the Han: Self, Truth, and Transcendence in Chinese and Western Culture*. Albany: State University of New York Press.

Hanshu 漢書. Comp. 1962. *Ban Gu* 班固 (32–92 CE). Beijing: Zhonghua shuju.

Hardy, Grant. 1999. *Worlds of Bronze and Bamboo: Sima Qian's Conquest of History*. New York: Columbia University Press.

Harris, William V. 1979. *War and Imperialism in Republican Rome, 327–70 B.C.* Oxford: Clarendon Press.

He Pingli 何平立. 2003. *Xunshou yu fengshan: fengjian zhenzhi de wenhua guiji* 巡狩與封禪：封建的文化軌跡. Jinan: Qi Lu shushe.

Hejduk, Julia Dyson. 2020. *The God of Rome: Jupiter in Augustan Poetry*. Oxford: Oxford University Press.

Hekster, Olivier and John Rich. 2006. "Octavian and the Thunderbolt: The Temple of Apollo Palatinus and the Roman Tradition of Temple Building," *The Classical Quarterly*, New Series, 56.1: 149–68.

Hobsbawm, Eric. 1992 (1983). "Introduction: Inventing Traditions," in *The Invention of Tradition*, Eric Hobsbawm and Terence Ranger, eds., 1–14. Cambridge: Cambridge University Press.

Hoffman Lewis, Martha W. 1952. "The College of Quindecimviri (Sacris Faciundis) in 17 B.C.," *The American Journal of Philology*, 73: 289–94.

Hoffman Lewis, Martha W. 1955. *The Official Priests of Rome under the Julio-Claudians: A Study of the Nobility from 44 B.C. to 68 A.D.* Rome: American Academy in Rome.

Hölkeskamp, Karl-Joachim. 1988. "Das Plebiscitum Ogulnium de sacerdotibus: Überlegungen zu Authentizität und Interpretation der livianischen Überlieferung," *Rheinisches Museum für Philologie*. Neue Folge, 131: 51–67.

Hölkeskamp, Karl-Joachim. 2004. *Senatus populusque romanus: die politische Kultur der Republik: Dimensionen und Deutungen*. Wiesbaden: Franz Steiner Verlag.

Hölkeskamp, Karl-Joachim. 2010. *Reconstructing the Roman Republic: An Ancient Political Culture and Modern Research*. Translated by Henry Heitmann-Gordon. Princeton, NJ: Princeton University Press.

Holleman, Aloysius Wilhelmus Jozef. 1973. "Ovid and the Lupercalia," *Historia: Zeitschrift für Alte Geschichte*, 2nd Qtr. 22.2: 260–68.

Hopkins, Keith. 2017. "From Violence to Blessing: Symbols and Rituals in Ancient Rome," in *Sociological Studies in Roman History*. Christopher Kelly, ed., 313–39. Cambridge: Cambridge University Press.

Hopkins, John North. 2016. *The Genesis of Roman Architecture*. New Haven, CT: Yale University Press.

Hsing, I-tien. 1980. "Rome and China: The Role of the Armies in the Imperial Succession. A Comparative Study." PhD Diss. University of Hawai'i at Manoa.

Hsu, Cho-yun. 1965. *Ancient China in Transition: An Analysis of Social Mobility, 722–222 B.C.* Stanford, CA: Stanford University Press.

Hsu, Cho-yun. 1999. "The Spring and Autumn Period," in *The Cambridge History of Ancient China: From the Origins of Civilization to 221 B.C.*, Michael Loewe and Edward L. Shaughnessy, eds., 545–86. Cambridge: Cambridge University Press.

Huainanzi 淮南子. Comp. Liu An 劉安 (d. 122 BCE) et al. 21 *juan*. See Liu Wendian.

Hulsewé, A. F. P. 1990. "A Striking Discrepancy between the Shih chi and the Han shu," *T'oung Pao*, 76.4–5: 322–23.

Hurlet, Frédéric. 2011. "Consulship and Consuls under Augustus," in *Consuls and Res Publica: Holding High Office in the Roman Republic*, Hans Beck, et al., eds., 319–35. Cambridge: Cambridge University Press.

Hurlet, Frédéric and Bernard Mineo, eds. 2009. *Le principat d'Auguste: Réalités et représentations du pouvoir autour de la Res publica restituta*. Rennes: Presses universitaires de Rennes.

Ing, Michael David Kaulana. 2012. *The Dysfunction of Ritual in Early Confucianism*. Oxford: Oxford University Press.

Jin Dejian 金德建. 1963. *Sima Qian suo jian shu kao* 司馬遷所見書考. Shanghai: Shanghai renmin chubanshe.

Jullien, François. 2000. *Detour and Access: Strategies of Meaning in China and Greece*. New York: Zone Books.

Jullien, François. 2004. *A Treatise on Efficacy: Between Western and Chinese Thinking*. Honolulu: University of Hawai'i Press.

Jullien, François. 2007. *The Impossible Nude: Chinese Art and Western Aesthetics*. Chicago: University of Chicago Press.

Kaneko Shūichi 金子修一. 2006. *Chūgoku kodai kōtei saishi no kenkyu*. 中國古代皇帝祭祀の研究. Tokyo: Iwanami Shoten.

Kearsley, Rosalinde. 2009. "Octavian and Augury: The Years 30–27 B.C.," *The Classical Quarterly*, 59.1: 147–66.

Kern, Martin. 1996. "In Praise of Political Legitimacy: The Miao and Jiao Hymns of the Western Han," *Oriens Extremus*, 39.1: 29–67.

Kern, Martin. 1997. *Die Hymnen der Chinesischen Staatsopfer: Literatur und Ritual in der Politischen Repräsentation von der Han-Zeit bis zu den Sechs Dynastien*. Stuttgart: Franz Steiner.

Kern, Martin. 2000. *The Stele Inscriptions of Ch'in Shih-huang: Text and Ritual in Early Chinese Imperial Representation*. New Haven, CT: American Oriental Society.

Kim, Hyun Jin. 2009. *Ethnicity and Foreigners in Ancient Greece and China*. London: Duckworth.

Kim, Moonsil Lee. 2014. "Food Redistribution during China's Qin and Han Periods: Accordance and Discordance among Ideologies, Policies, and their Implementation." PhD Diss. University of California, Santa Barbara.

Kings College London. *Digital Prosopography of the Roman Republic*. Accessible at www.romanrepublic.ac.uk.

Knoblock, John, trans. 1988. *Xunzi: A Translation and Study of the Complete Works*. Stanford, CA: Stanford University Press.

Knoblock, John, and Jeffrey Riegel, trans. 2000. *The Annals of Lü Buwei* 呂氏春秋. Stanford, CA: Stanford University Press.

Koo, Telly H. 1920. "The Constitutional Development of the Western Han Dynasty," *Journal of the American Oriental Society*, 40: 170–93.

Lagerway, John and Marc Kalinowski, eds. 2008. *Early Chinese Religion: Part One; Shang through Han (1250 BC–220 AD)*. 2 Vols. Leiden: Brill.
Lai Guolong. 2003. "The Diagram of the Mourning System from Mawangdui," *Early China*, 28: 43–99.
Laidlaw, James. 1999. "On Theatre and Theory: Reflections on Ritual in Imperial Chinese Politics," in *State and Court Ritual in China*, Joseph P. McDermott, ed., 399–416. Cambridge: Cambridge University Press.
Lange, Matthew. 2013. *Comparative-Historical Methods*. Los Angeles: Sage.
Leach, Neil, ed. 1997. *Rethinking Architecture: A Reader in Cultural Theory*. London: Routledge.
Legge, James, trans. 1885. *The Sacred Books of China, The Texts of Confucianism: The Li Ki. Sacred Books of the East*, F. Max Müller, ed. Vols. 27–28. Oxford: Clarendon Press.
Lewis, Mark Edward. 1990. *Sanctioned Violence in Early China*. Albany: State University of New York Press.
Lewis, Mark Edward. 1999. "The *Feng* and *Shan* Sacrifices of Emperor Wu of the Han," in *State and Court Ritual in China*, Joseph P. McDermott, ed., 50–80. Cambridge: Cambridge University Press.
Lewis, Mark Edward. 2006. *The Construction of Space in Early China*. Albany: State University of New York Press.
Lewis, Mark Edward. 2015. "Public Spaces in Cities in the Roman and Han Empires," in *State Power in Ancient China and Rome*, Walter Scheidel, ed., 204–29. Oxford: Oxford University Press.
Li Du-du 李都都, "Ganquan yu xi Han zhongqi de guojia jisi," 甘泉與西漢中期的國家祭祀, *Shihezi daxue xuebao (zhexue shehui kexue ban)* 石河子大學學報（哲學社會科學版）, 25.5 (2011)：114–19.
Li Feng. 2008. *Bureaucracy and the State in Early China: Governing the Western Zhou*. Cambridge: Cambridge University Press.
Li Ling 李零. 1995–1996. "An Archaeological Study of Taiyi (Grand One) Worship," in *Early Medieval China*, 2:1–39. Translated by Donald Harper. Also published in Chinese as "Taiyi chongbai de kaogu yanjiu" 太一崇拜的考古研究.
Li Ling 李零. 2006. *Zhongguo fangshu zhengkao* 中國方術政考. Beijing: Zhonghua shuju.
Liang Yun 梁雲. 2005. "Dui luanting shan jisi yizhi suo aidi de chubu renshi," 對鸞亭山祭祀遺址所在地的初步認識, *Zhongguo lishi wenwu*, 5: 15–31.
Liebeschuetz, J. H. W. G. 1979. *Continuity and Change in Roman Religion*. Oxford: Clarendon Press.
Liji jijie 禮記集解. 61 *juan*. 2002. *Xuxiu siku quanshu* 續修四庫全書. Vols. 103–04. Ed. Ruan Yuan 阮元 (1764–1849 CE). Shanghai: Shanghai guji chubanshe.
Linderski, Jerzy. 1985. "The *Libri Reconditi*," *Harvard Studies in Classical Philology*, 89: 207–34.
Linderski, Jerzy. 1986. "The Augural Law," in *Aufstieg und Niedergang der römischen Welt*. II.16.3: 2146–312. Wolfgang Haase, ed. Berlin: Walter de Gruyter.
Lintott, Andrew. 1999. *The Constitution of the Roman Republic*. Oxford: Clarendon Press.
Lintott, Andrew. 2010. *The Romans in the Age of Augustus*. Malden, MA: Wiley-Blackwell.
Lipka, Michael. 2009. *Roman Gods: A Conceptual Approach*. Leiden: Brill.
Liu Wendian 劉文典. 1978. *Huainan hong lie jijie* 淮南鴻烈集解. 2 Vols. Beijing: Zhonghua shuju.
Livy. 1924. *History of Rome, Volume III: Books 5–7*. Translated by B. O. Foster. Loeb Classical Library 172. Cambridge, MA: Harvard University Press.

Livy. 2017. *History of Rome, Volume IX: Books 31–34*. Edited and translated by J. C. Yardley. Introduction by Dexter Hoyos. Loeb Classical Library 295. Cambridge, MA: Harvard University Press.

Lloyd, Geoffrey E. R. 1996. *Adversaries and Authorities: Investigations into Ancient Greek and Chinese Science*. Cambridge: Cambridge University Press.

Lloyd, Geoffrey E. R. 2002. *The Ambitions of Curiosity: Understanding the World in Ancient Greece and China*. Cambridge: Cambridge University Press.

Lloyd, Geoffrey E. R. 2004. *Ancient Worlds, Modern Reflections: Philosophical Perspectives on Greek and Chinese Science and Culture*. Oxford: Oxford University Press.

Lloyd, Geoffrey E. R. 2006. *Principles and Practices in Ancient Greek and Chinese Science*. Aldershot: Ashgate/Variorum.

Lloyd, Geoffrey E. R., and Nathan Sivin. 2002. *The Way and the World: Science and Medicine in Early China and Greece*. New Haven, CT: Yale University Press.

Loar, Matthew P., Sarah C. Murray, Stefano Rebeggiani, eds., 2019. *The Cultural History Of Augustan Rome: Texts, Monuments, and Topography*. Cambridge: Cambridge University Press.

Loewe, Michael. 1974. *Crisis and Conflict in Han China, 104 BC to AD 9*. London: Allen & Unwin.

Loewe, Michael. 1986. "The Former Han Dynasty," in *The Cambridge History of China Volume 1: the Ch'in and Han Empires, 221 B.C.–A.D. 220*, Denis Twitchett and Michael Loewe, eds., 103–222. Cambridge: Cambridge University Press.

Loewe, Michael, ed. 1993. *Early Chinese Texts: A Bibliographical Guide*. Berkeley, CA: University of California Press.

Loewe, Michael. 1994. *Divination, Mythology, and Monarchy in Han China*. Cambridge: Cambridge University Press.

Loewe, Michael. 2000. *A Biographical Dictionary of the Qin, Former Han, and Xin Periods, 221 BC–AD 24*. Leiden: Brill.

Loewe, Michael. 2004. *The Men Who Governed Han China: A Companion to A Biographical Dictionary of the Qin, Former Han, and Xin Periods*. Leiden: Brill.

Loewe, Michael. 2015. "The Tombs Built for Han Chengdi and Migrations of the Population," in *Chang'an 26 BCE: An Augustan Age in China*, Michael Nylan and Griet Vankeerberghen, eds., 201–17. Seattle, WA: University of Washington Press.

Loewe, Michael and Edward L. Shaughnessy, eds. 1999. *The Cambridge History of Ancient China*. Cambridge: Cambridge University Press.

Loewe, Michael and Denis Twitchett, eds. 1986. *The Cambridge History of China Volume 1: The Ch'in and Han Empires, 221 B.C.–A.D. 220*. Cambridge: Cambridge University Press.

Lott, J. Bert. 2004. *The Neighborhoods of Augustan Rome*. Cambridge: Cambridge University Press.

Lu, Xing. 1998. *Rhetoric in Ancient China, Fifth to Third Century BCE: A Comparison with Classical Greek Rhetoric*. Columbia: University of South Carolina Press.

Luce, T. J. 1990. "Livy, Augustus, and the Forum Augustum," in *Between Republic and Empire: Interpretations of Augustus and His Principate*, Kurt Raaflaub and Mark Toher, eds., 123–38. Berkeley: University of California Press.

Lunyu zhushu 論語注疏. 2009. Beijing: Zhonghua shuju.

Lüshi chunqiu jiaoshi 呂氏春秋校釋. 1990. Compiled and annotated by Chen Qiyou 陳奇猷. Shanghai: Xuelin chubanshe.

Macmullen, Ramsey. 2000. *Romanization in the Time of Augustus*. New Haven, CT: Yale University Press.
Macrobius. 2011. *Saturnalia, Volume I: Books 1-2*. Edited and translated by Robert A. Kaster. Loeb Classical Library 510. Cambridge, MA: Harvard University Press.
Major, John S. et al., trans. 2010. *The Huainanzi: A Guide to the Theory and Practice of Government in Early Han China*. New York: Columbia.
Marincola, John, ed. 2007. *A Companion to Greek and Roman Historiography*. Malden, MA: Blackwell.
Marsili, Filippo. 2018. *Heaven Is Empty: A Cross-Cultural Approach to "Religion" and Empire in Ancient China*. Albany: State University of New York Press.
Martin, Thomas R. 2010. *Herodotus and Sima Qian: The First Great Historians of Greece and China, a Brief History with Documents*. Boston: Bedford/St. Martin's.
McDermott, Joseph P., ed. 1999. *State and Court Ritual in China*. Cambridge: Cambridge University Press.
McKnight, Brian E. 1981. *The Quality of Mercy: Amnesties and Traditional Chinese Justice*. Honolulu: University of Hawai'i Press.
McLynn, Neil. 2008. "Crying Wolf: The Pope and the *Lupercalia*," *Journal of Roman Studies*, 98: 161–75.
Mehl, Andreas. 2011. *Roman Historiography: An Introduction to Its Basic Aspects and Development*. Hans-Friedrich Mueller, trans. Malden, MA: Wiley-Blackwell.
Mellor, Ronald. 1999. *The Roman Historians*. London: Routledge.
Miller, John F. 2009. *Apollo, Augustus, and the Poets*. Cambridge: Cambridge University Press.
Morrison, Kathleen D. 2011. "Sources, Approaches, Definitions," in *Empires: Perspectives from Archaeology and History*, Susan E. Alcock, Terence N. D'Altroy, Kathleen D. Morrison, and Carla M. Sinopoli, eds., 1–9. Cambridge: Cambridge University Press.
Mouritsen, Henrik. 2001. *Plebs and Politics in the Late Roman Republic*. Cambridge: Cambridge University Press.
Mueller, Hans-Friedrich. 2002. *Roman Religion in Valerius Maximus*. London; New York, NY: Routledge.
Musial, Danuta. 2014. "The Princeps as the *Pontifex Maximus*: The Case of Tiberius," *Electrum*, 21: 99–106.
Mutschler, Fritz-Heiner. 2008. "Tacite (et Tite-Live) et Sima Qian: La vision politique d'historiens latins et chinois," *Bulletin de l'Association Guillaume Budé*, 2, 123–55.
Mutschler, Fritz-Heiner and Achim Mittag, eds. 2008. *Conceiving the Empire: China and Rome Compared*. Oxford: Oxford University Press.
Ngo, Van Xuyet. 1976. *Divination, magie et politique dans la chine ancienne*. Paris: Presses universitaires de France.
Nienhauser, William H. et al., trans. 1994. *The Grand Scribe's Records*. 7 Vols. Bloomington: Indiana University Press.
Nippel, Wilfried. 1995. *Public Order in Ancient Rome*. Cambridge: Cambridge University Press.
Niu Jingfei 牛敬飛. 2017. "Bei kuada de qian jiaosi shidai—cong "Qin-Han guojia jisi shigao" dui shiliao de wu yong shuo qi" 被誇大的前郊祀時代—從《秦漢國家祭祀史稿》對史料的誤用說起, *Qinghua Daxue xuebao (zhexue shehui kexue ban*, 1.32: 82–83.
Noreña, Carlos. 2011a. *Imperial Ideals in the Roman West: Representation, Circulation, Power*. Cambridge: Cambridge University Press.

Noreña, Carlos. 2011b. "Coins and Communication," in *The Oxford Handbook of Social Relations in the Roman World*, M. Peachin, ed., 248–68. Oxford: Oxford University Press.
Nylan, Michael. 1998–1999. "Sima Qian: A True Historian?" *Early China*, 23–24: 203–46.
Nylan, Michael. 2001. *The Five "Confucian" Classics*. New Haven, CT: Yale University Press.
Nylan, Michael. 2008. "The Rhetoric of 'Empire' in the Classical Era in China," in *Conceiving the Empire: China and Rome Compared*, Fritz-Heiner Mutschler and Achim Mittag, eds., 39–64. Oxford: Oxford University Press.
Nylan, Michael and Michael Loewe, eds. 2010. *China's Early Empires: A Re-appraisal*. Cambridge: Cambridge University Press.
Nylan, Michael and Griet Vankeerberghen, eds. 2015. *Chang'an 26 BCE: An Augustan Age in China*. Seattle, WA: University of Washington Press.
Ogilvie, R. M. 1970. *The Romans and Their Gods in the Age of Augustus*. New York: Norton.
Ord, Edmund Burke Holladay. 1967. "State Sacrifices in the Former Han Dynasties According to the Official Histories." PhD Diss. University of California, Berkeley.
Orlin, Eric M. 2002. *Temples, Religion, and Politics in the Roman Republic*. Leiden: Brill.
Ovid. 1931. *Fasti*. Translated by James G. Frazer. Revised by G. P. Goold. Loeb Classical Library 253. Cambridge, MA: Harvard University Press.
Pak, Chae-u 朴宰雨. 1994. "Shiji" "Hanshu" *bijiao yanjiu* "史記" "漢書" 比較研究. Beijing: Zhongguo wenxue chubanshe.
Pandey, Nandini B. 2018. *The Poetics of Power in Augustan Rome: Latin Poetic Reponses to Early Imperial Iconography*. Cambridge: Cambridge University Press.
Pankenier, David. 2004. "A Brief History of Beiji 北極 (Northern Culmen), With an Excursus on the Origin of the Character Di 帝," *Journal of the American Oriental Society*, 124.2: 211–36.
Parke, H. W. 1988. *Sibyls and Sibylline Prophecy in Classical Antiquity*. B. C. McGing, ed. London; New York, NY: Routledge.
Peralta, Dan-el Padilla. 2019. "Monument Men: Buildings, Inscriptions, and Lexicographers in the Creation of Augustan Rome," in *The Cultural History of Augustan Rome*, Loar et al., eds., 80–102. Cambridge: Cambridge University Press.
Peralta, Dan-el Padilla. 2020. *Divine Institutions: Religions and Community in the Middle Roman Republic*. Princeton, NJ: Princeton University Press.
Peterson, Jens Østergard. 1995. "Which Books Did the First Emperor of Ch'in Burn? On the Meaning of Pai Chia in Early Chinese Sources," *Monumenta Serica*, 43: 1–52.
Pighi, Ioannes Baptista. 1965. *De ludis saecularibus populi Romani Quiritium libri sex*. Amsterdam: Verlag P. Schippers NV.
Pina Polo, Francisco. 2011. *The Consul at Rome: The Civil Functions of the Consuls in the Roman Republic*. Cambridge: Cambridge University Press.
Pines, Yuri. 2002. *Foundations of Confucian Thought: Intellectual Life in the Chunqiu Period, 722–453 B.C.E.* Honolulu: University of Hawai'i Press.
Pines, Yuri. 2004. "Beasts or Humans: Pre-Imperial Origins of the Sino-Barbarian Dichotomy," in *Mongols, Turks, and Others: Eurasian Nomads and the Sedentary World*, Reuven Amitai and Michal Biran, eds., 59–102. Leiden: Brill.
Pines, Yuri. 2009. *Envisioning Eternal Empire: Chinese Political Thought of the Warring States Era*. Honolulu: University of Hawai'i Press.
Pines, Yuri. 2012. *The Everlasting Empire: The Political Culture of Ancient China and Its Imperial Legacy*. Princeton, NJ: Princeton University Press.

Pines, Yuri, Lothar von Falkenhausen, Gideon Shelach, and Robin D.S. Yates, eds. 2014. *Birth of an Empire: The State of Qin Revisited*. Berkeley: University of California Press.

Pippidi, D. M., ed. 1976. *Assimilation et résistance à la culture gréco-romaine dans le monde ancien*. Bucuresti: Editura Academiei.

Pliny. 1942. *Natural History, Volume II: Books 3–7*. Translated by H. Rackham. Loeb Classical Library 352. Cambridge, MA: Harvard University Press.

Plutarch. 1916. *Lives, Volume IV: Alcibiades and Coriolanus. Lysander and Sulla*. Translated by Bernadotte Perrin. Loeb Classical Library 80. Cambridge, MA: Harvard University Press.

Plutarch. 1919. *Lives, Volume VII: Demosthenes and Cicero. Alexander and Caesar*. Translated by Bernadotte Perrin. Loeb Classical Library 99. Cambridge, MA: Harvard University Press.

Plutarch. 1921. *Lives, Volume X: Agis and Cleomenes. Tiberius and Gaius Gracchus. Philopoemen and Flamininus*. Translated by Bernadotte Perrin. Loeb Classical Library 102. Cambridge, MA: Harvard University Press.

Polybius. 2011. *The Histories, Volume III: Books 5–8*. Translated by W. R. Paton. Revised by F. W. Walbank, Christian Habicht. Loeb Classical Library 138. Cambridge, MA: Harvard University Press.

Poo, Mu-chou. 1998. *In Search of Personal Welfare: A View of Ancient Chinese Religion*. Albany: State University of New York Press.

Poo, Mu-chou. 2014. "Religion and Religious Life of the Qin," in *Birth of an Empire: The State of Qin Revisited*, Yuri Pines, Lothar von Falkenhausen, Gideon Shelach, and Robin D. S. Yates, eds., 187–205. Berkeley: University of California Press.

Pregadio, Fabrizio, ed. 2008. *The Encyclopedia of Taoism*. London: Routledge.

Price, Simon R.F. 1984. *Rituals and Power: The Roman Imperial Cult in Asia Minor*. Cambridge: Cambridge University Press.

Puett, Michael. 2002. *To Become A God: Cosmology, Sacrifice, and Self-divinization in Early China*. Cambridge, MA: Harvard University Press.

Puett, Michael. 2008. "Human and Divine Kingship in Early China: Comparative Reflections," in *Religion and Power: Divine Kingship in the Ancient World*, Nicole Brisch, ed., 207–20. Chicago: Oriental Institute of the University of Chicago.

Puett, Michael. 2009. "Combining the Ghosts and Spirits, Centering the Realm: Mortuary Ritual and Political Organization in the Ritual Compendia of Early China," in *Early Chinese Religion, Part One: Shang through Han (1250 BC–220 AD)*, John Lagerwey and Marc Kalinowski, eds. Vol. 2, 695–720. Leiden; Boston, MA: Brill.

Puett, Michael. 2015. "Ghosts, Gods, and the Coming Apocalypse: Empire and Religion in Early China and Ancient Rome," in *State Power in Ancient China and Rome*, Walter Scheidel, ed., 230–59. Oxford: Oxford University Press.

Putnam, Michael C. J. 2001. *Horace's 'Carmen Saeculare': Ritual Magic and the Poet's Art*. New Haven, CT: Yale University Press.

Queen, Sarah A. and John Major, trans. 2016. *Luxuriant Gems of the Spring and Autumn: Attributed to Dong Zhongshu*. New York: Columbia University Press.

Raaflaub, Kurt A. 1996. "Born to Be Wolves? Origins of Roman Imperialism," in *Transitions to Empire: Essays in Greco-Roman History, 360–146 B.C.*, in Honor of E. Badian, Robert W. Wallace and Edward Monroe Harris, eds., 273–314. Norman: University of Oklahoma Press.

Raaflaub, Kurt A. and Mark Toher, eds. 1990. *Between Republic and Empire: Interpretations of Augustus and His Principate*. Berkeley: University of California Press.

Raphals, Lisa Ann. 2013. *Divination and Prediction in Early China and Ancient Greece*. Cambridge: Cambridge University Press.
Rappaport, Roy A. 1999. *Ritual and Religion in the Making of Humanity*. Cambridge: Cambridge University Press.
Rawson, Jessica. 1999. "Western Zhou Archaeology," in *The Cambridge History of Ancient China*, Michael Loewe and Edward L. Shaughnessy, eds., 352–449. Cambridge: Cambridge University Press.
Richardson, John S. 2012. *Augustan Rome 44 BC to AD 14: The Restoration of the Republic and the Establishment of the Empire*. Edinburgh: Edinburgh University Press.
Ridley, Ronald T. 2005. "The Absent Pontifex Maximus," *Historia*, 54.2: 275–300.
Riegel, Jeffrey K. 1993. "*Li Chi* 禮記," in *Early Chinese Texts: A Bibliographical Guide*, Early China Special Monograph Series No. 2, Michael Loewe, ed., 293–97. Berkeley: Society for the Study of Early China and Institute of East Asian Studies.
Robinson, Rebecca. 2018. "Spectacular Power in Early China and Ancient Rome," *The Journal of World History*, 29.3: 343–368.
Robinson, Rebecca. 2020. "To Reverently Bestow the Seasons: Calendrical Narratives in Early China and Rome," in *Intersections of Religion and Astronomy*, Aaron Ricker et al., eds., 27–35. Oxon: Routledge.
Robinson, Rebecca. 2021. "Employing Knowledge: Experts and Emperors in Qin, Han, and Rome," in *Rulers and Ruled in Ancient Greece, Rome, and China*, Hans Beck and Griet Vankeerberghen, eds., 369–96. Cambridge: Cambridge University Press.
Robinson, Rebecca. Forthcoming. "Repairing the Yellow River Breach at Huzi: Flood Control and Immortality during the reign of Han Wudi," *Etudes Chinoises*.
Roth, Harold D. 1987. "Fang-shih," in *Encyclopedia of Religion*, vol. 5, Mircea Eliade, ed., 282–84. New York: Macmillan.
Rüpke, Jörg, ed. 2007. *The Blackwell Companion to Roman Religion*. Malden, MA: Blackwell.
Rüpke, Jörg. 2008. *Fasti sacerdotum: A prosopography of pagan, Jewish, and Christian religious officials in the city of Rome, 300 BC to AD 499*. Translated by David Richardson. Oxford: Oxford University Press.
Rüpke, Jörg. 2012. *Religion in Republican Rome: Rationalization and Ritual Change*. Philadelphia: University of Pennsylvania Press.
Sage, Steven F. 1992. *Ancient Sichuan and the Unification of China*. Albany: State University of New York Press.
Sanft, Charles. 2008. "Progress and Publicity in Early China: Qin Shihuang, Ritual, and Common Knowledge," *Journal of Ritual Studies*, 22.1: 21–37.
Sanft, Charles. 2011. "Debating the Route of the Qin Direct Road (Zhidao): Text and Excavation," *Frontiers of History in China*, 6.3: 323–46.
Sanft, Charles. 2014. *Communication and Cooperation in Early Imperial China: Publicizing the Qin Dynasty*. Albany: State University of New York Press.
Santangelo, Frederico. 2016. "Enduring Arguments: Priestly Expertise in the Early Principate," *Transactions of the American Philological Association*, 146: 349–76.
Satterfield, Susan. 2016. "The Prodigies of 17 B.C.E. and the *Ludi Saeculares*," *Transactions of the American Philological Association*, 146: 325–48.
Sanfu huangtu 三輔黃圖. See Chen Zhi.
Scheid, John. 1975. *Les Frères Arvales: Recrutement et origine sociale sous les empereurs julio-claudiens*. Paris: Presses universitaires de France.

Scheid, John. 1978. "Les prêtres officiels sous les empereurs julio-claudiens," in *Aufstieg und Niedergang de römischen Welt*, II.16.1: 610–54. Wolfgang Haase, ed. Berlin: Walter de Gruyter.

Scheid, John. 1985. "Numa et Jupiter ou les dieux citoyens de Rome," *Archives de Sciences Sociales Des Religions*, 30e Année, 59.1: 41–53.

Scheid, John. 1990. *Romulus et ses frères: le collège des Frères Arvales, modèle du culte public dans la Rome des empereurs*. Rome: Ecole Français de Rome.

Scheid, John. 1998. "Déchiffrer des monnaies: réflexions sur la représentation figurée des Jeux séculaires," in *Images romaines: Actes de la table ronde organise à l'École normale supérieure, Tome 9*, C. Auvray-Assayas, ed., 13–35. Paris: Presses de l'École normale supérieure.

Scheid, John. 2003. *An Introduction to Roman Religion*. Janet Lloyd, trans. Bloomington, IN: Indiana University Press.

Scheid, John. 2007. "Sacrifices for Gods and Ancestors," in *The Blackwell Companion to Roman Religion*, Jörg Rüpke, ed., 263–71. Malden, MA: Blackwell.

Scheid, John. 2009. "Les restaurations religieuse d'Octavien/Auguste," in *Le principat d'Auguste: Réalités et représentations du pouvoir autour de la Res publica restituta*, Fréderic Hurlet and Bernard Mineo, eds., 119–28. Rennes: Presses universitaires de Rennes.

Scheidel, Walter, ed. 2009. *Rome and China: Comparative Perspectives on Ancient World Empires*. Oxford: Oxford University Press.

Scheidel, Walter, ed. 2015. *State Power in Ancient China and Rome*. Oxford: Oxford University Press.

Severy, Beth. 2003. *Augustus and the Family at the Birth of the Roman Empire*. New York: Routledge.

Shaughnessy, Edward L. 2006. *Rewriting Early Chinese Texts*. Albany: State University of New York Press.

Shiji 史記. Comp. Sima Qian 司馬遷 (145?–86? BCE). 1959. Beijing: Zhonghua shuju.

Shisanjing zhushu 十三經注疏. 1980. Ed. Ruan Yuan 阮元 (1764–1849 CE). 245 *juan*. Beijing: Zhonghua shuju.

Sobocinski, Melanie Grunow. 2006. "Visualizing Ceremony: The Design and Audience of the Ludi Saeculares Coinage of Domitian," *American Journal of Archaeology*, 110.4: 581–602.

Staack, Thies and Ulrich Lau. 2016. *Legal Practice in the Formative Stages of the Chinese Empire: An Annotated Translation of the Exemplary Qin Criminal Cases from the Yuelu Academy Collection*. Leiden; Boston: Brill.

Stadter, Philip A., ed. *Plutarch and the Historical Tradition*. Routledge, 2002.

Sterckx, Roel. 2011. *Food, Sacrifice, and Sagehood in Early China*. Cambridge: Cambridge University Press.

Suetonius. 1914. *Lives of the Caesars, Volume I: Julius. Augustus. Tiberius. Gaius. Caligula*. Translated by J. C. Rolfe. Introduction by K. R. Bradley. Loeb Classical Library 31. Cambridge, MA: Harvard University Press.

Sumi, Geoffrey S. 2005. *Ceremony and Power: Performing Politics in Rome between Republic and Empire*. Ann Arbor: The University of Michigan Press.

Syme, Ronald. 1980. *Some Arval Brethren*. Oxford: Clarendon Press of Oxford University Press.

Syme, Ronald. 2002 (1939). *The Roman Revolution*. Oxford: Oxford University Press.

Syme, Ronald. 2016. "Caesar as *Pontifex Maximus*," in *Approaching the Roman Revolution: Papers on Republican History*, Federico Santangelo, ed., 189–95. Oxford: Oxford University Press.

Tacitus. 1937. *Annals: Books 4–6, 11–12*. Translated by John Jackson. Loeb Classical Library 312. Cambridge, MA: Harvard University Press.

Tang Xiejun 唐燮軍 and Weng Gongyu 翁公羽. 2012. *Cong fenzhi dao jiquan: xi Han de wangguo wenti jiqi jiejue*. 從分治到集權：西漢的王國問題及其解決. Hangzhou: Zhejiang daxue chubanshe.

Tang Xiaofeng 唐曉峰. 2007. "Fenyin Houtu ci de diaocha yanjiu" 汾陰后土祠的調查研究. *Jiuzhou Vol. 4, Zhongguo dilixue shi zhuanhao* 九州。第四輯，中國地理學史專號, Tang Xiaofeng, ed., Beijing: Shang wu yin shu guan.

Tanner, Jeremy. 2009. "Ancient Greece, Early China: Sino-Hellenic Studies and Comparative Approaches to the Classical World, A Review Article," *Journal of Hellenic Studies*, 129: 89–109.

Tatum, W. Jeffrey. 2008. *Always I Am Caesar*. Malden, MA: Blackwell.

Taylor, Lily Ross. 1942. "The Election of the Pontifex Maximus in the Late Republic," *Classical Philology*, 37.4: 421–24.

Taylor, Lily Ross. 1966. *Roman Voting Assemblies from the Hannibalic War to the Dictatorship of Caesar*. Ann Arbor: University of Michigan Pres.

Tellegen-Couperus, Olga, ed. 2011. *Law and Religion in the Roman Republic*. Leiden, Brill.

Tellegen-Couperus, Olga. 2011. "Introduction," in *Law and Religion in the Roman Republic*. Olga Tellegen-Couperus, ed., 1–10. Leiden, Brill.

Thornton, John. 2013. "Pragmatic History," in *The Encyclopedia of Ancient History*, First Edition, Roger S. Bagnall, Kai Brodersen, Craige B. Champion, Andrew Erskine, and Sabine R. Huebner, eds., 5499–501. Malden, MA: Wiley-Blackwell.

Tian Tian 田天. 2013. "Chunqiu Zhanguo Qinguo ci si kao" 春秋戰國秦國祠祀考, *Zhongguo dianji yu wenhua* 中國典籍與文化, 1: 35–37.

Tian Tian 田天. 2014. "Xi Han Tai Yi jisi yanjiu" 西汉太一祭祀研究 "An Approach to Taiyi Sacrifice of the Western Han," *Shi Xue Yue Kan* 史学月刊, 4: 39–51.

Tian Tian 田天. 2015a. *Qin-Han guojia jisi shigao* 秦漢國家祭祀史稿. (*Qin and Han State Sacrifices: A Draft History*). Beijing: Xin zhi san lian shu dian.

Tian Tian 田天. 2015b. "The Suburban Sacrifice Reforms and the Evolution of the Imperial Sacrifice," in *Chang'an in 26 BCE: An Augustan Age in China*, Michael Nylan and Griet Vankeerberghen, eds., 263–92. Seattle: University of Washington Press.

Tian Yaqi 田亞岐. 1993. "Qin-Han zhi zhi yanjiu" 秦漢置時研究, *Kaogu yu wenwu*, 3: 53–59.

Trigger, Bruce. 2003. *Understanding Early Civilizations: A Comparative Study*. Cambridge: Cambridge University Press.

Vanggaard, Jens H. 1988. *The Flamen: A Study in the History and Sociology of Roman Religion*. Copenhagen: Museum Tusculanum Press.

Vankeerberghen, Griet. 2001. *The Huainanzi and Liu An's Claim to Moral Authority*. Albany: State University of New York Press.

Vankeerberghen, Griet. 2010. "Texts and Authors in the *Shiji*," in *China's Early Empires: A Re-appraisal*, Michael Nylan and Michael Loewe, eds., 461–79. Cambridge: Cambridge University Press.

Vankeerberghen, Griet. 2021. "Of Gold and Purple: Nobles in Western Han China and Republican Rome," in *Rulers and Ruled in Ancient Greece, Rome, and China*. Hans Beck and Griet Vankeerberghen, eds., 25–69. Cambridge: Cambridge University Press.

Varro. 1938. *On the Latin Language, Volume I: Books 5–7*. Translated by Roland G. Kent. Loeb Classical Library 333. Cambridge, MA: Harvard University Press.
Wallace, Robert W. and Edward Monroe Harris, eds. 1996. *Transitions to Empire: Essays in Greco-Roman History, 360–146 B.C.*, in Honor of E. Badian. Norman: University of Oklahoma Press.
Wallace-Hadrill, Andrew. 2008. *Rome's Cultural Revolution*. Cambridge: Cambridge University Press.
Wang Jing 王靜 and Liang Yong 梁勇. 2010. "Qin-Han shiqi fangshu, fangshi yu zhengzhi wenhua zhi guanxi" 秦漢時期方術，方士與政治文化之關係, *Journal of Hebei University (Philosophy and Social Science)*, 35.3: 39–43.
Watson, Burton, trans. 1993. *Records of the Grand Historian of China: Qin Dynasty*. New York: Columbia University Press.
Watson, Burton. 1993b (1961). *Records of the Grand Historian of China: Han Dynasty*. 2 Vols. Revised Edition. New York: Columbia University Press.
Wechsler, Howard J. 1985. *Offerings of Jade and Silk: Ritual and Symbol in the Legitimation of the T'ang Dynasty*. New Haven, CT: Yale University Press.
Weinstock, Stefan. 1971. *Divus Julius*. Oxford: Oxford University Press.
Weld, Susan R. 1997. "The Covenant Texts from Houma and Wenxian," in *New Sources of Early Chinese History: An Introduction to the Reading of Inscriptions and Manuscripts*, Edward L. Shaughnessy, ed., 125–60. Berkeley: Society for the Study of Early China and the Institute of East Asian Studies, University of California, Berkeley.
Wildfang, Robin Lorsch. 2006. *Rome's Vestal Virgins: A Study of Rome's Vestal Priestesses in the Late Republic and Early Empire*. London: Routledge.
Wilkinson, Endymion. 2013. *Chinese History: A New Manual*. Cambridge, MA: Harvard University Press.
Wiseman, Timothy Peter. 1995. "The God of the Lupercal," *The Journal of Roman Studies*, 85: 1–22.
Woolf, Greg. 1994. "Becoming Roman, Staying Greek. Culture, Identity and the Civilizing Process in the Roman East," *Proceedings of the Cambridge Philological Society*, 40: 116–43.
Woolf, Greg. 2001. "Inventing Empire in Ancient Rome," in *Empires: Perspectives from Archaeology and History*, Susan E. Alcock, Terence N. D'Altroy, Kathleen D. Morrison, and Carla M. Sinopoli, eds., 311–22. Cambridge: Cambridge University Press.
Woolf, Greg. 2008. "Divinity and Power in Ancient Rome," in *Religion and Power: Divine Kingship in the Ancient World*, Nicole Brisch, ed., 243–60. Chicago: Oriental Institute of the University of Chicago.
Wu Hung. 1988. "From Temple to Tomb: Ancient Chinese Art and Religion in Transition," *Early China*, 13: 78–115.
Xiang Jinwei 向晉衛, and Mu Wei 穆葳. 2015. "Qin Han Shiqi de Houtu Chongbai - Jianlun Fenyin Houtu Ci de Jianzhi Beijing 秦漢時期的后土崇拜 - 兼論汾陰后土祠的建置背景," *Nandu Xuetan (Renwen Shehui Kexu Xueban)*, 35.1: 16–20.
Xunzi zhuzi suoyin 荀子逐字索引. 1996. *The ICS Ancient Chinese Texts Concordance Series* 26, D. C. Lau, ed. Hong Kong: The Commercial Press.
Yakobson, Alexander. 1992. "Petitio et Largitio: Popular Participation in the Centuriate Assembly of the Late Republic," *Journal of Roman Studies*, 82: 32–52.
Yakobson, Alexander. 2014. "The First Emperors: Image and Memory," in *Birth of an Empire: The State of Qin Revisited*, Yuri Pines, Lothar von Falkenhausen, Gideon Shelach, and Robin D.S. Yates, eds., 280–300. Berkeley: University of California Press.

Yang Hua 楊華. 2011. "Qin Han diguo de shenquan tongyi: chutu jianbo yu 'Fengshan shu', 'Jiaosi zhi,' de duibi kaocha" 秦漢帝國的神權統一：出土簡帛與《封禪書》、《郊祀志》的對比考察. *Lishi Yanjiu* 5: 4–26.

Yao Shengmin 姚生民, "Xi Han Ganquan gong zai Ganquanshan xia" 西漢甘泉宮在甘泉山下, *Qin-Han Yanjiu*, 6 (2012): 66–70.

Yao Yuanyuan 姚媛媛. 2020. "Lun Handai de Fenyin Houtu jisi" 論漢代的汾陰后土祭祀, *Yuncheng xueyuan xuebao*, 38.1: 13–17.

Yates, Robin D. S. 2001. "Cosmos, Central Authority, and Communities in the Early Chinese Empire," in *Empires: Perspectives from Archaeology and History*, Susan E. Alcock, Terence N. D'Altroy, Kathleen D. Morrison, and Carla M. Sinopoli, eds., 351–68. Cambridge: Cambridge University Press.

Yates, Robin D. S. 2012–2013. "The Qin Slips and Boards from Well No. 1, Liye, Hunan: A Brief Introduction to the Qin Qianling County Archives," *Early China*, 35–36: 291–329.

Yü Ying-shih. 1987. "O Soul, Come Back!—A Study in the Changing Conceptions of the Soul and Afterlife in Pre-Buddhist China," *Harvard Journal of Asiatic Studies* 47: 363–95.

Zanker, Paul. 1988. *The Power of Images in the Age of Augustus*. Ann Arbor: University of Michigan Press.

Zhang Defang 張德芳. 2005."Xuanquan Han jian zhong de 'chuanxin jian' kaoshu" 懸泉漢簡中的'傳信簡'考述, in *Chutu wenxian yanjiu* 出土文獻研究 7. ed., Zhongguo wenwu yanjiusuo, 65–81. Shanghai: Shanghai guji chubanshe.

Zhang Shuguo 張樹國. 2009. "Han Wudi shidai guojia jisi de zhubu queli yu "jiaosi ge" shijiu zhang chuangzhi shi di kaolun" 漢武帝時代國家祭祀的逐步確立與"郊祀歌"十九章創制時地考論, *Hangzhou shifan daxue xuebao: Shehui kexue ban*, 2: 49–57.

Zhao, Suisheng. 1993. "Deng Xiaoping's Southern Tour: Elite Politics in Post-Tiananmen China," *Asian Survey*, 33.8: 739–56.

Zhongguo lishi ditu ji bianji zu 中國歷史地圖集編組. 1982. *Zhongguo li shi di tu ji* 中國歷史地圖集. *The Historical Atlas of China*. Shanghai: Ti tu chu ban she: Xin hua shu dian Shanghai fa xing suo fa xing.

Zhou, Yiqun. 2010. *Festivals, Feasts, and Gender Relations in Ancient China and Greece*. Cambridge: Cambridge University Press.

Zhuangzi zhuzi suoyin 莊子逐字索引 (A Concordance to the Zhuangzi). 2000. The ICS Ancient Chinese Texts Concordance Series, 43, D. C. Lau, ed. Hong Kong: The Commercial Press.

Zito, Angela. 1997. *Of Body and Brush: Grand Sacrifice as Text/Performance in Eighteenth-Century China*. Chicago: University of Chicago Press.

Index

For the benefit of digital users, indexed terms that span two pages (e.g., 52–53) may, on occasion, appear on only one of those pages.

Tables and figures are indicated by *t* and *f* following the page number

Actium, battle of, 57–58
Agrippa, Marcus, 56–57, 72–73, 80
amnesties, 11–12, 21, 75, 85, 86–88, 118–19
ancestors
　temples to, 60–61, 67–68
　worship of, 35–36, 60–61
animals
　display, 82–83, 85, 107–8
　sacrificial, 38–39, 40, 93–94, 96, 101–2, 108–9
Antony, Mark, 57, 73
Apollo
　temple of, 73, 111–12, 154n.27
Ara Pacis, 69–70, 110–11
Arval Brothers, 44–45, 56, 70–71, 72, 121
Arvales Fratres. *See* Arval Brothers
Attic Nights, 16–17
augures, 20–21, 41–44, 46, 57–58, 69, 99, 117–18, 121
augurium salutis. *See* Augury of Safety
Augury of Safety, 1, 2, 21–22, 98–101, 103
Augustus, 1, 2–3, 15–17, 18–22, 23, 26, 31, 33, 41–45, 47–48, 49–50, 52–59, 60–61, 68–71, 72–74, 75, 78–83, 87–88, 89–90, 97–104, 106–7, 109–13, 114–15, 116–18, 121–22, 123–24

Ban Biao, 12–13
Ban Gu, 12–13
Ban Zhao, 12–13
Beacham, Richard, 104
Beard, Mary, 41–43
Benjamin, Walter, 87, 153n.10
Brashier, Kenneth, 9, 128–29n.38
Bright Hall. *See mingtang*

Burbank, Jane, 4, 30–31

Caesar, Gaius, 121
Caesar, Julius, 18–19, 23, 25–26, 31, 44, 45, 52–55, 58–59, 70–71, 101–2, 106–7, 114–15, 117–18, 122
Caesar, Lucius, 121
Calendar, Roman, 41–43, 52–55, 70–71, 165n.130
Calvinus, 70–71, 166n.137
Campus Martius, 111–12
Carmen Saeculare, 16–17, 109–10
Cauldron, 96–97
Censorinus, 104
Chang'an, 18–19, 53*t*, 60–61, 62–63, 65, 68–69, 83–84, 92–93, 96, 118–19, 123–24
Changshan, kingdom of, 62–64
Cheng, Emperor of Han, 35–36, 83–84, 118–19
Cheng, King of Zhou, 37, 105
Chwe, Michael Suk-young, 77–78
Cicero, 16–17, 41, 43, 44, 99, 106
Claudius, 2–3, 22, 99, 100, 123
coins, 81–82, 112, 113, 121
comparative ancient history, 3–8
Compitalia, 1, 21–22, 80, 81, 98–99, 102–3
comptia, 80–81, 102
Confucians. *See* Ru
Confucius, 11–12, 105
Constantine, 123
consul, 18–19, 24–26, 43, 71, 71*t*, 72–73, 99, 106
Cooper, Frederick, 4, 30–31
cursus honorum, 18–19, 69

Dark Ram, 1, 90–91
decemviri, 43–44, 111–12
Diana, 111–12
Ding Furen, 52, 53*t*
Ding Gong, 53*t*
Dio, Cassius, 15–16, 123
Dionysius of Halicarnassus, 102
Director of Sacrifices, 1, 40, 67–68, 89–90, 95–96
Documents, the, 36–37, 62
Domitian, 123

Eco, Umberto, 77
emperor worship, 19–20, 81–82
epulones, 41, 43–44, 56, 71*t*, 72
erudites, 67–68, 105–6
excavated manuscripts, 13–14, 92

fangshi, 20–22, 50–52, 53*t*, 58–59, 65, 66, 84, 92–93, 96–97, 107–8, 114, 120
fang shu, 51
fasti (Ovid), 16–17
Fasti sacerdotum, 57
feng and *shan* sacrifices
  "Treatise on the," 19–20, 35–36, 38–39, 50, 60–61, 90–91, 92–93
feng Sacrifice, 35–36, 62–63, 105–6, 107–9, 113
Fenyin, 53*t*, 65, 94, 96–97, 107–8
First Emperor, the, 18, 23, 28–29, 31, 37–38, 58–59, 61, 65, 66, 82–85, 95, 104–6, 107–8, 114, 117
five phases, 7, 31–32, 62
Five Sacred Peaks, 61, 62, 63, 64*f*, 65, 107–8, 118–19
flamen Dialis, 1, 46–47, 70–71, 98, 101–2, 121–22
flamines, 41–43, 46–47, 140n.46
Flower, Harriet, 24, 80–81, 102

Games. See *ludi*
Ganquan, 53*t*, 65–66, 68, 91, 93–94, 95–97, 108–9, 118–19, 120
Gaozong, Emperor of Tang, 104–5
Gaozu, Emperor of Han, 18, 23, 28–30, 39
Geertz, Clifford, 76–77, 153n.4
Gellius, Aulus, 16–17, 44
gifts. See rewards
golden age, 21–22, 27–28, 33, 110–11

Goldstone, Jack, 5
Gongsun Qing, 53*t*, 65–66, 84, 85, 96–97, 107–8
Grand Diviner, 67–68
Grand Scribe, 11–12, 67–68
Great Unity, 1, 21–22, 52, 53*t*, 65–66, 68, 89–97, 107–9, 118–19
Greece, 3–4, 7, 9, 14, 16, 17, 109–10, 111–12
Guangwu, Emperor of Han, 104–5, 120–21
Guan Zhong, 105

Han
  dynasty, 12–13
  Eastern, 12–13, 22, 35–36, 104–5, 118–19, 120–21
  Western, 2–3, 11–13, 35–36, 60–61, 76–77, 118–19, 120
Hanshu, 12–13, 62–63, 65–66, 84, 91
Heng, Mt., 62–63
Hengg, Mt., 61, 62–64
Hengshan, kingdom of, 62–63
High Gods, 1, 21–22, 36, 39–40, 53*t*, 65, 89–91, 92–95, 96, 119, 139n.35
historical writing, 3, 5, 6–7, 10–12, 14–17, 18–19, 33, 80, 104–5
Horace, 15, 16–17, 109–10
Horse Traveller, 1, 90–91
Houtu. See Sovereign Earth
Huainanzi, 13
Hua, Mt., 61, 62–63
Huan, Duke of Qi, 105
Huo Guang, 118–19
Hurlet, Frédéric, 72–73

immortality, pursuit of, 50–51, 58–59, 66, 114, 116–17
immortal spirits, 145n.7, 147n.28
Imperial Cult, 19–20, 22, 23, 33, 35–36, 39–40, 47–48, 49, 50, 58–59, 67–68, 89, 90–92, 107, 118–19, 120, 123–24
imperial procession. See inspection tour
imperium, 24, 67–68, 72–73
inspection tour, 36–38, 50, 75–76, 84–85, 87, 109, 117, 120, 123–24

Janus, gates of, 99–100
Jiao, 1, 38–40, 90–91, 93, 94, 107–9, 138n.26

Jibei, kingdom of, 62–64
  king of (*see* Liu Kuan)
Jin, Shamaness, 53*t*, 96–97
Jing, Emperor of Han, 29–30
Juno, 111–12
Jupiter, 43, 46–47, 70–71, 111–12, 121–22

Kearsley, Rosalinde, 99–100
Kern, Martin, 37–38
Kongzi. *See* Confucius
Kuang Heng, 119, 120, 123–24
Kuan Shu, 1, 53*t*, 90, 96

labour service, 21, 75, 85, 87–88, 109
lares augusti, 21, 80, 81, 87–88, 98–99, 102–3
Lares Compitalia, 80
Lepidus, 55–56, 57, 69–71, 97–98, 110–11, 112–13
Lewis, Mark Edward, 29, 62, 105
lex Ogulnia, 41, 43–44
Liang Dynasty, 105
Liangfu, Mt., 105–6
Liji, 13, 62, 128–29n.38
Li Ling, 92
Ling, Lord of Qin, 39
Li Shaojun, 53*t*
Liu Bang. *See* Han Gaozu
Liu Ju, 118–19
Liu Kuan, 63–64
Liu Xiang, 120
Livy, 10–11, 15–16
Lloyd, Geoffrey, 3–4
Loewe, Michael, 118–20
Luan Da, 52, 53*t*
ludi, 2, 45, 47, 57, 98–99, 102, 111–12, 123
ludi saeculares, 1, 20–22, 43–44, 52–55, 69–70, 73, 89–90, 98, 103–4, 106–7, 109–11, 112–13, 114–15, 117–18, 123
Lupercalia, 1, 21–22, 98–99, 100–2, 103
Lüshi Chunqiu, 13

Macrobius, 16–17
Mandate of Heaven, 104–5, 120–21
Marsili, Filippo, 9
mingtang, 109
Misenum, Treaty of, 57, 71, 73
Miu Ji, 1, 53*t*, 90, 92–93

mountains and rivers, 36–38, 50–51, 61–62, 67–68. *See also* Five Sacred Peaks
Mu, Lord of Qin, 39
music, 37, 93–95, 108–9

Numa, 41, 70–71

Octavian. *See* Augustus
omens, 11–12, 38–39, 95, 104, 106–8, 123
Ovid, 16–17, 101–2

pax deorum, 34–35, 41, 46–47
Penglai, 65, 66
Philip, 123
Plutarch, 16, 41–43, 106
Pole Star, 92
Polybius, 10–11, 14, 24–25
Pompey, 25–26, 106
Pontifex Maximus, 41–43, 45, 52–56, 69–71, 73, 97–98, 109–11, 112–13, 117–18, 121–22
pontifical college, 41–43, 69–71, 121–22
pontifices, 20–21, 41–44, 57–58, 69, 70, 71, 71*t*, 117–18
Poo Mu-chou, 34–36
Pope Gelasius I, 100–1
populus Romanus, 31–32, 87, 112
priestly colleges, 16–17, 19–21, 22, 41–43, 44–45, 46, 47–48, 49–50, 52–59, 60, 72, 80, 97–98, 116–18, 121
priests, 19–21, 41–43, 45, 46–47, 52–55, 56, 57–58, 60–61, 70, 71, 71*t*, 72, 77, 81–82, 107
princeps. See Augustus
public building, 21, 75–76, 78, 79, 87

Qin
  direct road, 65
  empire, 18, 29, 38–39, 61, 75
  Shi Huangdi (*see* First Emperor)
  state, 29, 38–39, 119
  unification, 18, 27–28
quindecimviri sacris faciundis, 41, 43–44, 69

Red Star, 1, 90–91
regional lords, 2–3, 18, 23, 27, 36–37, 38–40, 50–51, 62–63, 65–66, 84–85, 108–9, 113

190   INDEX

regional lords and kings, 23, 84–85
religion
   Abrahamic, 9
   ancient world, 3, 5, 6–7, 9–11, 16–17, 30–31, 76–77, 85, 114–15
Renzong, Emperor of Song, 104–5
Res gestae divi Augusti, 16–17
rewards, 52, 84, 86–87
ritual, 9, 11–13, 20–21, 27, 36–39, 40, 41–43, 47, 50–51, 60–61, 67–68, 70–71, 76–78, 79–81, 82–85, 86, 87, 88, 89–90, 93–94, 105–6, 107–8, 113, 118–19, 120, 123
Roman Kings, 18–19, 24
Rome, city of, 15, 18–20, 21, 31, 49, 60–61, 68–69, 75, 79, 80–83, 87, 98–100, 113, 121–22, 123
   vici, 81, 102–3
Romulus, 70–71
Ru, 105–6, 107–8, 118–19, 120
Rüpke, Jörg, 16–17, 45–46

sacrificial tour. *See* inspection tour
sacrifice, 1, 2, 9, 11–12, 16–17, 19–22, 26, 34–41, 44–45, 46–47, 49–52, 53t, 58–59, 60–66, 67–68, 70–71, 74, 75, 77, 82–87, 88, 89–97, 102, 117, 118–19, 120–22, 123
saeculum, 69–70, 104, 106–7, 111–13, 123
Sanft, Charles, 37–38, 84–85
Saturnalia, festival, 102
Saturnalia, poem, 16–17
Scheidel, Walter, 5
Second Emperor, 29, 39
Secular Games. *See ludi saeculares*
Senate, 2–3, 6–7, 16, 19–20, 24–25, 26, 41–45, 46, 56–57, 70–71, 72, 73, 79, 80, 81–82, 87–88, 99–100, 102, 106, 109–10, 122
Septimus Severus, 123
Shangdi. *See* High Gods
shan sacrifice, 19–20, 35–36, 38–39, 50, 52, 53t, 60–61, 84–85, 89–93, 96–97, 103–5, 106–8, 112, 113–14, 117, 120–21, 123
Shaoweng, 53t, 65, 145n.7
Shiji, 1, 11–13, 19–20, 36, 37–38, 47–48, 50, 51, 62–63, 85, 92, 96, 105, 108–9

Shun, 36–37, 62–63
Sibylline books, 43–44, 73, 106–7, 111–12, 152n.71, 152n.73, 163n.101
Sima Qian, 1, 10–12, 15, 19–20, 35–37, 38–39, 40, 47–48, 50–52, 58–59, 61, 62, 66, 84, 90–91, 95, 97, 105, 107–8, 114, 116–17
Sima Tan, 11–12, 164n.109
Sivin, Nathan, 3–4
Song, Mt., 61, 62–63, 67–68
Sovereign Earth, 1, 21–22, 52, 53t, 65, 89–92, 93–94, 95–97, 118–19
Spring and Autumn Period, 27–29, 38–39
Suetonius, 1, 16, 52–55, 97–100, 101–2, 103, 116–17, 121–22
Sulla, 25–26, 44, 52–56, 106
Superintendent of Ceremonial, 40, 47–48, 51, 67–68, 91, 123–24
Syme, Ronald, 44–45

Tacitus, 10–11, 16
Tai, Mt., 61, 62–64, 84, 105–6, 107–8, 109, 120–21
Taiyi. *See* Great Unity
Tang Dynasty, 2–3
Tanner, Jeremy, 7
taxation, 21, 29
temple, 21, 26, 29, 34–35, 46–47, 60–61, 67–68, 73, 75, 77, 78–81, 87–88, 102–3, 111–12, 121–22, 123
Three Unities, 1, 90–91
Tian Tian, 68, 120
Tiberius, 22, 121–22
Titus, 15, 52–55, 121
Trigger, Bruce, 7–8

universal drinking, 86–87

Vestal Virgins, 41–43, 45, 52–55
Virgil, 111–12

Wang Shuo, 53t
Warring States period, 18, 27–29, 38–39, 61
Wei river, 29, 39–40, 91
Wei, Empress of Han, 118–19
Wen, Emperor, 39–40, 58–59, 62, 67–68, 91, 96–97

Wen, Lord of Qin, 38–39
wine, 67–68, 93–94, 108–9
Wu, Emperor, 1, 2–3, 11–14, 18–22, 23, 28–30, 33, 35–36, 47–48, 49, 50–51, 53*t*, 58–59, 60, 61, 62–69, 64*f*, 74, 75, 78, 82–83, 84–85, 86–88, 89–92, 93–94, 95, 96–97, 103–6, 107–8, 109, 113–15, 116–19, 120–21, 123–24
Wuxing. *See* five phases

Xiang, Lord of Qin, 38–39
Xinyuan Ping, 96–97
Xiongnu, 18, 65–66, 95, 118–19, 149n.29, 149n.31
Xuan, Emperor of Han, 65–66, 118–19
Xuanzong, Emperor of Tang, 104–5

Yates, Robin D.S., 31
Yellow Thearch, 33, 53*t*, 62–64, 65–66, 96–97, 105, 114
Yin-Yang, 119
Yong, 36, 38–40, 65, 68, 84, 90–91, 92–94, 96, 105–6
Yong Zhi, 53*t*
Youshui Fagen, 53*t*
Yuan, emperor of Han, 118–19
Yu Chu, 52, 53*t*

Zanker, Paul, 79–80
Zhang Cang, 39
Zhao, Emperor, 63–64, 118–19
Zhidao. See Qin: direct road
Zihou, 107–8